REHABILITATION OF MEMORY

REHABILITATION OF MEMORY

BARBARA A. WILSON

Foreword by Leonard Diller

THE GUILFORD PRESS
New York   London

To Mick

Printed in the United States of America
Last digit is print number 9 8 7 6 5 4 3 2

Library of Congress Cataloging in Publication Data

Wilson, Barbara A.
    Rehabilitation of memory.

    Bibliography: p.
    Includes index.
    1. Brain — Wounds and injuries — Complications and
sequelae.   2. Memory, Disorders of — Diagnosis.
3. Memory, Disorders of — Patients — Rehabilitation.
4. Rehabilitation — Research.   I. Title.
RD594.W55   1987   616.85′232   86-7636
ISBN 0-89862-678-1 (cloth)
ISBN 0-89862-513-0 (paper)

ACKNOWLEDGMENTS

This book is based on my Ph.D. thesis (Wilson, 1984b). The work was carried out at Rivermead Rehabilitation Centre in Oxford, England, between October 1979 and July 1984. The studies were designed and implemented by me, with the following exceptions: The Rivermead Behavioural Memory Test (RBMT), described in Chapter 5, was designed jointly with Zafra Cooper; approximately two-thirds of the assessments and reliability studies described in Chapter 5 were carried out by Zafra Cooper, Helen Kennerley, and Helen Hutchins; Alan Baddeley was jointly responsible with me for the design of the treatment of the young head-injured woman which is described in Chapter 8; David Thomas executed most of the work described in Experiment 4 in Chapter 9 while under my supervision; Denise Peixoto tested approximately one-third of the subjects in Chapter 9.

Some of the work described in the book has already been published. Experiment 1 in Chapter 6 appeared in *Behavioural Psychotherapy*, 1981, 9, 338–344; a version of Chapter 7 appeared in *Cortex*, 1982, 18, 581–594. The data in Chapter 8 are to appear in G. Pavlides and D. Fisher (Eds.), *Dyslexia: Neuropsychology and Treatment* (London: Wiley) in a chapter written jointly with Alan Baddeley.

In addition, some of the data have been presented at conferences. A description of the RBMT was included in a paper entitled "Implications of Recent Neuropsychological Findings for Rehabilitation," presented at a meeting of the Society for the Study of Alcoholism, Boston, May 1984. A version of this paper, entitled "Identification and Remediation of Everyday Problems in Memory Impaired Adults," is to be published in O. Parsons, N. Butters, and P. Nathan (Eds.), *Neuropsychology of Alcoholism: Implications for Diagnosis and Treatment* (New York: Guilford Press). Further data on the RBMT were presented at the British Psychological Society (Cognitive Section) Annual Conference, Oxford, September 1984. Alan Sunderland has given permission to use his stories in the RBMT, and Gay Snodgrass has given permission to use her pictures.

The treatment of a young man who was shot in the head, referred to in Chapter 8, was presented at the Second World Congress on Dyslexia, Halkidiki, Greece, June 1983. These data, together with those from the treatment of the young woman who sustained a severe head injury in a horse-riding accident reported in Chapter 8, were also included in a paper presented at a joint meeting of the Dutch Psychonomic Society and the British Experimental Psychology Society, Amsterdam, July 1984.

The data from Experiment 2 in Chapter 9 were included in a paper entitled "Differences among Amnesias and between Amnesics: The Role of Single-Case Methodology in Theoretical Analysis and Practical Treatment" written jointly with Alan Baddeley and presented at the Princeton Conference on Amnesia, April 1983.

An earlier version of Chapter 10 was presented at the Fifth Annual European Conference of the International Neuropsychological Society, Deauville, France, June 1982.

Finally, several people have helped me in pursuing the work connected with this book during the past few years. Max Coltheart and Graham Powell, my Ph.D. supervisors, gave me guidance and encouragement. Alan Baddeley and Gerry Goldstein have provided useful comments and discussion. Zafra Cooper, Helen Kennerley, Helen Hutchins, and David Thomas have given their time and support during much of the practical work at Rivermead Rehabilitation Centre. Elizabeth Warrington loaned some material for testing the young woman described in Chapter 8. My husband, Mick, has undertaken the typing with good humor, patience, and sound judgment, and my daughter, Anna, showed much fortitude in chasing up many of the references. Dr. Elizabeth Rushworth, Medical Director of Rivermead, gave permission to publish data on the patients, and the therapists at Rivermead filled in the checklists described in Chapter 5. Above all, the patients at Rivermead have given me their cooperation and forbearance. To all these people I offer my sincere thanks.

—Barbara Wilson, *February 1986*

FOREWORD

Who would have thought as recently as 15 or 20 years ago that a book like this could be written? Problems with memory could be discussed by psychodynamic psychologists in terms of their meanings and significance or by neurologists and neuropsychologists as markers of brain damage. However, examining failure in a brain-damaged person as a live problem, not for the sake of testing a theory or demonstrating a diagnosis but for the purpose of trying to help a victim, was unthinkable. While the experimental study of memory has had a respectable, rich, albeit complex, history over the last century, the remediation of memory problems had been deemed to be a somewhat shady enterprise, belonging to the Sunday newspaper supplements rather than to medicine and science. This has been the case since a well-known mnemonist of the last century, who enthralled audiences by teaching them to improve their memory, was taken to be a fraud. Indeed, the name of the mnemonist, Dr. Feinagel, has become part of our daily vocabulary.

Rehabilitation workers have been equally cautious and avoidant in coming to grips with the cognitive consequences of brain damage. When they focused on the more tangible sequelae of motor disorders following central nervous system damage, their concern with activities of daily living and functional assessment was translated into consideration of activities which were motorically based, such as driving, feeding, grooming, and walking. These activities were measurable, easily related to sensory-motor disturbances and gradable in terms of level of assistance needed for independence. Language disorders were also identified as domains of diagnosis and treatment. However, memory problems were identified and considered as givens with no further thought as to how to pursue systematic methods for their amelioration. Furthermore, the methods in the clinic and the laboratory did not seem to have a practical usefulness in daily life. How could one measure memory deficit in functional as opposed to psychometric terms? What percentage of memories of actual experiences are forgotten? The analysis of memory problems in the laboratory seems several steps removed from memory failure in naturalistic situations. Rehabilitation workers have a strong interest in the behavior of people in their natural environments.

They also share Dr. Wilson's basic beliefs which can be paraphrased as "whatever the problem and however severe it is, there is always something to be done which can improve matters and every treatment procedure should be properly evaluated." But until now, rehabilitation workers, as hard-nosed empiricists driven by ideals, have lacked the tools and the concepts to deal with the situation of memory failure. Dr. Wilson has provided such tools.

How would one go about ameliorating or improving or even preparing a person with brain damage to live with a memory problem? Dr. Wilson recognizes that a contemporary approach to this problem must combine several subfields—cognitive psychology, neuropsychology, and behavioral psychology. It is at once apparent that mastery of these fields is a formidable and imaginative enterprise—drawing on a range of scholarship as well as personal experiences. Any attempts at solution, particularly if they are stated in specific terms with specific examples, are bound to fly in the face of conventional wisdom, stirring up new clinical paths and avenues for experiment. On the theoretical level, the process of interventions opens up new areas for study. In a sense the differences in perspective between the prevailing views in clinical neuropsychology and an interventionist approach parallels the difference between an academic approach to the study of politics and the approach of the local politician who is in daily contact with his constituents. Both have validity. Both can learn from each other.

Dr. Wilson's attempt to frame the treatment of memory by theories radiating from three fields offers clarity and a network of ideas, but avoids the cookbook approach. Her recounting of first-hand experiences, failures as well as successes, shows a healthy respect for the complex phenomena she is addressing. Her willingness to test the efficacy of the techniques gives some hope that we may be in a position to deliver scientifically based practical approaches to problems which have seemed intractable since ancient times. Students in the field will be helped by the specific descriptions of problems, the procedures, and the simple tools which have been developed to alleviate the problems.

Dr. Wilson's clinical studies suggest that there is a field of special education for adults with acquired brain damage which is waiting to emerge from the different links of clinical and scientific experiences.

—Leonard Diller, *NYU Medical Center*

CONTENTS

· I ·

INTRODUCTION

·1·

THE RATIONALE FOR THIS VOLUME

THE BRAIN-INJURED POPULATION

Many people who survive insults to the brain remain cognitively impaired to some degree or other. In Great Britain, for example, about 1000 people each year sustain severe head injuries from which they will not recover sufficiently to return to work. About 36% of these will experience major difficulties with memory (Schacter & Crovitz, 1977). There are also some 93,000 people in Great Britain who are severely disabled as a result of stroke (Weddell & Beresford, 1979). A considerable number of these will be left with cognitive disorders, such as, for example, material-specific memory problems, or even global amnesia if the stroke is bilateral or there have been previous cerebral vascular accidents (CVAs). Cognitive difficulties may also result from intracerebral tumors; intracranial infections, such as encephalitis; degenerative diseases, such as Alzheimer disease or Huntington chorea; toxic disorders, such as carbon monoxide poisoning; nutritional disorders, such as those associated with Korsakoff syndrome; or anoxia, sustained, perhaps, during cardiac arrest or an anesthetic accident. These and other conditions that are associated with cognitive impairment are described by Lishman (1978).

The survivors of these conditions place a great burden upon their communities; upon their national health services and other agencies attempting to care for them; and, perhaps most of all, upon their immediate families. Owing to lack of resources and sometimes lack of interest or understanding, many are inappropriately placed in geriatric units, psychiatric wards, or hospitals for the mentally handicapped. Others may be confined to their homes and neglected by the outside community in the mistaken belief that nothing can be done for them.

Even for those patients lucky enough to receive some form of therapeutic intervention, there is often a lack of understanding of appropriate measures to ameliorate some of their difficulties. Inappro-

3

priate ameliorative strategies may be tried as a result of ignorance of the theoretical principles that underpin work in this field. Similarly, attempts to evaluate treatment effectiveness may be misguided and therefore unhelpful.

Professional staff working with these groups may be so influenced by the organic nature of the cause of the problems that they regard them as untreatable. For example, a relatively recent chapter on unilateral neglect (Heilman, 1979) states that the person with neglect should be approached from his or her "good" side, that the patient's locker should be on the nonneglected side, and that all communication should take place on that side. The assumption here is that, because neglect results from an organic/physical cause, all treatment will be ineffective. In fact, the recommendations described above (which have, incidentally, been made by one of the world's leading experts in neglect) are quite contrary to current rehabilitative practices that are informed by research. The work of Diller and his colleagues in New York (Diller & Weinberg, 1977) indicates that many patients with the neglect syndrome can be taught to orient to stimuli in their neglected field. Thus, it should not be assumed that, because it is impossible to regenerate a part of the brain that has been damaged, it will be impossible to improve cognitive functioning normally associated with that part of the brain.

In contrast to those who believe that little or nothing can be done to help the brain-damaged, there are those who believe that it is possible to restore lost functioning. Relatives and patients, lacking knowledge in this area, are ready to believe that memory or language functioning can be restored to premorbid levels with the application of the appropriate drug or the passage of a certain amount of time. Such recovery is rarely the case (see, e.g., Milner, Corkin, & Teuber, 1968; Sarno & Levita, 1981). Some therapists working in this field have also indicated their lack of knowledge when they have attempted to improve memory functioning in severely amnesic patients by playing memory games such as "pelmanism" (pairs) and "Kim's game."[1] A more

1. "Pelmanism" is a game where several cards are placed face downward on the table. Each player in turn is allowed to turn over two cards. If these make a pair (e.g. 2 kings or 2 eights) the player keeps the pair. If not, the cards are turned over face down and the next player tries to collect a pair. The skill is in trying to remember the position of previously turned cards. The winner is the player with the greatest number of pairs. In "Kim's game" a tray of objects is shown to the subject for some 20 or 30 seconds. The tray is then removed and the subject tries to remember as many of the objects as possible. Sometimes a delay is built in before recall; sometimes cues are provided (e.g. "What was in the top right hand corner?").

realistic approach would encourage specification of objectives connected with the amelioration of some of the problems faced by brain-damaged people and their families. (E. Miller, 1978). Such an approach informs the treatment that is described throughout this book. It does not, of course, rule out all hope for substantial recovery on the part of some patients (though these are likely to remain a small minority).

GENERALIZATION AND REHABILITATION

Even if therapists do find ways to help the memory-impaired they are still faced with problems of generalization. Generalization is of crucial importance in rehabilitation and should be an integral part of each and every treatment program. There are several kinds of generalization to be considered—generalization across subjects, across behaviors, and across settings.

Generalization across subjects means that procedures which work for one subject can be expected to work with other subjects. This can rarely be taken for granted in rehabilitation. Even when research has established that one particular strategy is significantly superior to another it does not follow that every individual will benefit from that superior strategy. Furthermore, most treatment research studies are carried out with people who have one particular deficit, such as the classic amnesic syndrome or Broca aphasia. Many patients undergoing rehabilitation, however, have several problems or cognitive deficits, making it less likely that they will respond to treatment in a way similar to patients in the research studies. What therapists need to do is use research findings to help them select potential treatment techniques and then evaluate each patient's responses to the selected treatments. Ways this might be done are discussed in Chapter 4. The topic of generalization across subjects is also referred to again later in this chapter. (See section on research design).

Generalization across behaviors refers to situations in which a strategy taught to help with one problem is used to help with another problem. An example would be teaching a patient to use visual imagery for names and finding the patient used the method to remember a shopping or "things-to-do" list. It is unlikely, though, that many will spontaneously do this, and if generalization of this nature is considered to be desirable then it will probably need to be built into the treatment program by therapists in the same way generalization is sometimes built into programs with the mentally handicapped (Carr,

1980). To date, however, there seem to be no findings from investigations into such generalization in adults with acquired brain damage.

Generalization across settings refers to the situation where a strategy taught in one setting is used in other settings. For example, if a patient is taught a method for remembering prose and uses this method at home for review purposes, generalization across settings has occurred. Again, this rarely appears to happen spontaneously with the kind of brain-damaged patients discussed in this volume who have been seen at Rivermead Rehabilitation Centre in Oxford. Nevertheless, failure to generalize does not mean that the treatment method is a failure. Penicillin, for example, is known to be an effective drug for certain infections but if people do not take the drug on the occasions when it is prescribed the penicillin will not be effective. This does not mean that penicillin itself is no good. Similarly, if visual imagery is an efficient way to learn names but people do not use it, then we should not infer that the strategy is no good for learning names. It does mean, however, that therapists have to consider what they are going to do about a patient's failure to use the strategy.

Several solutions are possible. First, it may be necessary to teach relatives and/or staff to apply a strategy when the need arises. If a patient is able to learn information in one way, then when it is necessary to teach similar information the appropriate means are there. Second, as stated above, it is possible on some occasions to *teach* generalization. For example, the treatment could take place in a variety of settings. Thus, if a patient is taught to use an electronic memory aid in occupational therapy, the next step might be to use the aid in physiotherapy and then in speech therapy and so on. Eventually the patient could be encouraged to use the aid at home. The wider the range of settings the more likelihood there is of the strategy generalizing to other settings (Carr, 1980). Similarly, a patient could be shown how to use PQRST (described in Chapters 7 and 9) for newspaper stories and then be encouraged to use the strategy for articles in magazines, chapters in books, and even studying for examinations.

Persuading patients to put into practice the strategies they have been taught may be more difficult. Again, several options are open. It is possible to put some patients on a behavioral program to reinforce the use of memory aids and mnemonics. Appropriate goals might include: "teaching Mrs. X to refer to her notebook after each meal" or "increasing the numbers of times Mr. Z spontaneously uses the PQRST in history review." The use of timers together with prompting and fading

(Carr, 1980) would perhaps be one way of achieving success. Alternatively, a chaining method could be used whereby a particular task is broken down into a series of smaller units and taught one at a time.

In other cases it might be necessary to allow more time before expecting the strategies to be used spontaneously. Some patients are slow to start but if given sufficient time they can sometimes quite suddenly begin to put into practice the skills they have been previously taught. For example, one man, a patient from Rivermead, frequently argued with his wife over whether or not he had taken a bath. Because of his amnesia he could not remember and believed he had bathed recently. His wife knew better but could not convince him. It was suggested that he keep a "bath diary" recording dates and times of baths, but he kept forgetting to record the times. With the help of his wife, frequent reminding, and keeping the diary above the sink in the bathroom, he began to note his bath times and eventually the strategy became well enough established for him to use it to maintain a regular bath schedule.

Generalization may sometimes be contraindicated. In point, it may be necessary to abandon a particular strategy in favour of another when a patient shows signs of distress. M. L., for example (described in Chapters 6 and 9) hated visual imagery and his comment every time he worked with imagery was "Where's the logic in that?" Although he learned the names of staff by using imagery he became angry whenever the method was presented. He was much happier using other strategies in which he could "see the logic in it." In his case visual imagery was not recommended to his relatives when the time came for his discharge from the center. At what point a therapist abandons a strategy in favour of another will usually be guided by observation, clinical experience, and intuition, but there is little doubt that a method which causes a patient some discomfiture and even distress will be unlikely to lead to generalization.

If there is a major strand running through my comments on generalization it is that we should not *expect* generalization to occur. If it does occur spontaneously then that should be seen as a bonus. If it does not, then it might be possible to include it as part of the treatment program. If the program fails, then therapists should recognise that it is perhaps sufficient that an effective learning method has been discovered for a patient to practise in specific circumstances. Furthermore, the particular method may well be one that others in the patient's community can implement if necessary.

THEORY AND RESEARCH

Major Theoretical Approaches

In attempting to reduce cognitive deficits and, in particular, memory deficits, there are at least three branches of psychology that provide fruitful starting points. Neuropsychology provides (1) information regarding localization of function within the cerebrum; (2) investigations of particular etiologies (e.g., Korsakoff syndrome, encephalitis, and closed head injury [CHI]); and (3) techniques for testing or eliminating additional deficits. Cognitive psychology provides (1) theories about the nature of human memory; (2) theoretical interpretations of amnesia; and (3) information about the learning abilities of amnesic patients. Behavioral psychology provides (1) behavioral assessment techniques for assessing everyday problems resulting from cognitive deficits; (2) treatment techniques, such as shaping, chaining, and modeling, to help reduce cognitive problems; and (3) single-case methodology for evaluating treatment of individuals.

Section II of this book, "Theoretical Foundations," provides the reader with an overview of the theoretical frameworks, methodologies, and previous research findings that have influenced the development, design, and application of the investigations forming the content of Section III, "Memory Rehabilitation Studies." The three chapters in Section II cover the major contributory disciplines of neuropsychology, cognitive psychology, and behavioral psychology. Due recognition is given to the unique contributions made by each of these disciplines to the study and practice of memory therapy. Emphasis is also placed upon the strength of their influence when ideas, principles, and practices from all three areas are combined in research projects aimed at revealing new knowledge about ways in which memory-impaired people can be helped to alleviate or even overcome some of their everyday memory problems. It is perhaps the first time that such an attempt has been made to select from three major disciplines those concepts and practices that, when combined, can inform the methods we use to assess and treat the memory-impaired. The specific contributions of the major theoretical disciplines to the studies presented in this volume are considered in the chapters reporting research and are reviewed in the concluding chapter.

It follows, therefore, that a proper reading of Section III requires prior reflection upon the content of Section II. However, some readers are likely to be very familiar with one or more of the disciplines described in Chapters 2 through 4, and may have "taken on board" the relevant concepts and practices in their own work. Such readers should feel free to bypass one or more of the chapters in Section II and go straight on to a reading of Section III. The important point to stress at the outset is that Section II has been prepared in the belief that specialists might find it a useful exercise to reflect upon ways in which their disciplines can be interlinked with others in order to achieve greater effectiveness when assessing and treating patients whose problems should not be regarded from one perspective alone.

While the aims of the studies composing Section III may be said to speak for themselves, consideration of these studies should be prefaced with a word about research design.

Research Design

The studies reported in this volume include single case, small group (under 10 subjects), and large group (20 or more subjects) studies, demonstrating the fact that different designs are required to answer different questions. Single-case studies can tell us how individuals respond to treatment, while group studies allow for more general statements about particular populations.

There is usually no need to convince psychologists or other therapists of the value of group studies. All recognize their usefulness and are familiar with the rationale of such designs. With regard to single-case studies, however, it is not uncommon to hear the view that they are unscientific or that their findings are not applicable to anyone other than the individuals being studied. Two famous examples may suffice to contradict this view: Broca's patient "Tan" and that of H. M., the temporal lobectomy patient studied by Milner and colleagues. Small-group studies are also criticized for being incapable of generating broad findings that are applicable to a large population. However, as demonstrated throughout this work, the reverse is true in many cases: Significant results can only be obtained in small group studies when almost all the participating subjects show the desired effect. In contrast, large-group studies may involve several individuals who fail to demonstrate the desired outcome, yet statistically significant results may still be obtained because sufficient numbers of the remaining subjects do show this effect. The obscuring of individual differences that follows such large-group designs may mean that the findings that are generated are not applicable to the kind of patient population included in the sample. Significant results from small group studies, however, are much more generally applicable to the *particular* population involved in the investigation, *and to those whose diagnosis is similar.*

Take for example one of the studies to be described in Chapter 9. Eight head-injured subjects took part in an experiment to see which of two methods led to better recall of verbal material. Each one of the patients forgot less material using the PQRST method (a method involving deeper levels of thinking) then when using repetition. This suggests that most head-injured patients who fall within the same age range and show similar results on pretreatment measures will do better with PQRST than with repetition. In contrast, findings from a large group study such as that reported in Chapter 11 are less generally applicable. This study compared the effectiveness of four different mnenomic strategies for learning lists of words. Some individuals performed very well using one method but performed poorly on another. This preference was reversed for other individuals. The outcome was that successes and failures canceled each other out and led to nonsignificant results between three of the four strategies. What we know from this study is that individuals differ in their preference and their ability to benefit from a particular strategy. However, the design used in Chapter 11 enabled us to counter-balance the order in which mnemonic strategies were introduced—something which cannot be done so easily in single-case or small-group studies.

In rehabilitation we need to understand "[w]hat specific treatment is effective with a specific type of client under what circumstances" (Hersen & Barlow, 1976, p. 13). This quotation provides a neat description of a theme that runs throughout this work. The treatment referred to by Hersen and Barlow is frequently best established through research dependent upon single-case designs. Replication with larger group studies may be a desirable corollary, however, and there are several good reasons why large-group studies should be included in rehabilitation research, representing in some situations the preferred methodology over single-case designs. First, they are used to answer different questions. For example, the question asked in the group study in Chapter 10 is "Can we predict which patients will benefit from visual imagery?" This is a rather different question from that asked in studies reported in Chapter 6, "Can patients learn people's names by means of visual imagery?" The former aims to find a screening method for selecting patients for a particular treatment. The latter aims to find out whether the treatment itself is effective. The former question might have been answered by performing a series of case studies, but this would have been very time consuming. Designed as a group study classifying patients according to severity of impairment, it was possible to see clear differences between the three groups in a relatively short time.

Large-group studies are also useful for comparing several treatments when one of the treatments may in fact influence another. Thus, if a particular mnemonic device is introduced and found by subjects to be effective, they may use this mnemonic device at a later stage when the experimenter wants them to use a different strategy. Within a single-case design, only one strategy can be used first, but within a group design it is possible to counterbalance the order of the mnemonic strategies and thus erase possible order effects. For example, Chapter 11 describes a study in which four mnemonic strategies (first-letter cueing, method of loci, visual imagery, and story) are compared. Had the story method always been presented first it would not be clear whether the method itself was better, or whether subjects benefited because they were less fatigued, or whether they realized the method was helping and actually used this method in the tasks requiring other strategies. Because the order of the mnemonic strategies was systematically changed, the evidence is in favor of the method itself being beneficial. Such counterbalancing is not possible in single-case designs.

Similarly, group designs should be used when an interaction effect may be expected to occur. As Kazdin (1982) reminds us, single-case designs do not lend themselves readily to analysis of combined effects. For example, in the study of mnemonic strategies described in Chapter 11, brain-damaged patients and normal controls were compared in their use of four strategies. Differences were found in measures of retention between the groups of subjects and among the strategies; there was also a significant interaction between group and strategy. That is to say, the methods that worked best for one group were not identical to the methods that worked best for the other group.

The implication contained in the foregoing argument is that both single-case and large-group studies are important methodologies for evaluating the effectiveness of treatment, each providing complementary ways of seeking answers to questions. The present work has attempted to examine various approaches to rehabilitating the memory-impaired through the use of methodologies appropriate to the kinds of questions asked.

·II·

THEORETICAL
FOUNDATIONS

·2·

NEUROPSYCHOLOGY

LOCALIZATION STUDIES

The areas of the brain that are most frequently reported as being involved in memory functioning are (1) the hippocampal formations within the temporal lobes—that is, the hippocampal or parahippocampal gyrus, and the hippocampus; (2) the fornix; (3) the mammillary bodies; and (4) the thalamus, and, in particular, the dorsomedial nuclei of the thalamus. Hecaen and Albert (1978) state that a continuous pathway of connections exists: parahippocampal gyrus–hippocampus–fornix–mammillary bodies–mammillo-thalamic tract–anterior thalamic nuclei–cingulate gyrus–parahippocampal gyrus. This pathway forms one of the inner circuits of the limbic system.

The four major areas can be more fully described as follows:

1. *The hippocampal formations.* The parahippocampal gyrus lies on the inferior surface of the temporal lobe near the middle of the brain. The anterior portion of this gyrus curves around the hippocampal fissure to form the uncus. The hippocampus lies in the inferior horn of the lateral ventricle, with the anterior end close to the uncus.

2. *The fornix.* This is the major efferent fiber system of the hippocampus. The tails or crura of the fornix join together to become the body of the fornix, which later divides again into the anterior columns of the fornix before connecting with the anterior commissure and the mammillary bodies.

3. *The mammillary bodies.* These are part of the uppermost portion of the brain stem, the diencephalon. The uppermost surface of the diencephalon forms part of the floor of the lateral ventricle, and it is on this floor that the mammillary bodies lie.

4. *The thalamus.* This is also part of the diencephalon, and is one of its principal components. It lies on both sides of the midline at the rostral end of the brain stem, and contains several nuclei that project to most parts of the cortex and midbrain.

15

What evidence is there that these structures are involved in memory? With regard to the hippocampal formations, the best-documented evidence probably comes from the studies of H. M. and a number of other patients operated on for intractable epilepsy or severe psychiatric disturbance (Penfield & Milner, 1958; Scoville, 1968; Scoville & Milner, 1957). At the age of 27 years, H. M. received bilateral temporal lobe ablations in an attempt to stop previously uncontrolled seizures, which had developed when he was 16 years old. Once he had recovered from surgery, it became apparent that he was unable to learn new information; that he also had a retrograde amnesia (RA); and that he showed all the features of a classic amnesic syndrome. Scoville and Milner (1957) also described eight psychotic patients who had received the same operation, in an attempt to reduce their thought disorders. When the lesions involved the hippocampus, severe amnesia developed. When the hippocampus was spared, and the operation was confined to the uncus and amygdala, amnesia was not present. The authors concluded that an intact hippocampus was essential for normal memory functioning. Surgical procedures in all these cases were radical, involving the medial surfaces of both temporal lobes. Furthermore, the lesions destroyed the anterior two-thirds of the hippocampus and the parahippocampal gyri. The length of each lesion was 8 cm. Unilateral temporal lobectomy did not result in such a devastating memory impairment.

Further work by Milner (1965, 1968, 1971) has demonstrated material-specific deficits following unilateral temporal lobectomy. Removal of the left temporal lobe results in deficits in verbal memory, while patients with right temporal lobectomies are more impaired in remembering nonverbal material, such as faces, patterns, and mazes. These temporal lobectomies, performed in Montreal, have involved a number of neuroanatomical structures, but the evidence strongly suggests that the hippocampus is the most crucial organ for adequate memory functioning, and that the degree of deficit correlates with the amount of hippocampus removed. Corsi (1969) found that among patients with left temporal ablations, those with extensive hippocampal involvement were more impaired on short-term verbal-memory tasks than were those patients with little or no hippocampal involvement. With maze-learning tasks, Milner (1965) and Corkin (1965) found that patients with right temporal lobectomies were impaired only if they had extensive hippocampal lesions. The same was true with recognition of photographs (Corkin, 1968). Lesions involving the amygdala, uncus, and neocortex, while sparing the hippocampus, did not produce noticeable deficits on either verbal or nonverbal tasks.

Damage to the temporal–hippocampal structures can result from causes other than surgical procedures. Victor, Angevine, Mancall, and Fisher (1961) reported a case of a patient who suffered a CVA in which both posterior cerebral arteries were occluded. This resulted in a profound deficit of recent memory and an RA. His general intellectual level was found to be above average. The neuropathology in this case was a bilateral infarction involving the hippocampal formation, the fornix, and the mammillary bodies. The uncus and amygdalae were unaffected. A Korsakoff-type syndrome has also been reported following bilateral lesions of the posterior cerebral arteries (Hecaen & Albert, 1978). Some cases of dementia may also be due to posterior cerebral artery infarction (K. Walsh, 1978). Walsh states that after a period of confusion and visual difficulty, the patient may remain disoriented and may appear to suffer from dementia. Psychological examination usually reveals severe amnesia, with intact performance on standard intellectual tests. Many of these patients do become demented, and this is likely to be caused by subsequent infarctions. However, the patient who suffered bilateral infarction of the posterior cerebral arteries, described in Chapter 7, remained intellectually intact (apart from memory functioning) 3 years after his stroke (Baddeley & Wilson, in press). The posterior cerebral arteries feed several cerebral areas, including the medial surface of the temporal lobes where the hippocampi are situated.

Severe head injury is another common cause of memory deficit (e.g., W. R. Russell, 1971). It usually results in diffuse cerebral damage, but it has been suggested (Hecaen & Albert, 1978) that the tips and the undersurfaces of the temporal lobes may be more susceptible to damage. If this is true, then the memory impairment may also indicate hippocampal involvement.

Encephalitic patients are another group who may develop amnesia. There is much evidence to suggest that encephalitis can result in extensive medial temporal lobe lesions (e.g., Brierley, Corsellis, Hierons, & Nevin, 1960; Drachman & Adams, 1962), although the viruses causing encephalitis do not always attack this area (Lishman, 1978).

Korsakoff, head-injured, and postencephalitic patients may all show amnesia following damage to other neurological structures, but there is certainly strong evidence from a variety of sources that the hippocampi are implicated in memory processes.

Evidence for the importance of the second structure involved in memory—namely, the fornix—is harder to find. The fornix may be regarded as the bridge between the temporal lobes and the diencephalon. Warrington and Weiskrantz (1982) suggest that amnesia is a result of a disconnection syndrome, and that the disconnected pathways are in the fornix–mammillary body route. The amnesias associated with lesions in the diencephalon are discussed below, but as the fornix connects the two, then it is possible that fornical damage also results in amnesia.

Parkin (1984) suggests that damage to the fornix rarely results in amnesia. He quotes several studies to support this: For example, Woolsey and Nelson (1975) described a patient with a tumor that caused bilateral destruction of the fornix and no memory loss. Dott (1938) recorded two asymptomatic cases showing lesions of the fornix. Sometimes a transient memory impairment has been described (Apuzzo et al., 1982); and one study (Cameron & Archibald, 1981) describes an operation in which the left fornix was divided, resulting in a selective impairment in learning and retaining new information.

Several split-brain studies are quoted by Parkin (e.g., Zaidel & Sperry, 1974) in which the fornix was involved. Most patients performed normally on tests of memory, although a few showed mild memory deficits. When severe amnesia is reported after fornical damage, it is not clear to what extent other structures or processes have been involved. In some cases, an impediment is likely to have occurred because of damage around the third ventricle (Victor, cited in Sweet, Talland, & Ervin, 1959). An interesting case was reported by Hassler and Riechert (1957) of a patient who suffered right fornical damage with no memory loss. Following a left fornical lesion some 11 months later, however, he became amnesic. Unfortunately, this man only lived for 8 days after the operation, so it is possible (1) that the amnesia was transient and/or (2) that it was due to other residual effects of the surgery (e.g., bleeding, edema, or changes in intracranial pressure). Even in the case reported by Heilman and Sypert (1977) in which amnesia was said to follow a tumor in the fornix, leaving the hippocampus and diencephalon intact, it is possible that surgical procedures resulted in other impairments that could have been responsible for the memory impairment. Gade (1982) described a surgical procedure used for clipping anterior communicating artery aneurysms. The procedure did not implicate any of the structures normally associated with memory functioning, yet severe amnesia resulted in certain cases.

The conclusion to be drawn, therefore, is that lesions of the fornix do not seem to produce memory deficits of a comparable severity to those following damage to the hippocampus. Squire and Moore (1979), in a study of 50 cases where fornical damage was reported, found that memory loss occurred in only 3 of them.

The mammillary bodies, in contrast, do seem to be crucially involved in memory. These, together with the dorsomedial thalamic nuclei, are the most commonly reported structures involved in Korsakoff syndrome. Gudden (1896; quoted in Brierley, 1977) was probably the first to suggest that the mammillary bodies were implicated in the syndrome. Delay and Brion (1969) believe that the mammillary bodies are always involved, and Victor, Adams, and Collins (1971) believe that they are almost always involved. Mair, Warrington, and Weiskrantz (1979) state that, although large numbers of Korsakoff patients do show changes in the mammillary bodies, considerable variation in pathology is seen. In addition to alcoholic Korsakoff patients, amnesia has been reported in five cases of surgical lesions involving the mammillary bodies (Kahn & Crosby, 1972), and in a case of an intracerebral cyst that was pressing on these structures (Rizzo, 1955). Tumors in this area have also led to memory difficulties (Assal, Probst, Zander, & Rabinowicz, 1976). Thus, even though severe memory impairment can occur without the involvement of mammillary bodies, they do appear to be among the most critical structures in memory functioning.

The fourth structure involved in amnesia is the thalamus. One of the largest studies carried out on the Wernicke–Korsakoff syndrome was by Victor et al. (1971). The authors found that the dorsomedial nuclei of the thalamus was involved in 88% of the 43 cases examined. The pulvinar was the second most frequently damaged area of the thalamus. Other thalamic nuclei were also implicated, but to a lesser extent. One of the best-known cases of thalamic damage is N. A. (Teuber, Milner, & Vaughan, 1968). This man suffered a stab wound to the left dorsal thalamic region at the age of 22 years (Squire & Moore, 1979). Several cases of amnesia associated with thalamic tumors have also been described (e.g., McEntee, Biber, Perl, & Benson, 1976; Sprofkin & Sciarra, 1952). Lishman (1978) also reminds us that thalamic tumor can lead to rapidly developing dementia.

In addition to tumors associated with the thalamus, there are those associated with the third ventricle, also a part of the diencephalon. Williams and Pennybacker (1954) studied four such cases, all of whom showed an amnesic syndrome. Nielsen (1958), Angelergues

(1969), and Delay, Brion, and Derouesne (1964) all provide further evidence of amnesia associated with third-ventricle tumors.

The evidence presented in this section demonstrates that the medial temporal lobes, and the diencephalon, are both involved in human memory. Damage to either of these structures can result in the amnesic syndrome. Amnesia following diencephalic damage is more common, at least as far as Korsakoff patients are concerned (Victor et al., 1971). Within the diencephalon, the two most frequently affected structures are the mammillary bodies and the dorsomedial nuclei of the thalamus. There would appear to be little to choose between them with regard to their importance in memory. It is known that amnesia can follow lesions in either structure, but it is not yet known whether lesions in both structures result in more severe amnesia (Squire & Zola-Morgan, 1983).[1]

SPECIFIC DISORDERS GIVING RISE TO MEMORY IMPAIRMENT

The most frequent causes of permanent organic memory impairment are (1) chronic alcohol abuse; (2) head injury; (3) temporal lobe surgery; (4) encephalitis; (5) cerebral vascular disorder; (6) tumors; and (7) degenerative disorders. Cerebral damage may be focal or diffuse in all of these afflictions.

Chronic Alcohol Abuse

Chronic alcohol abuse may give rise to the Wernicke–Korsakoff syndrome. Wernicke encephalopathy is an acute reaction to severe thiamine deficiency (Lishman, 1978). The symptoms include ocular-motor abnormalities, ataxia of gait, confusion, and disorientation. It is commonly associated with alcohol abuse, but it can also result from carcinoma of the stomach, or can even follow severe malnutrition. Originally, the connection between Wernicke encephalopathy and Korsakoff syndrome was not recognized, but by 1956 Malamud and Skillicorn had demonstrated that Wernicke and Korsakoff patients

---

1. While knowledge of these structures is potentially important for rehabilitation, it is not directly relevant to the rehabilitation reported later in this book.

only differed in the acuteness or chronicity of disorder, with Korsakoff syndrome being the residual and often permanent effect. Wernicke encephalopathy, therefore, is now seen as a precursor of the Korsakoff syndrome.

Korsakoff first described the syndrome, in which the central feature is severe amnesia, in 1887 (cited in Victor et al., 1971). The disorder is one of the most frequent causes of amnesia, and is probably the most studied. It differs from confusional states in that there is clarity of consciousness and intact perception (Hecaen & Albert, 1978). Unlike demented patients, Korsakoffs show relatively intact intellectual functioning as measured by standard tests of intelligence (Talland, 1965). Striking personality changes are often reported. Butters (1979), for example, states: "Regardless of the patient's premorbid personality, he is extremely passive, malleable and emotionally flat in the chronic Korsakoff state" (p. 453).

The nature of the memory deficit in the Korsakoff population has been extensively examined (Butters, 1984; Butters & Cermak, 1976; Cermak & Butters, 1973). Although the core features are present, differences between Korsakoffs and other amnesics have been demonstrated. For example, Butters (1984) compared Korsakoff patients with patients suffering from Huntington disease. The memory quotient (MQ) levels were similar in both groups, but dramatic differences were noticed in procedural-learning tasks: Korsakoffs were able to acquire and retain mirror-reading skills, while Huntington patients found this very difficult; and in recognition tasks, Huntingtons approached normality while Korsakoffs were impaired.

Differences have also been reported in the length of RA, with relatively circumscribed RA following temporal lobectomy and more extensive RA seen in Korsakoff patients (Parkin, 1984). However, the evidence for this is inconclusive, and one reported patient (Wilson, 1982) had a considerable RA of some 12 or more years prior to stroke. This patient did not appear to have diencephalic damage. Short-term memory (STM) deficits have been found in Korsakoff patients (Kinsbourne & Wood, 1975; Piercy, 1978) but not in other amnesics (Baddeley & Warrington, 1970). Increased sensitivity to interference is also widely reported (Butters, 1979), although Mair et al. (1979) reported two exceptions to this. Their Korsakoff patients were able to perform very well on the Peterson task. Finally, differences have been reported in frontal lobe signs. Squire (1982) gave a group of Korsakoff patients three tests for detecting frontal lobe damage: the Wisconsin

Card Sorting Test (Milner, 1963); the word fluency test (Benton, 1968); and the Embedded Figures Test (Corkin, 1979). The Korsakoff patients showed impaired scores on all tests. The scores correlated well with release from proactive inhibition (i.e., interference from previously encountered material). Watkins (1975) has demonstrated that Korsakoffs fail to show release from proactive inhibition. Thus, failure to show release from proactive inhibition may represent an underlying frontal lobe dysfunction—a finding supported by the work of Moscovitch (1982), who demonstrated that nonamnesic patients with a unilateral frontal lobotomy also failed to show release from proactive inhibition. In contrast, H. M. (Milner *et al.*, 1968) performed normally on frontal lobe tasks, as did Cermak's (1976) postencephalitic patient, S. S.

There would, then, appear to be differences between Korsakoff patients and other amnesics. However, the picture may not be as clear-cut as the literature reported above suggests. Korsakoff patients vary considerably in the nature and extent of their cognitive deficits. Victor *et al.* (1971) showed that in a group of Korsakoffs, several different cerebral structures may be involved, and Mair *et al.* (1979) found normal performance on the Peterson task. Findings that performance is normal on general intelligence tests are also open to question, as two Korsakoff patients tested by me showed an abnormal verbal–performance discrepancy on the Wechsler Adult Intelligence Scale (WAIS) (Wechsler, 1955).

Head Injury

The earliest known scientific document is believed to be the Edwin Smith Surgical Papyrus, found by Smith in Luxor in 1862 (K. Walsh, 1978). The papyrus is between 2500 and 3000 years old, and contains 48 case descriptions of treatment. Eight of these cases refer to head injuries, and it is apparent that the physician recognized that head injury could affect other parts of the body. More recently, Schacter and Crovitz (1977) mention 19th-century reports of memory impairment following CHI. Lishman (1978) states that amnesia is much less common after crushing or penetrating injury than after CHI, due, he believes, to the lesser likelihood of shearing stress occurring throughout the brain. The sequelae resulting from head injury may be due both to direct physical damage to the brain, and to secondary factors, such as vascular disturbance, anoxia, and cerebral edema. In addition, penetrating injury may give rise to intracranial infection. The amount of direct physical damage sustained depends on the kind of injury the individual receives. CHI is probably the most common type of injury (Lishman, 1978), and factors determining the nature and extent of the damage include whether or not the head was free at impact, and the direction, force, and velocity of the blow. In cases where the head is at rest, the maximal damage will be at the site of impact; in cases where the head is moving, the "contrecoup" effect (i.e., damage to the side opposite to the point of impact) is likely to be the most pronounced (Bloomquist & Courville, 1947).

Contrecoup effects are particularly likely to occur in the temporal and orbital regions, and may result in loss of neurons, followed at a later stage by areas of subcortical demyelination. Minute lesions in the corpus callosum are also reported (Oppenheimer, 1968).

Both acceleration and deceleration injuries lead to swirling movements throughout the brain, with rotational and linear tearing causing damage to nerve fibers. Vascular damage can result in widespread, small hemorrhages and areas of infarction throughout the brain. These may be caused by rises in intracranial pressure, spasm of blood vessels, embolism, and hypotension. Bleeding may occur into the cerebrum itself, or into the subarachnoid space, leading to intracerebral, subdural, or extradural hematomas. Cerebral edema or swelling may occur, causing raised intracranial pressure, and anoxia can cause lesions in Ammon's horn (in the temporal lobes) and in the basal ganglia. If the patient survives, there may be cerebral atrophy, distortion of brain tissue, enlargement of the ventricles, and various other permanent changes (Lishman, 1978).

Both focal and diffuse effects may contribute to memory disorder following head injury. Lishman believes that the temporal lobes are particularly vulnerable, being "tightly enclosed in a bony framework," with the result that the medial temporal structures may be liable to "disproportionate damage when the brain is set in sudden motion" (1978, p. 193). In the majority of cases, permanent severe memory impairment, with intact functioning in other areas, does not occur. When it does, it is reasonable to suppose that focal damage has occurred. Diffuse damage may, if severe, lead to posttraumatic dementia, with general intellectual impairment (Joynt & Shoulson, 1979).

Following head injury, there is a period of impaired consciousness, then a period of confusion and impaired memory known as "posttraumatic amnesia" (PTA). Length of coma and PTA have both been correlated with degree of recovery (Evans, 1981). PTA may be defined as "the time from the moment of injury to the time of resumption of normal continuous memory" (Lishman, 1978, p. 201). During this period the patient is confused and disoriented. RA is present, and there is impairment in the ability to store and retrieve new information.

One of the main problems in studying PTA is the lack of agreed-upon criteria for assessing its presence or absence. W. R. Russell (1932), for instance, asked the patient, "When did you 'wake up'?" That is, "When did you stop being confused and start to remember coherently?" In 1946, W. R. Russell and Nathan were of the opinion that the patient is usually able to date the time from which continuous memory is present. Schacter and Crovitz (1977) believe the idea of continuous memory to be important, because recovery from PTA may be sporadic, with "islands" of normal memory functioning interspersed with confusion. Other authors have used "PTA" synonymously with "coma" (e.g., Klove & Cleeland, 1972). Still others have differentiated between disorientation and amnesia in the posttraumatic period (B. E. Moore & Ruesch, 1944). Sisler and Penner (1975) have argued that there are three distinct components of PTA: namely, disorientation, anterograde amnesia (AA), and RA. It would appear that PTA does not necessarily begin at the moment of injury. In a study of American footballers, Yarnell and Lynch (1973) questioned four players who were concussed during play. When questioned immediately following the blow, all realized what had happened to them, and three of them could describe the situation of the game immediately preceding the blow. When questioned again between 3 and 20 minutes later, all had forgotten this information. This suggests that information was registered but was not consolidated or retrieved appropriately.

When RA after head injury is temporary, it will shrink with recovery. Temporary RA often begins with a memory loss extending over a period of weeks, months, or years prior to the injury. Permanent RA, on the other hand, may extend for as little as a few seconds or minutes. In very severe head injury, however, the permanent RA may also cover weeks or months before the trauma. W. R. Russell (1932) reported a good correlation between length of unconsciousness and length of RA, but did not undertake a statistical analysis. Sisler and Penner (1975) provided evidence to suggest that the unidirectional shrinkage of RA may not always occur: In a sample of 24 CHI patients, 5 showed no change in RA, 8 showed shrinkages, 5 showed increases, and 6 showed both increases and shrinkages. Informal interviews with CHI patients at Rivermead suggest that such variability is not uncommon. As with PTA, measurement of RA is not consistent across studies. Indeed, tools for measuring RA are rather sparse, and all have limitations (Squire & Cohen, 1982).

With regard to permanent memory impairment following head injury, the best predictor would appear to be length of PTA. W. R. Russell and Nathan (1946) found a positive correlation between PTA and permanent RA. W. R. Russell and Smith (1961) demonstrated that 56% of patients with a PTA of more than 7 days developed a memory or calculation defect, while only 8% of patients with PTA of less than an hour did so. Brooks (1972, 1974) found that the relationship between PTA and memory impairment depended upon the age of the patients. Another factor that appears to be influential is the amount of time that has passed between the injury and the actual testing. E. Smith (1974) found no correlation between PTA and memory performance on the Wechsler Memory Scale (Wechsler, 1945) in a large group of CHI patients when she tested them 10–20 years after injury. In contrast, Klove and Cleeland (1972) found there was a significant correlation when testing was carried out within months of head injury. Brooks (1972, 1974) tested patients between 6 and 12 months after injury. However, the case for correlations being found after relatively early testing is not a straightforward one. Dailey (1956), Wowern (1966), and Norrman and Svahn (1961) all tested CHI patients several years after injury and were able to find an effect of length of PTA. Schacter and Crovitz (1977) suggest that these discrepancies may result from differences in measuring PTA, from the presence of focal damage in some samples and the absence of focal damage in others, and from differential effects caused by variations in age.

The percentage of patients left with memory impairment once PTA has ended varies considerably from one study to another. About 36% of the patients studied by W. R. Russell (1932) were described as having defects of memory, but information is not provided on the memory assessments given. W. R. Russell and Smith (1961), in a much larger study, reported memory deficits in 23% of the patients, but, again, no descriptions of assessment procedures were provided. Bennett-Levy (1982) found that impairment consistently occurred when PTA was greater than 3 weeks, but rarely occurred with shorter periods of PTA. Subjective reports of memory problems have ranged from 10% in children (Klonoff & Paris, 1974) to 16% in adults (Lidvall, Linderoth, & Norlin, 1974). In more recent studies that have included subjective reports, Sunderland, Harris, and Baddeley (1983) found that head-injured patients were not as good as their relatives in reporting memory failures, and McKinlay and Brooks (1984) also found discrepancies between patients' and relatives' subjective assessments of impaired memory. The question of assessment of memory functioning is considered in Chapter 5. It is sufficient to state here that even if only 10% of CHI patients are left with memory impairments, this results in large numbers in the community—given that some 100,000 people receive head injuries each year in the United Kingdom alone. (For readers interested in more detailed accounts of head injury, three recent books are recommended. These are by Brooks, 1984; E. Miller, 1984; and Levin, Benton, and Grossman, 1982.)

Temporal Lobe Surgery

The evidence of severe amnesia following bilateral temporal lobectomy comes from the work of Milner and her colleagues in Montreal (Milner, 1966, 1970; Penfield & Milner, 1958; Scoville & Milner, 1957). H. M., and eight other patients who underwent this operation, were studied. The researchers suggest that it is the subcortical part of the temporal lobe—namely, the anterior section of the hippocampus—that is the crucial area, as amnesia does not result from lesions involving the uncus or the amygdala, provided the hippocampus is spared.

Unilateral temporal lobectomies lead to material-specific memory impairments, as noted earlier (see p. 16). Left temporal lobectomy patients have greater difficulty learning and retaining verbal material, such as paired associates, prose passages, or Hebb's recurring digit sequences (Milner, 1971). Electrical stimulation of patients awaiting unilateral temporal lobectomy has also resulted in material-specific deficits (Fedio & Van Buren, 1974). Stimulation of the left temporal lobe leads to a number of naming errors in addition to impaired recall. The interesting finding in this study was that two areas were found within the left temporal lobe that produced two different kinds of memory deficit. Stimulation of the anterior section resulted in AA, while stimulation of the posterior section produced an RA. Thus, if the anterior portion was stimulated while the patient was correctly naming a picture, the patient would often be unable to recall this picture on a later trial without stimulation. Conversely, stimulation of the posterior section of the temporal lobe resulted in problems in recalling a picture presented on the *preceding* trial, also without stimulation.

Patients with unilateral right temporal lobectomies are usually unimpaired on verbal tasks, but have difficulty (compared to patients with left temporal lobectomies) in knowing whether or not they have seen a geometric shape before (Kimura, 1963), and in learning visual or tactile mazes (Corkin, 1965; Milner, 1965). Similar deficits have been found with recognition of tonal patterns (Milner, 1967) and recognition of faces (Milner, 1968). The severity of all these deficits has ben found to correlate with the extent of hippocampal lesions (Milner, 1974). Lesions that involve the amygdala, the uncus, and the neocortex, but do not involve the hippocampus (or involve very little of it), do not cause noticeable defects on verbal or nonverbal tasks.

With regard to the nature of the memory impairment in cases of bilateral hippocampal damage, there have been no reports of confabulation or poor insight (Parkin, 1984), but differing reports as to the extent of RA. Milner *et al.* (1968), for example, claimed that H. M. had an RA for 2–3 years prior to surgery. However, Corkin, Cohen, and Sagar (1983) have re-examined H. M.'s retrograde deficit, and report a milder deficit extending back a further 8 years and into his school days. Sagar (personal communication) reported that in a test of autobiographical memory, H. M. was unable to recall one event after the age of 16 years, the time at which his severe epilepsy developed. The operation occurred when H. M. was 27 years old. Events prior to the age of 16 years were recalled much more readily. Milner (1959), reporting on other bilateral temporal lobectomies, described an RA for 4 years in one case and 3 months in another. However, the problems in assessing RA apply here as much as they do with regard to head-injured patients. AA is, of course, present and severe in bilateral temporal lobectomies involving the hippocampi, but performance on immediate memory tasks, such as digit span, is apparently normal (Prisko, 1963).

Encephalitis

Encephalitis is an inflammation of the brain caused by a virus. If meningeal irritation is also present, then the disease is sometimes called meningoencephalitis. Several types of encephalitis exist (see Robbins, 1958, for a description of these); however, for the purposes of this volume, the relevant varieties are the sporadic virus infections of the central nervous system (e.g., herpes simplex and herpes zoster) and postinfection encephalitis (e.g., that following influenza or vacci-nation). The typical picture of most forms of encephalitis is of a rapidly developing illness, with headache, prostration, vomiting, and irritabil-ity. Impaired consciousness is usually encountered, although this may range from mild sleepiness to deep coma (Lishman, 1978). Delirium and epilepsy are common in some varieties. Focal neurological signs vary greatly, depending on the major site of inflammation. (For exam-ple, if the brain stem is the most affected area, then quadriplegia and dysarthria may well result; however, when the main site of infection is the temporal lobes, then a classic amnesic syndrome may be observed.) In some cases, no residual effects may be seen. In others, permanent sequelae range from mild neurological signs to severe global intellectual impairment. Of six postencephalitic patients treated at Rivermead in a 2-year period, there were two with severe global intellectual impair-ment, two with quadriplegia and dysarthria but with no noticeable cognitive deficits, one with moderate memory impairment, and one with an amnesic syndrome.

The etiology is often unknown. For example, the four posten-cephalitic amnesic patients reported by Rose and Symonds (1960) were of "a non-specified aetiology" (p. 15). However, the virus most often implicated in the human amnesic syndrome is herpes simplex, with its characteristic preference for the temporal lobes and orbital structures of the frontal lobes (Lishman, 1978). Herpes zoster virus can also lead to amnesia (P. Hall, 1963). It has been reported that herpes simplex produces massive lesions in the temporal lobes, including the hippocampus, while leaving the diencephalon reasonably unaffected (Brierley *et al.*, 1960; Davies, Davis, Kleinman, Kirchner, & Taveras, 1978; Drachman & Adams, 1962). Thus, one would expect amnesic deficits to be predominantly of the type found after temporal lobe surgery, and less like those seen in Korsakoff patients with dienceph-alic damage. Parkin (1984) provides support for this point of view. He has reviewed the literature and argues that postencephalitic amnes-ics do not confabulate, and have reasonable insight once the acute stage has passed. In this sense, they are more similar to the temporal lobectomy patients than to Korsakoffs. However, with regard to RA, the picture is not so straightforward. In the case of patient S. S., for instance, his RA was extensive and lasted as long as many Korsakoff patients. Another postencephalitic patient is reported with an RA of 30 years. The four patients reported by Rose and Symonds (1960) also showed long RAs, ranging from 3 to 16 years. In contrast, the postencephalitic patient to be described in Chapters 6 and 9, and previously reported by Baddeley and Wilson (1983), had an RA of only 2 years.

AA would appear to vary among postencephalitic amnesics. Cermak and O'Connor (1983) found that S. S. was unable to retain anything beyond the limits of his STM. Procedures such as chunking enabled S. S. to increase his working memory, but once this was surpassed, retrieval of information was virtually impossible. L'Hermitte and Signoret (1972) compared a group of 10 Korsakoff patients with 3 postencephalitic patients. The Korsakoffs were able to reach criterion on an object- and position-learning test within 20 trials. Two of the three postencephalitic patients failed to reach criterion in this period. Furthermore, the errors made by the postencephalitics were different in that they tended to forget the objects, while the Korsakoffs tended to place the object in the wrong position. One of the postencephalitics, however, learned as readily as the Korsakoffs, although she forgot much more rapidly than they did. Such variability is hardly surprising, given the nature of the disease, which is sometimes extensive and may include diencephalic structures (Brierley et al., 1960).

In STM tasks, some postencephalitic patients perform better than some Korsakoffs. This was demonstrated with S. S. (Cermak, 1976), a patient of Starr and Phillips (1970), and three other postencephalitic patients (Butters & Cermak, 1980). S. S. also showed less sensitivity to interference than Korsakoffs (Cermak, 1976), and showed a normal release from proactive inhibition, unlike Korsakoffs (Cermak & O'Connor, 1983). The postencephalitic patient (Baddeley & Wilson, 1983), though, did not show normal release from proactive inhibition. However, it is surely dangerous to generalize too far from what has been a relatively small number of postencephalitic amnesics. Given that herpes simplex can attack other parts of the brain in addition to the temporal lobes, then there may well be postencephalitic patients showing a wide variety of cognitive deficits in general, and memory impairments in particular.

Cerebral Vascular Disorders

The two main kinds of cerebral vascular disorders are those resulting from hemorrhage and those resulting from infarction, or blocking of the vessels. The term "stroke" is used for both these processes, and refers to "a focal neurological disorder of abrupt development and due to a pathological process in the blood vessels" (Lishman, 1978, p. 451). Hemorrhages may be intracerebral, or may occur in the subarachnoid space. Infarction may be due to thrombosis of the cerebral blood vessels, or to emboli that lodge in them.

From the point of view of the human amnesic syndrome, three types of CVA are considered: (1) infarction of the posterior cerebral arteries; (2) subarachnoid hemorrhage; and (3) infarction associated with transient global amnesia.

Infarction of the Posterior Cerebral Arteries

Infarction of the posterior cerebral arteries leading to amnesia was reported by Victor et al. (1961). The patient was functioning at an above-average level of intelligence overall, but demonstrated "a profound defect in recent memory and inability to learn new facts and skills . . . He also showed an incomplete retrograde amnesia, covering the two year period prior to the onset of his illness" (p. 261). The memory deficits remained for 5 years, until the patient died. A postmortem showed old bilateral infarctions in the inferomedial portions of the temporal lobes. Several other cases with postmortem evidence of bilateral infarctions in the posterior cerebral arteries have been reported since (e.g., Boudin, Brion, Pepin, & Barbizet, 1968; Dejong, Itabashi, & Olson, 1969). D. F. Benson, Marsden, and Meadows (1974) reported the acute onset of amnesia in 10 patients associated with bilateral or unilateral visual-field defects and infarctions in the posterior cerebral arteries.

Visual-field defects appear to be prevalent, and were also present in the case reported in Chapter 7. D. F. Benson et al. (1974) questioned whether amnesia could result from a unilateral infarction. This had been suggested, for example, by Geschwind and Fusillo (1966), and Mohr, Leicester, Stoddard, and Sidman (1971), following damage to the left side only. However, K. Walsh (1978) believes this may have been due to testing procedures that emphasized verbal-memory tasks. Walsh describes a patient with a unilateral lesion who showed most of the features of the amnesic syndrome, but whose difficulty with verbal material was much more severe than with nonverbal material. Without neuropathological evidence, it is always possible that some impairment has been sustained by the supposedly unaffected hemisphere. D. F. Benson et al. (1974) felt that the evidence regarding unilateral damage and amnesia was insufficient to permit conclusions to be drawn. Patients who demonstrate amnesia without significant other deficits are seen infrequently.

Subarachnoid Hemorrhage

About 8% of cerebral vascular disorders are due to subarachnoid hemorrhage (Walton, 1971). Despite their small numbers, they are important because they tend to affect a younger age group who are less likely to suffer from more widespread cerebral vascular disease. The usual cause is rupture of an intercranial aneurysm, which bleeds into the subarachnoid space surrounding the brain. Sometimes a subarachnoid hemorrhage results from a ruptured angioma, but in some 15–20% no structural cause can be found at all (Walton, 1971). Aneurysms are usually found at the forks of cerebral arteries, and certain sites are more commonly involved than others. The anterior communicating artery is one site frequently associated with ruptured aneurysm. This lies between the frontal lobes and is close to the anterior hypothalamus. Other commonly involved sites are the middle cerebral artery and the posterior communicating artery. In most of the subarachnoid hemorrhages seen at Rivermead, the anterior communicating artery is involved. In addition to the hemorrhage, ischemia (restricted blood flow) may result from spasm or occlusion of associated vessels (Lishman, 1978).

Shortly after the hemorrhage, a picture resembling Korsakoff syndrome is sometimes seen, with disorientation, confabulation, and impaired memory. Walton (1953), for example, described several cases, some of which did not develop amnesia until several days or weeks following the hemorrhage. This may have been due to vascular spasm or to hydrocephalus developing (Theanders & Granholm, 1967). In Walton's cases, recovery was often abrupt. In their study of 56 survivors of subarachnoid hemorrhage, Theanders and Granholm found communicating hydrocephalus in five patients, four of whom had experienced severe memory impairment that often lasted months or even years. Three of these improved remarkably after having a shunt inserted. Thus, it would appear that memory impairment following subarachnoid hemorrhage may be either temporary or permanent. Sweet, Talland, and Ballantine (1966) and Talland, Sweet, and Ballantine (1967) have reported persistent memory impairment following operations on the aneurysms. Operations are performed to tie the neck of the aneurysm in an attempt to prevent further hemorrhaging. Gade (1982) followed patients who had been operated on for anterior communicating artery aneurysms and found that one particular operative procedure was very likely to produce an amnesic syndrome, while a more common operative procedure rarely led to this syndrome.

Infarction Associated with Transient Global Amnesia

In 1956, Bender described an isolated episode of confusion with amnesia. Since then, several cases of transient global amnesia have been reported (Fisher & Adams, 1964; Patten, 1971; Shuttleworth & Wise, 1973; R. S. Wilson, Koller, & Kelly, 1980). Transient global amnesia is almost certainly due to a cerebral vascular cause, the symptoms and signs being characteristic. There is sudden onset after the patient has usually been well. The episode may begin with a brief clouding of consciousness, which soon passes (Hecaen & Albert, 1978). The amnesia is the central feature, with both RA and AA being observed. The episode typically lasts for several hours, although in some cases this may be longer, and ends in complete recovery. The RA may cover a period of only a few hours, or may last for several weeks. This shrinks, however, leaving only a brief RA on recovery. Insight is believed to be good, even during the attack; speech remains unimpaired; and few abnormalities have been noted. There have been few neuropsychological studies carried out during episodes of transient global amnesia, probably because most people recover before this can be arranged. However, R. S. Wilson et al. (1980) were able to conduct some neuropsychological assessment. Their patients had a transient RA for events of the previous day, and a patchy RA for the previous 2–3 years. A profound AA was noted, but STM was spared. There have been few anatomical studies, as most patients survive, but clinical investigations (Heathfield, Croft, & Swash, 1973) suggest that transient global amnesia results from bilateral temporal or thalamic lesions, due to ischemia in the posterior cerebral arteries. From the point of view of rehabilitation, patients with transient global amnesia are not seen, as they recover spontaneously. Some, however, may proceed to suffer a full-blown CVA (Whitty & Lishman, 1966).

There is too little evidence from stroke patients to compare the nature of their deficits with those of Korsakoffs, patients with temporal lobectomies, or postencephalitic amnesics, although the patient described in Chapter 7 did not confabulate, had reasonable insight, normal STM, extensive RA, and a profound AA.

Tumors

"Tumor" is a general term referring to any abnormal swelling. "Cerebral tumors" usually refers to a neoplasm or new growth (K. Walsh, 1978). Intellectual deficits are commonly noticed in patients, and may be steadily progressive or may fluctuate from one occasion to another (Lishman, 1978). Focal changes are observed more frequently than in generalized dementia because of the nature of the lesions. The type of deficit will depend on (1) intracranial pressure; (2) the nature of the tumor; (3) the location of the tumor; and (4) the individual's response to the tumor. Raised intracranial pressure is responsible for many of the symptoms (Brain, 1963) and for fluctuating levels of consciousness. Malignant tumors, such as gliomas, typically lead to greater cognitive impairment than benign tumors, such as meningiomas. Tumors in the third ventricle are particularly likely to result in an amnesic syndrome (Williams & Pennybacker, 1954). Premorbid personality is also likely to determine how an individual will respond to the situation.

Frontal lobe tumors are likely to be mistaken for dementia (Sachs, 1950), particularly when both lobes are involved and the tumor develops in the midline (Strauss & Keschner, 1935). Memory impairment may also be seen in isolation. Hecaen and Ajuriaguerra (1956), for example, found amnesia in 70 out of 80 frontal tumor cases. Lack of insight is characteristic in frontal patients (Lishman, 1978), and therefore frontal amnesics are comparable to Korsakoff and other diencephalic amnesics in this respect. Patients with corpus callosum tumors are also likely to show severe memory impairment (Selecki, 1964), with a rapid progression to general intellectual deficits. General impairment is also commonly seen in temporal lobe tumors, although one reported patient (see Wilson, 1981b, and Chapter 6, this volume) had been treated for a left temporal lobe tumor, which resulted in a severe but specific verbal-memory deficit. Parietal tumors are less likely to result in impaired memory (Keschner, Bender, & Strauss, 1938), although other cognitive deficits are frequently observed (e.g., unilateral neglect and dysphasia), depending on which hemisphere is more affected. Occipital tumors can also lead to memory disturbances

(Keschner *et al.*, 1938). The percentages of patients showing impairment of memory following tumors in different lobes in the Keschner *et al.* study were as follows: frontal, 50%; temporal, 57%; parietal, 25%; and occipital, 45%.

Tumors of the third ventricle are frequently associated with amnesia. Sprofkin and Sciarra (1952) reported three cases presenting with a Korsakoff syndrome but without a history of alcohol abuse. Williams and Pennybacker (1954), in a large study of 180 cerebral tumors, found that over half the patients with marked memory impairment had tumors involving the third ventricle. This group included the four with the classic amnesic syndrome described in the section on localization studies. A further 32 patients with diencephalic and third-ventricle tumors were studied by Williams and Pennybacker, and these were compared with a group having tumors in the posterior fossa in an attempt to control for the effects of raised intracranial pressure. The former group continued to show a greater incidence of memory disorders.

Tumors of the posterior fossa (e.g., the cerebellum, cerebellopontine angle, and brain stem) are less likely to result in cognitive deficits than those tumors described above, unless the raised intracranial pressure is such that hydrocephalus occurs (Lishman, 1978). Of the patients treated for memory impairment at Rivermead, tumor patients are the third most common group, following those with head injuries and CVAs. This does not reflect the frequency of occurrence in the general population. In the U.S., for example, a higher proportion of patients would suffer memory impairments following alcohol abuse.

Degenerative Disorders

The most frequently encountered degenerative disorders are the dementias. "Dementia" can be defined as abnormal loss of intellectual functioning. Thus, it covers several diagnostic disorders, including severe head injury, encephalitis, and multi-infarct disorder. However, in this section the term "dementia" is used for progressive degenerative disorders—in particular, Alzheimer disease, Pick disease, and Huntington chorea. These are described only briefly, for none of the patients described in this book suffered from progressive brain damage.

Alzheimer disease is the most common of the progressive dementias, and is found in some 10% of the population over 65 years old

(Joynt & Shoulson, 1979). Alzheimer disease and senile dementia are indistinguishable; whether the disease occurs before or after the age of 65 years, the same senile plaques and neurofibrillary tangles are observed (Walton, 1971). Often the earliest cognitive sign is memory impairment, although, as Geschwind (1975) has pointed out, there is great variability from one individual to another, and not all will show memory disorder. However, the picture of a typical Alzheimer patient is one that includes defects in orientation, judgment, memory, and abstract thinking (Joynt & Shoulson, 1979). These are often followed by a more rapid intellectual deterioration, and the appearance of symptoms indicating focal cerebral lesions. Parietal lobe signs are prominent—for example, disorders of language, praxis, and perception. In the final stages of the disease, Alzheimer patients are bedridden, doubly incontinent, and show a profound apathy (Lishman, 1978). Death follows from 2 to 5 years after onset. Although Alzheimer disease is primarily a cortical dementia, some subcortical involvement may be present.

Pick disease usually starts in the frontal lobes (Walton, 1971). It is less common than Alzheimer disease, and sometimes both are included under the one heading of Alzheimer. Early abnormalities often include changes of personality and social behavior rather than memory and intellect, although these will follow in due course. Some patients show perseverative speech, while others will become mute. The spatial and apraxic deficits typically seen in Alzheimer disease are unlikely to be present in the early stages of Pick disease, although in time these develop, and the two groups of patients may become indistinguishable.

Huntington chorea is an inherited disorder that usually begins to manifest itself when patients are in their 40s, but there are wide individual variations. The characteristic features are slowing of thought and motor performance, with memory impairment (M. L. Albert, Feldman, & Willis, 1974), facial grimacing, and uncontrollable movements. These movements typically precede the dementia by several years, although it is not unknown for the cognitive deficits to occur first (Lishman, 1978). The caudate nuclei and subcortical structures are involved to a greater extent in Huntington than in Alzheimer or Pick disease (Joynt & Shoulson, 1979). Psychotic disorders may also become apparent; both manic–depressive psychosis and schizophrenic-like hallucinations have been reported in Huntington patients (McHugh & Folstein, 1975). Language is likely to be intact for a much longer period than in the cortical dementias, although dysarthria is not uncommon. Memory defects are found, however, in keeping with other forms of dementia. AA is often the most prominent cognitive deficit in recently diagnosed Huntington patients (Butters, Sax, Montgomery, & Tarlow, 1978). M. S. Albert, Butters, and Brandt (1981) have also reported striking differences in the RA of Huntington and Korsakoff patients. The former showed a long RA without a temporal gradient; that is, they were equally affected for all time periods sampled. The Korsakoffs, on the other hand, did show a temporal gradient, with earlier memories being selectively spared. M. S. Albert *et al.* also found that the RA deficit was present in recently diagnosed patients, as well as those in whom the disease had been present for some years.

Joynt and Shoulson (1979) state that the rate of intellectual decline is slower in Huntington disease than it is in Alzheimer or Pick disease. Even so, the final result is similar, with the exception of preserved language in the Huntington group.

Conclusion

The seven diagnostic groups of patients discussed in this section are not the only people in whom memory impairment may be found. Those with cerebral anoxia (e.g., resulting from cardiac arrest, cyanide poisoning, anesthetic accidents, etc.) are also at high risk of such impairment. Patients undergoing electroconvulsive therapy (ECT) show both AA and RA. Survivors of carbon monoxide poisoning can be left with profound cognitive impairment, and malnutrition can also result in memory impairment. Nevertheless, the main groups have been described, and all the patients to be referred to later in this book fall into one or other of these categories, with the exception of two subjects in Chapter 10 who became amnesic after anoxic episodes following cardiac arrest.

NEUROPSYCHOLOGICAL ASSESSMENT

In assessing a brain-damaged individual, the neuropsychologist may be investigating deficiencies of language, memory, perception, reasoning, emotion, planning, and self-control. It is in such areas that brain damage manifests itself (Lezak, 1976). Yates (1966) has pointed out that brain damage may result in a general deterioration of all aspects of functioning; in a differential effect, where some abilities will be impaired more than others; or in a highly specific effect, depending on the nature, site, and extent of the damage. The emphasis of assessment in neuropsychology has been intellectual, and, according to Lezak, "Out of all these data have evolved numerous reliable and well-standardized techniques for identifying, defining, grading, measuring, and comparing the spectrum of intellectual behaviors" (1976, p. 71). K. Walsh (1978) would not appear to agree wholeheartedly with her. He quotes several authors who point out some of the failings of neuropsychological tests. Heilbrun (1962), for example, believes that too many tests are validated on populations known to have neurological impairment, rather than cases where the diagnosis is uncertain at the time the tests are administered. For predictive validity, it is necessary to do prospective rather than retrospective studies.

Kinsbourne (1972) points out that the practice of using impaired test performance to diagnose a specific behavioral deficit is unhelpful and can be misleading, because it has been observed that many kinds of deficit are capable of producing a similar test score. Poor scores on digit span tasks, for example, could be due to impaired STM, dysphasis, anxiety, or even impaired hearing. A. D. Smith (1975) gives another example when he refers to the Digit–Symbol subtest of the WAIS. In order to complete this test, it is necessary to integrate visual–perceptual, ocular–motor, fine motor, and cognitive skills. Low scores on this test could be due to an impairment of any one of these skills, or to a combination of any number of them. Elithorn (1965) suggests yet another problem with neuropsychological assessment when he states that too many tests are concerned with whether or not the subject can reach the goal, rather than on how the subject approaches the task, or by how much or how little the subject fails to reach the goal. Lezak (1976) says that brain damage always implies behavioral impairment, although A. Smith (1962) has drawn attention to the fact that sometimes neurological lesions are revealed after death, although they were totally unsuspected during life. However, as K. Walsh (1978) points out, such patients might have been diagnosed during life had they been subjected to the appropriate assessment procedures. As neuropsychology has grown, it has been able to detect impairment in more and more areas of the brain.

However, the idea of brain damage as a unitary concept still persists. K. Walsh (1978) suggests that it is naive to expect single or simple tests to determine whether or not brain damage has occurred.

Given that brain damage covers lesions of different sizes and different etiologies in different locations, then a more comprehensive and sophisticated assessment should be undertaken. In cognitive rehabilitation, it is necessary to have as clear and accurate a picture as possible of the patient's cognitive strengths and weaknesses, as both the treatment technique chosen and the response to treatment will be influenced by these findings. Patient O. E., for example, (to be described in Chapter 6) had a severe face-recognition problem that hampered his ability to remember names of people. C. M., however (also to be described in Chapter 6), had a very specific verbal-memory deficit, but good perceptual and other cognitive abilities. Different treatment procedures were necessary for these individuals. The assessment of memory itself is, of course, also extremely important, and this is dealt with in Chapter 5.

How does one decide whether or not performance on a test is normal? Lezak (1976) describes several comparison standards, falling into two main categories—namely, "normative" (i.e., derived from a population) or "individual" (i.e., derived from the patient's history or present characteristics). Normative comparison standards would include (1) the population average (e.g., in the WAIS, one can compare an individual's score with others of a similar age in the general population); (2) species-wide performance (e.g., we would expect all normal 2- and 3-year-old children to talk in two- and three-word phrases, and all normal adults to be able to locate a touch on the skin); and (3) customary standards, which are normative standards that have been set arbitrarily (e.g., 20-20 vision). A customary standard is not an average, but it is met or surpassed by different percentages of people, depending on age.

Normative standards are widely used in psychology, particularly in the measurement of intellectual functioning and educational achievement. The disadvantages of such a comparison standard, however, arise when a patient shows a decline from a previously normal level of competence. Normative comparisons in such a case provide little or no information about the pattern or extent of the impairment. A previously normal reader, for example, may, following a stroke, score below the first percentile in comparison with other adults; however, this statement does not describe the nature of the reading impairment at all. The patient may comprehend words but may not be able to read aloud; he or she may have an acquired dyslexic syndrome, such as deep dyslexia (in which semantic errors are frequent and the reader has greater difficulty in reading verbs or prepositions than in reading nouns) or surface dyslexia (which is an impairment in reading irregular words). A further difficulty with using an average score for the population as the comparison standard is that half the general population does *not* perform in the average range. Thus, unless one knows how the brain-damaged person performed prior to the brain damage, it is meaningless to compare that person to the general population. If the patient performs at the 50th percentile, it will not be known whether this suggests no impairment or a significant degree of impairment.

Individual comparison standards are usually more appropriate when one is interested in determining whether or not a psychological skill has changed. This can be done by administering tests to the same individual on different occasions and comparing the test scores on each occasion. Provided that adequate information exists about practice effects, or that satisfactory alternative forms are available, this procedure may be helpful in detecting changes, although sometimes such test procedures only reveal gross alterations.

In addition to comparison standards, skills or functions can be assessed in different ways. Direct assessment of the skill may be the procedure of choice. For example, testing a person's ability to cook a meal can be assessed by simply getting that person to cook a meal. This requires normative standards in order to know whether the cooking of the meal is indeed normal or "impaired." Another direct measurement technique is the "before-and-after" assessment. Such a procedure might be adopted, for instance, to test a person before and after a temporal lobectomy. There is less need for normative standards here, as the comparisons can be made between the two sets of results. It is rarely the case, however, that premorbid information is available. Indirect measurement is usually required in order to assess premorbid ability, and sometimes common sense can be employed to achieve this end. For example, it would be reasonable to assume that a university lecturer was of above-average premorbid intelligence. However, this could not be assumed in the case of a truck driver, who might have had above-average, average, or below-average intelligence prior to insult. Other indirect measures will then be needed.

Lezak (1976) puts forward some assumptions underlying the principle of indirect measurement of premorbid ability. She writes; "[T]he performance level of most normally developed, healthy persons on any single test of an intellectual function or skill probably provides a reasonable estimate of their performance level on all other kinds of intellectual tasks" (p. 77). The corollary assumption she adds is that any marked discrepancies between the levels of performance "are evidence of disease, developmental anomalies, cultural deprivation, emotional disturbance, or some other condition that has interfered with the full expression of that person's intellectual potential" (p. 77). Thus, marked discrepancies between performances on different tests of cognitive functioning may be seen as abnormal. It is probably dangerous to take this view too uncritically, for Field (1960) has shown that some individuals in the general population do show large discrepancies between verbal and performance scores (e.g., on the WAIS).

Given that a discrepancy arises, how should the premorbid level of functioning be estimated? Some tests exist to predict premorbid intellectual ability, such as the National Adult Reading Test (H. E. Nelson & O'Connell, 1978). This test is probably a good indicator, provided no developmental or acquired dyslexia is present. Jastak (1949) has argued that the least depressed abilities are the best remaining behavioral representatives of premorbid potential. No one would seriously argue that brain damage improves intellectual functioning, so the best performance from an individual may either be equal to or less than the premorbid level. If it is not possible to determine the premorbid level from existing material, then one can only estimate on the basis of the best score.

Selection of tests for the brain-damaged may also present problems. Many have sensory or motor handicaps, and some will be too severely intellectually impaired to be subjected to conventional test procedures. It is possible to devise or adapt tests for people who cannot speak, see, hear, or move. It is possible to allow extra time for someone with ataxia; to reposition material for someone with unilateral neglect; and to administer tests that are normally used with children or the mentally handicapped to those with severe intellectual impairment. The norms will not always be appropriate, and it may not be possible to answer the questions as accurately as one would wish. When this happens, the neuropsychologist may wish to use other assessment procedures. These are described in Chapter 4. The main questions to ask when administering a neuropsychological assessment in order to design a cognitive rehabilitation program are the following: What is the nature of the memory impairment; what other impairments does the particular person have that may affect response to treatment; and what cognitive strengths are present?

In cognitive remediation, it is usually more effective to use a person's strengths in order to bypass the weaknesses than it is to try to resolve the weaknesses themselves. The areas that will be of primary interest to the cognitive therapist (in addition to general intellectual functioning) are language, perception, and the functions attributed to the frontal lobes (which include self-regulation, planning, and problem solving). The presence or absence of these cognitive abilities will influence the nature of the memory impairments, the selection of intervention procedures, and the response to these treatment procedures.

·3·

COGNITIVE PSYCHOLOGY

THE NATURE OF HUMAN MEMORY

From the work of Ebbinghaus (1885/1964) to the present day, cognitive psychologists have devoted much attention to memory research. In spite of differences of opinion, there is considerable agreement about the structure of human memory (Baddeley, 1982b). Atkinson and Shiffrin (1968) proposed that memory could be divided into three broad categories: sensory memory, STM, and long-term memory (LTM). Although this system has proved to be oversimplified, it represents, nevertheless, a useful model that enables discussion to continue meaningfully.

Sensory Memory

The initial processing of information received by the sensory organs is presumed to be carried out by very brief sensory-memory stores (Craik, 1979). The store that has been studied in most detail is that dealing with vision, and is often known as "iconic memory" (see Coltheart, 1972, for a detailed description). The auditory equivalent, which has been studied in far less detail, is known as "echoic memory." No comparable memory store has been described for touch, taste, or smell. It would appear that iconic memory enables us to interpret a series of still frames as moving pictures. A visual image can be perceived if it is presented for a few milliseconds (Sperling, 1960), but it starts to decay shortly after this (Haber & Standing, 1969). It is not yet clear whether iconic memory is located in the eye itself—that is, in the retina or the rods (Sakitt, 1976)—or in the central nervous system (Craik, 1979). Echoic memory enables us to perceive speech sounds (Craik, 1979). Breakdown in either of these systems would almost certainly result in perceptual problems, causing difficulty in integrating or interpreting sensory information into meaningful data. As this book is primarily concerned with memory deficits, sensory memory is not discussed further here.

Short-Term Memory

STM is regarded as a limited-capacity, temporary store that holds information for a few seconds. Other terms that are sometimes used are "primary memory," "immediate memory," or "working memory." Baddeley (1984) suggests that "primary memory" should be used for the simple unitary system described by Atkinson and Shiffrin (1968), and that the term "working memory" should refer to a more complex set of interacting, temporary storage systems.

The evidence for separating STM and LTM comes from several sources. First, there appears to be two separate components of memory that can be elicited by certain tasks. One component is short-term and transient, while the other is long-term and more durable. A way of demonstrating the two components is to apply the free-recall test (see, e.g., the work of Postman & Phillips, 1965). If a list of unrelated words is presented for immediate recall and in any order, then the words presented early in the list tend to be recalled well (the primacy effect), and those presented last also tend to be recalled well (the recency effect). By delaying recall for 15 or 20 seconds, while at the same time preventing rehearsal through the use of a counting or subtracting task (Peterson, 1966), the recency effect can be abolished. The primacy effect, however, remains. This would support the idea of a distinction between the two stores. The items in the durable LTM store are unaffected, while the last few items (in the STM store) are forgotten. Further supporting evidence for this argument comes from other tasks that have no effect on recency but that enable the earlier items to be remembered more easily. For example, if words are read at a slower rate, the primacy effect is enhanced; familiar words and high-imagery words also lead to better recall. However, none of these tasks will influence the recency effect—that is, the STM store.

The second main source of evidence for the distinction between STM and LTM comes from differences in coding (Baddeley, 1982b). STM uses acoustic or articulatory coding, and LTM uses semantic coding (Baddeley, 1966; Conrad, 1964). Thus, in a short list presented for immediate recall, more errors will be made with words that sound alike than with words that sound dissimilar. However, if a longer list is presented, and a delay is introduced before recall, then meaning rather than sound becomes important, and more errors will be made among words with similar meanings. The third main source of evidence for the STM–LTM distinction comes from studies of amnesic patients, and discussion of this evidence is included in Chapter 2.

An additional question with regard to STM/primary memory has to do with whether or not this system is unitary. Atkinson and Shiffrin (1968) believed this to be so; they also believed that information could only enter the LTM store by way of the STM store. Several pieces of research in subsequent years have suggested that this is not, in fact, the case. For example, Atkinson and Shiffrin's model assumed that information was held in the temporary store primarily by subvocal rehearsal. The longer information was held in the STM store, the more likely it was to transfer to the durable LTM store. However, Craik and Watkins (1973) observed no relationship between rehearsal time and amount learned. Baddeley and Hitch (1974) also cast doubt on Atkinson and Shiffrin's model, which predicted that if a subject was asked to learn some material and given a second task to do at the same time, then the recency effect should be wiped out. This was because the STM store was of limited capacity and could only hold a small amount of material. In the Baddeley and Hitch experiment, however, subjects were given a telephone number to remember while learning a list of words. This impaired long-term learning but had no effect on recency. Finally, of course, if it is necessary for information to pass through STM before entering LTM, then patients with impaired STM should show abnormal long-term learning. A few people, however, show impaired STM as measured by digit span, but do not demonstrate a severe deficit in LTM (Shallice, 1979; Shallice & Warrington, 1970). As a result of these findings, Baddeley and Hitch decided to abandon the concept of a single, unitary primary-memory system in favor of an alliance of temporary storage systems, which they termed "working memory." This system is coordinated by a "central executive," which is served by a series of "slave" systems.

This executive appears to be a controller of attention and planning, with two of the most investigated slave systems consisting of the "articulatory loop" and the "visual–spatial scratch pad." The former is a system that uses subvocal speech, and is responsible for the acoustic characteristics of many STM tasks. This is probably the deficit responsible for K. F.'s (Shallice & Warrington, 1970) difficulty in repeating back digits. Impairments of the visual–spatial scratch pad have yet to be identified, but they are likely to manifest themselves in difficulty in performing spatial-memory tasks—for example, a block-tapping task such as that described by Milner (1972). Possibly, some of the features of the neglect syndrome may also be due to a deficit in the visual-spatial scratch pad. The unusual-views test described by Warrington (1982) could also depend on the visual–spatial scratch pad for adequate interpretation.

Baddeley (1984) suggests that the problems seen in patients with dementia together with frontal lobe damage (personal communication) represent a breakdown of working memory, but that in these cases it is due to a fault in the central executive.

LTM or Secondary Memory

Some of the characteristics of LTM have already been mentioned: It is a durable store, retaining information for varying periods of time, ranging from minutes to decades; it has large, possibly unlimited capacity; and it codes information prinicipally by meaning rather than by speech characteristics. Most of the patients described in this book showed LTM impairments. Like STM, LTM is not a unitary system. There are two broad distinctions that can be made; these are the distinctions between visual and verbal memory, and between semantic and episodic memory.

Visual and Verbal Memory

Few people would deny that we can remember things we cannot easily verbalize—for example, a particular person's face, or the sound of a certain musical instrument. Tastes and smells can also be remembered, although it would be difficult to describe these. Paivio (1969) and Yuille and Paivio (1967) have also demonstrated that imageability affects memory for words; that is, words that are difficult to picture or imagine (e.g., abstract words like "honesty" or "justice") are harder to remember in a recall task than words more easily imagined or pictured (e.g., concrete words like "spaceship" or "jungle"). They did, of course, control for frequency of use in language. These findings are cited as evidence for separate visual- and verbal-memory stores. Further evidence comes from neuropsychological studies. Milner (1971), for example, has demonstrated that unilateral left temporal damage leads to verbal-memory deficits, while unilateral right temporal damage is more likely to result in weakened memory for faces and designs.

Semantic and Episodic Memory

Tulving (1972) was the first to suggest that LTM consists of semantic and episodic memory. "Semantic memory" refers to memory for knowledge—for example, remembering that Chesapeake Bay retrievers are the only dogs with webbed feet; that the tallest dog is the Irish wolfhound; or that bananas are fruit. It is not necessary to remember when this information was acquired or who was present at the time. In contrast, "episodic memory" is much more autobiographical, and includes such things as remembering what one did last Christmas, or when one's last credit card bill was paid. It is usually much more important to remember the particular occasion during which an event occured. Initially, one probably has to rely on episodic memory in order for information to enter semantic memory, but eventually (probably after a wide range of experiences) the information becomes part of one's semantic-memory system. Amnesic patients would appear to have impaired episodic memory (e.g., Baddeley, 1982a; Kinsbourne & Wood, 1975) and intact semantic memory (Baddeley & Warrington, 1970). However, it is not possible to increment the semantic memory of amnesics without a great deal of effort (Cermak & O'Connor, 1983; Wilson, 1982). Thus, in terms of adding new information, amnesic patients show difficulty with both episodic and semantic tasks.

Summary

In summarizing this section, it can be said that human memory appears to consist of sensory-memory stores (iconic and echoic memory); a short-term working memory that is coordinated by a central executive with the help of subsidiary slave systems; and a long-term store consisting of several components, including visual and verbal memory, and semantic and episodic memory.

THEORETICAL INTERPRETATIONS OF AMNESIA

The human anmesic syndrome is characterized by (1) "profound difficulty in learning and remembering new information of nearly all kinds" (Meudell & Mayes, 1982, p. 203); (2) difficulty in remembering some information acquired before the onset of the syndrome; (3) normal STM, when this is measured by digit span or the recency effect in free recall; and (4) normal and nearly normal functioning of other cognitive abilities.

Baddeley (1982a) distinguishes between primary and secondary amnesia. "Primary amnesia" refers to those features of the classic amnesic syndrome described above, while "secondary amnesia" refers to a whole range of memory problems that are secondary to some defect in the ability to process information. For example, a patient with prosopagnosia may have difficulty learning the names of new acquaintances because their faces are perceived inadequately. Similarly, an aphasic patient may perform poorly on verbal-learning tasks because of the overriding language deficit. Although most researchers try to select patients with "pure" amnesia, we do not know to what extent the "pure" and "impure" (or primary and secondary) amnesias overlap (Meudell & Mayes, 1982). Furthermore, in clinical practice there are far more people who show "impure" or secondary amnesias than who show a classical amnesic syndrome (Baddeley, 1982a). In fact, the classical syndrome is very rarely observed; by contrast, the number of patients with memory problems linked with additional cognitive or information-processing deficits is large. Such patients include those with dementia, head injury, Korsakoff syndrome, and subarachnoid hemorrhage. However, Baddeley (1982a) suggests that in the current state of knowledge it is worth generalizing from a model of the classic amnesic syndrome to other forms of memory disturbance, even though differences will almost certainly be found between "pure" amnesics and those with additional problems. This suggestion is made in the belief that models are tools that help us to understand where we are in an area of inquiry, and to guide us in developing arguments. For these reasons, the models of human amnesia are considered here, even though the majority of patients to be described later in this book did not show "pure" amnesia.

There are three main theoretical approaches to the study of amnesia: those that explain the syndrome as an encoding deficit; those that attribute it to storage problems; and those that suggest it is due to a deficit of retrieval. Each of these is considered in turn.

Encoding-Deficit Theories

Meudell and Mayes (1982) subdivide encoding-deficit theories into (1) failure of effortful processing and (2) failure of automatic processing. Butters and Cermak (1975) are among the chief proponents of the view that amnesia is a result of failure to pay adequate attention to the meaningful aspects of stimuli. They argue that amnesic patients encode at a shallow level—for example, using visual or phonological rather than semantic aspects. As noted above, LTM is dependent upon semantic coding; therefore, failure to use this method of coding will result in poor learning. There is certainly some evidence that impaired semantic processing occurs in Korsakoff patients. Cermak, Butters, and Moreines (1974), for example, demonstrated no release from proactive inhibition following a change of semantic category. This finding suggests that the subjects were not utilizing the semantic characteristics of the words. However, as Baddeley (1982a) points out, this could have been due to a secondary information-processing deficit, rather than representing a crucial feature of the amnesic syndrome itself. Moscovitch (1982) found that the same phenomenon occurred with frontal patients who were *not* amnesics. If semantic or effortful encoding is not occurring in amnesic patients, then inducing them to encode semantically should lead to better learning. The evidence for this is scant. Mayes, Meudell, and Neary (1978) tested Korsakoff patients by inducing shallow or deep encoding. In the shallow-encoding condition, the letters of the words to be remembered were written in different colors. Subjects had to report the colors used. In the deep-encoding condition, subjects were requested to supply the word to be remembered in answer to questions. (For example, "It's a frame covered with paper and flown by children on windy days. What is it?") There was no evidence that deeper processing differentially affected the learning of the amnesic patients. In later studies, Mayes, Meudell, and Neary (1980) equated level of learning in amnesics and controls by testing after different delays. They achieved similar results, suggesting that amnesic patients do not forget because of poor encoding strategies. Nevertheless, this may be a *contributing* factor in some patients, particularly those with Korsakoff syndrome.

Another kind of effortful processing is seen in the ability to form and use imagery. It has been suggested that a deficit in this ability could explain the human amnesic syndrome (Baddeley, 1973). In an experiment designed to test whether or not amnesic patients could benefit from visual imagery, Baddeley and Warrington (1973) showed that imagery did not help amnesics learn lists of four unrelated nouns. Controls, however, were helped. In contrast, Cermak (1975) found that with *two* nouns, Korsakoff patients, as well as controls, benefited from imagery. Jones (1974) found that two amnesic patients could readily form and describe the images they produced, but that these images did not help them learn paired associates. Thus, the evidence we have so far does not support the idea that an impairment in imagery per se is present in the amnesic syndrome. Any difference between amnesics and controls in their use of imagery is unlikely to be the cause of amnesia. It is more likely to be a result of the syndrome.

Failure of automatic processing has been suggested as the mechanism underlying amnesia. Hasher and Zacks (1979) have argued that some information, such as time when material is presented, or frequency with which it is presented, are encoded automatically, without cognitive effort. Huppert and Piercy (1978b) postulate that a failure in these automatic processes is responsible for the amnesic syndrome. They asked subjects, first, to say whether or not they had seen a series of slides on the day of testing or on the previous day; and, second, to say whether or not the slides had been seen once before or three times before. Amnesic subjects were unable to distinguish between recency and frequency, while control subjects were able to make this distinction. Huppert and Piercy argue that amnesics are unable to assign a temporal context to the item. Meudell and Mayes (1982) argue that this might be the result of a weak memory rather than an abnormal memory. Thus, if normals were tested after a longer delay, thereby equalizing learning, they might also show the same effect and be unable to assign a temporal context to the material.

If the encoding theories are correct, and if material learned prior to the onset of amnesia is encoded normally, there should be no RA present. This is obviously not the case. Meudell and Mayes (1982) describe some attempts to reconcile RA with encoding deficit theories.

M. S. Albert, Butters, and Levin (1979) have suggested two possible explanations for RA in alcoholic patients. First, such patients may have acquired less information over a lengthy period of time because of a progressive deficit in information processing, associated with alcohol abuse and malnutrition. In this event, RA would be secondary to the primary amnesic deficit. In cases of acute onset, RA might be associated with semantic-coding deficits, provided that the deficient semantic processes operate at retrieval as well as at acquisition. Such amnesics should be helped by semantic cues at the time of retrieval. However, M. S. Albert *et al.* (1979) found that amnesics were helped no more than controls in the experiments they carried out. Secondly, the RA might occur because different anatomical circuits are involved in RA and AA. Although there is some evidence for a double dissociation of RA and AA, such evidence is only tentative, and may reflect insensitive tests (Meudell & Mayes, 1981).

Storage-Deficit Theories

There are two types of storage-deficit theory: one claiming that amnesia is due to a more rapid rate of forgetting, and the other suggesting that amnesia is due to a failure of consolidation. The former interpretation assumes that a memory trace is formed adequately but decays much more rapidly in amnesic subjects. Huppert and Piercy (1978a) provided evidence against this view. They equated level of retention for pictures after a 10-minute delay in amnesics and control subjects by giving the former group a longer exposure time. They then studied the rate of forgetting after 1 day and 1 week. The rates of forgetting were comparable in both groups. Brooks and Baddeley (1976) did not equate subjects for initial learning and used amnesics with different etiologies, yet they, too, found no evidence for more rapid forgetting in amnesics. There is some slim evidence that certain patients with CHI (Sunderland *et al.* 1983), and patients who have recently received ECT for depression (Squire, 1981), do forget at an abnormally rapid rate. Baddeley, however, has stated (personal communication) that further work with head-injured patients has failed to replicate the findings.

The second of the storage hypotheses claims that failure to consolidate the memory trace is the mechanism underlying the human amnesic syndrome. Milner (1966) held this view, but Weiskrantz (1978) argues convincingly against it. He suggests that evidence from four different tasks shows that amnesia is not due to a failure of consolidation. The tasks indicate (1) that amnesics show prior-list intrusions in recall situations; (2) that amnesics are able to benefit from some cues, such as the first three letters of a word; (3) that amnesics often show normal learning on some perceptual tasks, such as frag- mented pictures; and (4) that there is some dissociation between amnesics' ability to carry out certain activities (e.g., pursuit rotor and mirror writing) without being able to remember that the particular activities have been performed on earlier occasions. In each of these instances, some consolidation has, presumably, taken place in order for the effects to have occurred. Baddeley (1982a) states that a general- consolidation hypothesis is no longer acceptable, because amnesic patients can learn certain tasks effectively. Meudell and Mayes (1982), on the other hand, argue that the evidence used against the consolida- tion hypothesis may in fact be a *result* of amnesia, rather than the cause of it. That is, the effects of prior-list intrusions, cueing, and so forth, may occur because of a failure to consolidate the memory trace effi- ciently. When this happens, the "weak" memory of amnesics results in their showing prior-list intrusions and all the other phenomena cited by Weiskrantz (1978) as evidence against the storage-deficit hypothe- ses. Meudell and Mayes attempt to use evidence from electroencepha- lographic (EEG) studies to support their view, but there is so little known about the relationship between EEG findings and memory that this support remains unconvincing. As Meudell and Mayes themselves point out, "it remains to be determined whether post stimulus EEG power is directly related to memory or not" (1982, p. 230). The conclu- sion, therefore, must be that the storage-deficit hypothesis cannot explain the human amnesic syndrome.

Retrieval-Deficit Hypotheses

Several retrieval-deficit hypotheses exist. Meudell and Mayes (1982) subdivide them into those affecting AA and those affecting RA.

Retrieval-Deficit Theories of AA

In the category of theories relating to AA would come, for example, the theory orginally put forward by Warrington and Weiskrantz (1970), who argued that the poor performance of amnesic patients is due to excessive interference from irrelevant traces. Their argument rested on three pieces of evidence: (1) the partial-cueing effect—that is, presenting the first three letters of a word—leads to improved recall. Warrington and Weiskrantz suggested that this happens because constraints are placed on the number of competing responses. The fact that amnesics can learn easy associations on paired-associate learning tasks was believed to be due to the same process. (2) The numbers of prior-list intrusions shown by amnesic subjects were seen as irrelevant competing responses, preventing normal recall. (3) The relatively normal performance of amnesic patients on fragmented-picture tasks was believed to occur because fragmented pictures are highly resistant to proactive inhibition.

Meudell and Mayes (1982) have put forward three reasons why the excessive interference postulated by Warrington and Weiskrantz may occur: (1) because information decays abnormally slowly; (2) because amnesics have difficulty judging familiarity of items (Gaffan, 1972); and (3) because amnesics are deficient at context retrieval. There is little evidence to support the hypothesis of abnormally slow decay. As noted earlier, the rate of forgetting between amnesics and controls does not appear to differ. The familiarity view of Gaffan (1972) suggests that long-term learning includes two separate components: one involving the formation of associative links, and the other involving judgments of familiarity. Gaffan indicated that amnesic patients are defective in their ability to assess familiarity, but that they are capable of learning associations. Brooks and Baddeley (1976) found the reverse to be true with their amnesic patients. The work of Huppert and Piercy (1976) has also indicated that the associative component is defective, and not the familiarity component. The idea that amnesics are deficient at context retrieval was suggested by Winocur and Kinsbourne (1978) when they found that changing the environment led to better recall of a paired-associate list by amnesic patients. Control subjects were unaffected by the change, probably because of ceiling effects. Control subjects might have been influenced had the tasks been more difficult.

The major weakness in the tests of these interference hypotheses is that they did not control for memory strength (Meudell & Mayes, 1982). Perhaps normals, tested after a longer delay, would perform like amnesics. The findings, then, would argue in favor of the observed phenomena resulting from "weak" memory traces rather than from an abnormal retrieval mechanism. Work completed by Mayes and Meudell (1981a, 1981b) and Mayes *et al.* (1980) suggests that normals do indeed behave like amnesics when tested after long delays. Meudell and Mayes have argued that amnesics do necessarily have a specific retrieval deficit. It is simply that their memories are weaker than those of controls when tested at the same retention intervals. They also suggest that when certain tasks are performed normally by amnesics, it should not be inferred that this is because the particular tasks avoid retrieval processes. Such success may be due to the fact that different parts of the brain are employed on these occasions.

By 1982, Warrington and Weiskrantz had abandoned their interference theory and suggested, instead, that amnesia is the result of a disconnection syndrome. They also argued that different neuropathological pathways are involved. An alternative explanation for the relatively normal performance described above is that the amnesic subjects were showing evidence of procedural learning, which normal subjects find, on the whole, relatively easy. Even the Tower of Hanoi puzzle (described on p. 56), which is not, in itself, an easy task, has a fairly straightforward set of rules that can be readily learned and applied by most people of average intelligence.

If procedural learning is easy for most people without amnesia, then performance on these tasks by amnesics should never equal the performance of normal subjects. The evidence here is ambiguous. Brooks and Baddeley (1976) did find normal learning on a pursuit-rotor task, while most other studies have indicated some impairment on such tasks (e.g., Corkin, 1968; Weiskrantz & Warrington, 1979). Perhaps there are patients for whom procedural learning is well within the normal range, and others for whom it is not. Two of our patients (Baddeley & Wilson, 1983) appeared to show normal procedural functioning, while a third patient, with amnesia and severe bilateral frontal lobe damage, showed an abnormal performance. There may be a correlation between performance on procedural-learning tasks and the presence or absence of information-processing deficits. In addition, there may be differences among the procedural-learning tasks themselves. This hypothesis needs to be explored. However, in support of such an idea, it is pointed out that the frontal lobe patient mentioned above, showed normal learning on a pursuit-rotor task but impaired learning on a jigsaw puzzle and on a mirror-reading task.

There are other tasks, of course, where amnesics show no impairment at all, such as a normal language functioning or piano playing (Starr & Phillips, 1970). Meudell and Mayes suggest that this may occur for the same unknown reason that some episodic memories are preserved. H. M., for example, remembers that President Kennedy was assassinated (Milner, *et al.*, 1968). Also, these tasks may be the ones that were very overlearned prior to the onset of amnesia (Huppert & Piercy, 1981). Another reason is that many of these skills are part and parcel of the semantic-memory system, and it has already been shown that semantic memory in amnesics is largely intact.

Retrieval-Deficit Theories of RA

Retrieval-deficit theories of RA claim that access to premorbid memories is impaired because of a retrieval deficit. If this hypothesis is correct, then RA should always occur; furthermore, it should occur for all premorbid memories, and not only for those close in time to the onset of the illness or disability that led to the amnesia. This does not appear to be true for many amnesic patients, although some studies are difficult to interpret because certain remote memories have been rehearsed more frequently, and are of much greater significance than other more recent memories.

Sanders and Warrington (1971) argue that if remote and recent events are equated for difficulty, then there is no differential preservation of remote memory in amnesic patients. Unfortunately, in their study the difficult events were at floor level for amnesic subjects, so it was not possible to demonstrate whether or not remote memory was more impaired. In a later study (Sanders & Warrington, 1975), prompts were used in order to avoid the floor effect. In this condition, the performance of amnesic subjects was similar to that of controls.

M. S. Albert *et al.* (1979) found a temporal gradient of events indicating that older memories were spared more than recent memories. Squire and Chace (1975) also demonstrated that recent memories were impaired in depressed patients who had received ECT. M. S. Albert *et al.* argue that RA occurs as a secondary consequence of a learning disorder. This could certainly explain a long RA with a temporal gradient in conditions such as Korsakoff syndrome. It does not explain the long RA seen, for example, with the stroke patient described in Chapter 7, who was unable to recall which of his two daughters had been born first. (One had been born 8 years and one 12 years prior to the patient's stroke.) This man also believed he lived in a house that in fact he had moved from years before.

The differential effects of recent and remote memories do cause difficulty for the retrieval-deficit hypotheses. In some cases of severe head injury, there would appear to be very little RA in the face of severe amnesia (Wilson, in press). However, even though remote memory is typically spared in amnesia, there are no studies reported in which amnesic patients have shown normal retrieval for any time period tested (Meudell & Mayes, 1982).

This might argue for some impairment in the retrieval process. In a study of autobiographical memory in amnesic patients, we (Baddeley & Wilson, in press) found that wide differences between amnesics did emerge. M. L., for example, a postencephalitic, "pure" amnesic (described in Chapters 6 and 9) showed normal autobiographical memory for events that had occurred up until a year or so before the onset of his illness. He had little difficulty recalling certain events to do with his Army days, his marriage, and holidays with his children. He provided rich detail and recalled these details consistently when asked about certain incidents on separate occasions. F. D., however, a bilateral stroke patient, (described in Chapter 7) also with a "pure" amnesia, had great difficulty recalling past events, and could not remember such things as whether he went into the Navy before or after going to college. This problem was perhaps due to a specific retrieval deficit, whereas M. L.'s problem may have been due to another underlying mechanism altogether, such as failure of consolidation.

Most of the evidence to date, though, does not strongly support a retrieval deficit as the underlying cause of amnesia. Meudell and Mayes (1982) argue that normal people show the characteristics of amnesic patients if they are tested for information that they have largely forgotten. Baddeley (1982a) believes that none of the theories so far described can adequately account for the amnesic syndrome. He believes this is due to "our inability to conceptualize adequately the complex processes of normal human memory" (p. 333). He also suggests that the clue to a reformulated theory of amnesia lies in the fact that amnesics are capable of learning, provided they are tested in the appropriate way. Thus, the amnesic patient can acquire new information, but may never recall having been exposed to that information before. From a rehabilitation point of view, this may prove to be one of the keys to reducing the problems faced by amnesic patients and their families.

THE LEARNING ABILITIES OF AMNESIC PATIENTS

In 1953 Scoville operated on H. M., who is probably the most thoroughly investigated and written-about amnesic of all time. In a later paper, Scoville and Milner (1957) stated that H. M. had "a complete loss of memory for events subsequent to his bilateral medial temporal lobe resection" (p. 11). This description, however, proved to be inaccurate. It was later demonstrated (Milner *et al.*, 1968) that H. M. could acquire new motor skills and learn some very simple visual and tactile mazes. In 1981, Cohen and Corkin also reported on H. M.'s ability to learn the Tower of Hanoi puzzle. This puzzle consists of a series of wooden blocks and pegs. The blocks are of different sizes, with the largest at the bottom and the smallest at the top. All are arranged on one peg. The subject's task is to move the blocks from the starting peg (on the left) to the finishing peg (on the right) so that sizes are in the correct order, with the largest still at the bottom and the smallest on top. There are two rules: First, only one block may be moved at a time; second, a larger block may never be placed on a smaller block. Thus the puzzle is a complex cognitive task, and one that patients with frontal lobe damage find extremely difficult to complete (Shallice, 1982). In spite of his profound amnesia, H. M. successfully completed it; furthermore, he was able to solve the puzzle in fewer moves over successive days. Yet on each occasion he did not remember having tackled the puzzle before. Cohen and Corkin (1981) stated that H. M. was able to acquire the procedural knowledge necessary for learning the puzzle, despite the fact that he could not remember any of the occasions when he had acquired the skills needed to solve the puzzle. This separation of learning into procedural versus declarative may prove to be particularly important in the treatment of disorders of memory.

There is considerable evidence from other sources suggesting that amnesic patients can, indeed, learn some tasks, either in a normal manner and at normal rates, or at least with far greater success than they show on some long-term episodic-memory tasks. One frequently reported illustration of this is when Claparede (1911/1951) concealed a pin in his hand and then shook hands with a Korsakoff patient. The next day he went to shake hands with her again, whereupon she refused; however, she was apparently unable to remember the earlier occasion, and could not explain her reluctance to shake hands. In a series of experiments, Weiskrantz and Warrington (1979) demonstrated eyelid conditioning in two amnesic patients. No episodic recall was apparent, even after many learning trials. In addition to conditioning, a number of studies have demonstrated intact or relatively intact motor learning. The Milner *et al.* (1968) study with H. M. has already been mentioned. Starr and Phillips (1970) also found that amnesic patients were able to learn Porteus mazes, that they retained this learning after a 2-week delay. A similar finding occurred in the Brooks and Baddeley (1976) investigation. The latter study also showed normal pursuit-rotor learning in their group of three Korsakoff and two postencephalitic patients. As mentioned in the preceding section, the Brooks and Baddeley study was the only one to report entirely normal motor learning in amnesic patients. The amnesic patient described in Chapter 7 showed consistent and marked improvement on a pursuit-rotor task, but as no normal controls were included it is not known to what extent this improvement can be described as "normal." A patient reported by Newcombe and Ratcliff (1979) was unable to learn a simple task in which she was required to place a few items in a particular order inside a box. This same patient, however, was able to learn an apparently more complex assembly task. This was probably due to the fact that the former task involved spatial memory (there was no automatic process of going from one step to another), and it was also analogous to a difficult paired-associate learning task known to be almost impossible for amnesics to acquire. The assembly task, on the other hand, involved procedural memory, and was thus similar to a jigsaw assembly task that Brooks and Baddeley (1976) found to be rather easily learned by amnesic patients: One step leads to another, and thus such tasks may be seen as akin to the easy or close paired-associate learning tasks that amnesics are able to learn.

As well as jigsaw assemblies, other perceptual activities have been learned by amnesic people. Williams (1953) showed that her patients could learn to reproduce line drawings easily, provided they were prompted with fragments of the original drawings. This finding was replicated by Warrington and Weiskrantz (1968), who further demonstrated that it was not only with line drawings that learning occurred: Presenting fragments of words achieved the same end. Thus, the effect is not limited to nonverbal material. There are several other perceptual tasks on which amnesic patients readily show improvement. These include perception of random-dot stereograms (Ramachandran, 1976), detection of anomalies in pictures (Warrington & Weiskrantz, 1973), and perception of "Mooney's Closure Faces" (Hiles, quoted in Baddeley, 1982a).

Verbal tasks, too, can be learned under certain conditions. Cohen and Corkin (1981) note that amnesic patients can learn to read mirror-reversed words at a rate indistinguishable from that of normal control subjects, and can retain the improvement over 3 months. Improvement on mirror reading was also shown to occur in the two pure amnesics we described (Baddeley & Wilson, 1983), although the frontal amnesic did not show such improvement. Paired-associate learning can also occur under certain conditions. It has long been established that amnesic patients can learn pairs of words that have some logical association or relationship (e.g., "north–south," "fruit–apple," (Erickson & Scott, 1977), but are unable to learn unrelated pairs (e.g., "cabbage–pen," "school–grocery"). Winocur and Weiskrantz (1976) demonstrated good paired-associate learning when semantic or phonological associations were present. Warrington and Weiskrantz (1982), in a further exploration of paired-associate learning in amnesics, found that performance by amnesics and controls was similar when the associated pairs were rhymes. Controls were superior, however, when the pairs were semantically connected, and when the pairs consisted of a noun and a verb. Baddeley (1982a) also reports some unpublished studies in which an amnesic patient was given scrambled sentences and asked to put the words into correct order. Improvement occurred steadily with each presentation, and this advance was maintained after a week's delay.

The final study to be described in this section is that of Jacoby and Witherspoon (1982). They selected a number of homophones (e.g., "reed" and "read"), and subjects were asked to identify the less common of the two homophones by means of a series of elicitations (for the example above, "What is the part of a clarinet that vibrates?"). In the next stage of the experiment, subjects were asked to recognize the words they had produced from a list containing both the original words and distractors. Not surprisingly, this proved difficult for the amnesic patients, and they performed poorly. However, when the subjects were then asked to spell the list of words, including those that had previously been presented, they showed a clear tendency to spell the homophone they had recently defined (i.e., the less common of the two words). Both amnesics and controls showed this tendency, which suggests evidence of learning among amnesics, despite their inability to recognize the target words.

There are, then, a number of tasks that are not difficult for amnesics to learn. What might these tasks have in common? Baddeley (1982b) states: "In all these cases, the subject tends to show unmistakable evidence of learning, but no evidence that he consciously remembers performing the task on which he shows learning" (p. 68). In another review of the topic, Baddeley (1982a) points out that it is not necessary for subjects to be aware of whether or not the material has been encountered previously; they simply have to perform the task to the best of their ability. As indicated earlier, this could be crucially important in rehabilitation, for several reasons.

First, it may be possible to teach memory-impaired persons skills to enable them to live more normal lives—for example, programming memory aids to remind them to do certain things. If such skills can be presented to the patients in a format similar to jigsaw assembly, or pursuit-rotor tasks, they should be acquired relatively easily. Second, it may be possible to teach relatives to provide better retrieval cues in order to gain access to what has been learned. For example, prompting with the initial letter often helps a patient retrieve a name he or she is unable to remember. This is a similar strategy to cueing with the first three letters of a word, as described by Warrington and Weiskrantz (1968). It might be more helpful to teach relatives to phrase questions in a more appropriate way. On one occasion, a Rivermead patient was asked, "Do you remember who came to see you yesterday, and where you went?" She answered, "No." The question was then rephrased: "When Roy came yesterday, where did he take you?" To this question, the patient correctly replied, "The Theater."

A third way in which the procedural-learning tasks can benefit rehabilitation is in guiding workers in the field as to what strategies are likely to work. In the area of visual-imagery research, for instance (to be described more fully in Chapter 6), there are conflicting findings regarding the ability of amnesic patients to use this technique in order to improve learning. One solution might be to ensure that visual images are related or highly associable, given that work on paired associates shows such associations can be learned. Thus, an amnesic patient who may find it impossible to remember an image associating the word "bun" with the word "car," might be helped to remember if given the words "bun" and "sausage"—because of the connection with "hot dogs."

In this chapter, we have been reviewing research that has revealed a small range of learning abilities in amnesic patients. Further work in treatment and assessment should lead to the discovery of other alternatives that should widen this range. Of course, a major breakthrough will occur if ways are found of "proceduralizing" many of the tasks that amnesics now seem incapable of remembering.

·4·

BEHAVIORAL PSYCHOLOGY

BEHAVIORAL ASSESSMENT

The distinction between behavioral assessment and behavioral treatment techniques (to follow in the next section) is an artificial one. As Goldfried and Sprafkin (1976) point out, there is a direct relationship between the two, and problems arise in determining when assessment ends and treatment begins. In clinical practice, the two are indistinguishable. Nevertheless, for purposes of discussion, it is perhaps better to talk about behavioral assessment and behavioral treatment as two separate topics. This first section covers two major areas: the nature of behavioral assessment and behavioral assessment procedures.

The Nature of Behavioral Assessment

Hersen and Bellack (1978) state that "the area of behavioral assessment is new" (p. 18). R. O. Nelson and Hayes (1979b), on the other hand, argue that "in some sense, behavioral assessment is not a new field at all" (p. 1). In fact, both points of view are credible. The goals of behavioral assessment have been the same throughout the 50 years or so of the history of behavior therapy. However, until the late 1960s, assessment was more indirect and informal, with a greater emphasis on the development of successful treatment techniques and intervention strategies. Two seminal papers appeared in 1968 and 1969, the first by Baer, Wolf, and Risley, and the second by Kanfer and Saslow. These may be seen as heralding the beginning of a more formal and specific approach to behavioral assessment. The emphasis over the 1970s and 1980s has been on improving the following three areas: (1) the identification and measurement of variables that control behavior; (2) the selection of successful treatment techniques; and (3) evaluation of treatment (R. O. Nelson & Hayes, 1979b).

How does behavioral assessment differ from traditional or conventional assessment techniques? If assessment is defined as "the systematic collection, organization and interpretation of information about a person and his situations" (Sundberg & Tyler, 1962), then obviously both assessment approaches overlap. Both are means of collecting, organizing, and interpreting information. To some extent, techniques for carrying out these procedures are also shared, as both approaches use interviews, questionnaires, and observations (R. O. Nelson & Hayes, 1979a). Nevertheless, there are some important differences. In many assessment procedures, the response obtained in test situations are seen as signs of some underlying disorder or deficit. Thus, poor performance on a paired-associate learning task may be seen as evidence supporting the diagnosis of an amnesic syndrome. In contrast, a behavioral assessment samples behavior in a particular situation. For example, if an amnesic patient frequently repeats the same question, the assessor might wish to discover how frequently this question is repeated within a given period of time. It is also important, however, to look at changes in frequency under certain stimulus conditions: For example, does the rate increase or decrease (1) at different times of the day, (2) in different settings, or (3) when different staff members or relatives are present? Both approaches are useful, depending on the questions being asked.

Implicit in the traditional approach is the view that behavior is a reflection of an underlying cause, or impairment, or personality trait. Implicit in the behavioral approach is the view that behavior is influenced by environmental circumstances. To put it another way, a conventional assessment is more concerned with what a person *has*, whereas behavioral assessment is more concerned with what a person *does* (Mischel, 1968). In terms of cognitive rehabilitation after brain damage, it is important to find answers to both of these questions; results from neuropsychological or standardized investigations and from behavioral investigations are seen as complementary.

Further differences between the two approaches may be seen in the beliefs about the stability of behavior. Thus, conventional assessment procedures assume that the behavior they are observing in a test situation is stable or relatively stable. It is not expected that a person's estimated IQ will fluctuate a great deal from morning to afternoon, or from Wednesday to Saturday. For certain behaviors, this is likely to be true: A person with a classic amnesic syndrome will almost certainly be unable to recall a prose passage after a delay, whether the person is tested on the ward or at home, or in the morning or afternoon. For other behaviors, however, this may not be the case. If someone shows evidence of unilateral neglect, for example, that person may neglect different portions of a page of script, depending on time of day, state of fatigue, lighting conditions, preparation beforehand, and so forth. Assessment in such a case will need to take account of these fluctuations. Furthermore, the extent to which these conditions handicap an individual (or create problems for staff members and relatives supporting the individual) is not likely to be fixed and permanent. A behavioral approach, therefore, recognizes the variability of behavior under different circumstances.

The purposes of assessment will differ according to whether a standardized or behavioral approach is being adopted. The former is more concerned with diagnosis and labeling, while the latter is usually employed in order to design treatment (Ciminero, Calhoun, & Adams, 1977). Thus, in the behavioral approach the purposes of assessment will be (1) to identify problems for treatment; (2) to determine particular characteristics of problems; and (3) to evaluate the effectiveness of treatment. Because of these contrasting aims, assessment is likely to be carried out at different times in each of the approaches. Standardized testing, with its *indirect* relationship to treatment, will almost certainly be completed prior to (and possibly following) treatment; behavioral methods, with a *direct* relationship to treatment, will almost certainly be undertaken throughout the treatment process, and in fact will be regarded as part and parcel of the treatment (Ciminero et al., 1977). One other major difference to be noted is that standardized testing deals specifically with the patient, with little or no attention being paid to the environment; by contrast, behavioral assessment often focuses on the environment or setting in which the behavior occurs. For a discussion about the relationship between behavioral and neuropsychological assessment, the reader is referred to Goldstein (1984).

What model can be used to help us understand behavioral assessment? The early stimulus–response views of behavior were soon found to be too simplistic, and it became necessary to encompass an interactionist point of view—that is, a view recognizing that behavior is influenced both by environmental factors and by organismic variables (see, e.g., Mischel, 1968). Probably the most influential model of behavioral assessment based on the interactionist perspective is the so-called "SORC" model of Kanfer and Saslow (1969) and Goldfried and Sprafkin (1976). This model assumes that behavior is determined by the following:

1. *Stimulus* events, such as physical, social, or internal events. A physical event, for example, might be the presence of a thing or an action that triggers a reaction. A social event could be an attitude expressed by one's colleagues. An internal event could be a feeling such as hunger or fear. Such stimulus events are modified by organismic variables.

2. *Organismic* variables, or those that are due to the biological condition of the person involved (e.g., physical handicap, hemianopia, or dysphasia).

3. *Responses*, which are observable or in some other way measurable behaviors of the individual concerned. These responses may be (a) motor (e.g., smiling, foot tapping, or talking); (b) cognitive (e.g., rating oneself as anxious or depressive); or (c) physiological (e.g., increasing one's heart rate or skin conductivity).

4. *Consequences* that follow from responses. These might be (a) self-generated (e.g., feeling less anxious or depressed); (b) physical (e.g., obtaining something to eat); or (c) social (e.g., being praised by a staff member). Consequences may be immediate or delayed, and may lead to secondary gains. Thus, an immediate consequence of forgetting what to do in a therapy session might be extra attention from the staff members, who supply reminders. A delayed consequence might be sympathy from other patients and visitors because of constant forgetting. A secondary gain might result from being moved to a more protected and less stressful environment.

In summary, the SORC model predicts that behavior is a function of the specific situations or events that precede the behavior, together with the individual's genetic predisposition, physiological state, and past learning of behavior. These determine what responses occur, and it is from among these responses that the problems for treatment will be selected. These, in turn, are maintained by the consequences of the responses—that is, the events that follow the problem behaviors.

In the early days of the behavioral method, "behavior" typically meant overt motor behavior. Currently, most behavioral therapists include physiological, emotional, and cognitive behaviors in the definition. Provided that the behavior can be measured in some objective and replicable manner (either by direct observation, rating scales, questionnaires, checklists, or physiological recording equipment), then it can be subjected to a behavioral assessment and treatment (R. O. Nelson & Hayes, 1979b).

Physiological, emotional, and cognitive behaviors require consideration in the field of cognitive rehabilitation. For example, it is possible that level of anxiety affects memory in brain-damaged patients, just as it does in the non-brain-damaged population (M. W. Eysenck, 1979). It might be desirable in some cases, therefore, to assess anxiety physiologically by means of the galvanic skin responses (GSR) of memory-impaired patients in situations where their defective memory causes everyday problems. Rating scales could be provided for patients to rate their anxiety under different stimulus conditions, and memory performance on specified everyday tasks could provide measures of the kinds of memory failures experienced. Treatment could focus on any or all of these aspects. Biofeedback, for instance, might reduce GSR; relaxation exercises might reduce anxiety; and memory therapy might improve everday memory functioning. The findings of Rachman and Hodgson (1974) suggest that, in fear-evoking situations, overt behavioral changes precede physiological changes, which in turn precede the self-report measures. If this were found to be the case in the kinds of situations described above, it would be expected that improvements in everyday memory functioning would occur before the GSR rates improved. The last measures to change would be scores on anxiety rating scales.

Behavioral assessment has also provided cognitive rehabilitation with a number of techniques for measuring behavior. J. F. Hall (1971) subdivides these into three main types: automatic recording, measurement of permanent product, and observational recording. From the point of view of rehabilitation, observational recording is the most relevant. (See Yule & Carr, 1980, for a full description of this technique.) It can be further subdivided into the following categories:

1. Continuous recording is recording everything a person does in a given situation; this is usually impossible over any extended period of time, although sometimes videotapes or audiotapes may be used to achieve this end.

2. Event recording is a method whereby a target behavior is defined and every instance of that behavior is recorded. Thus, for example, it would be possible to record each time a patient failed to put on the brake of a wheelchair before transferring to another chair. For some highly frequent behaviors, though, such as the number of

times an anomic aphasic is unable to articulate certain nouns, it is very difficult or impossible to count accurately. It is usual to limit event recording to a certain proportion of the day. As Yule and Carr (1980) point out, this can lead to problems. One might be sampling a part of the day when the problem behavior is particularly likely (or unlikely) to occur. This may give a false picture of the severity of the problem. In this case, the solution would be to ensure that the period sampled is representative of the whole day, or to change the sampling periods in order to cover a wide range of situations.

3. Duration recording is necessary with some behaviors because it is important to know how long they last. For example, duration recording would involve timing such behaviors as how long a person can concentrate on a given task, or how long a person takes to read a passage. One disadvantage is that it is not always easy to decide when a particular behavior stops and starts. (For instance, if one is measuring time on task, and the patient being observed looks at the ceiling, it may not be clear whether the patient is not "on task" or whether he or she is thinking about the next step in the activity.)

4. Interval recording is a convenient method of sampling behavior. The total observation period is divided into time intervals, and the observer notes whether or not the target behavior occurs at all in each interval. This method is particularly useful for certain behaviors, such as repetition of the same story or joke, or "tip-of-the-tongue" phenomenon. Interval recording has an added advantage in that it can indicate both severity and duration of a behavior. A major disadvantage, however, lies in the fact that it requires the undivided attention of the observer (J. F. Hall, 1971). Another disadvantage is that the method only *estimates* the frequency and severity of behavior, and cannot therefore be regarded as an accurate record. For example, in a given interval, a question will be recorded once only—whether it occurs 50 times or only once—or else it will become event recording and liable to the problems outlined above.

5. Time sampling occurs when the observer records only at the end of a predetermined interval. The length of the interval depends on the target behavior itself, and on the time available to the observer. Thus, one might decide to observe whether or not a person is in the correct room at the end of every 15-minute period during the morning, or whether the person is present for meals in the canteen at the start of each meal. The advantage of this method is that it does not need continuous recording, although it does require precise timing in order

to avoid biasing the results (Yule & Carr, 1980). However, a study by Murphy and Goodall (1980) found time sampling to be a more accurate reflection of the true rate of occurrence of target behavior than interval recording.

Single-case studies are the one other procedure that behavioral assessment has provided for cognitive rehabilitation. These have proved to be invaluable in treatment evaluation; because of their importance in rehabilitation, they are considered separately in a later section of this chapter.

Behavioral Assessment Techniques

L. R. Hay (1982) classifies assessment procedures into self-report measures and behavioral observation procedures.

Self-Report Measures

Self-report measures include (1) interviews; (2) questionnaires, rating scales, and checklists; and (3) self-monitoring.

Behavioral Interviewing. Morganstern (1978) states that the purpose of a behavioral interview is to gain a thorough functional analysis of the problematic behavior. A functional analysis involves determining the antecedents of the problem behavior, describing the problem behavior precisely and unambiguously, and identifying the consequences that maintain the behavior (Kiernan, 1973). Lazarus (1973) claims that the greatest impediment to successful treatment is inadequate assessment of the problem behavior.

Unfortunately, behavioral interviewing has not been subjected to the same amount of empirical investigation as have certain other methods. There would appear to be a lack of research into the effectiveness of the various components in the behavioral interview (Haynes, 1978). In 1979, W. M. Hay, Hay, Angle, and Nelson found considerable agreement between interviews with regard to the *number* of problems identified, but low agreement with regard to their *nature*. Kanfer and Saslow (1969) suggest that assessors should ascertain whether the problems are behavioral excesses or deficits. They also stress the importance of determining the skills, talents, strengths, and assets of each individual.

From the point of view of cognitive rehabilitation, determining an individual's strengths as well as weaknesses is particularly important. Early in the rehabilitation process, therapists are likely to attempt to restore lost functioning—that is, to tackle the weaknesses or deficits directly. At a later stage, however, particularly when clinical psychologists are involved, the treatment emphasis shifts, and an ameliorative approach is likely to be adopted. Such an approach will bypass the impaired functions as attempts are made to find alternative solutions that will make functioning less problematic. To do this with some degree of success, it is essential that the individual patient's strengths be utilized. On a more general point, behavioral interviewing with the majority of memory-impaired people is unlikely to provide a great deal of useful information concerning everyday problems. This is because such people tend to forget their memory failures or show poor insight into the nature of their difficulties. However, interviewing relatives may provide accurate information, as they are likely to be aware of many of the memory failures (Sunderland *et al.*, 1983).

Questionnaires, Rating Scales, and Checklists. Questionnaires, or self-descriptive rating scales, have been used since the early days of psychology (e.g., Galton, 1907). After an unpromising beginning, when behaviorists held such self-reports in low esteem, they have now become acceptable and regarded as valuable tools in behavioral assessment. Although Haynes (1978) is of the opinion that they vary in their reliability and validity (which is only to be expected), Cautela and Upper (1978) hold the view that the reliability and validity of self-report procedures appear to be as high as or even higher than those found in interview studies. The same finding would appear to hold true in comparison with physiological measures, at least as far as the measurement of physical pain is concerned. Cautela and Upper quote Hilgard, who wrote, "I wish to assert flatly that there is no physiological measure of pain which is either as discriminating of fine differences in stimulus conditions, as reliable upon repetition, or as lawfully related to change conditions, as the subject's verbal report" (Hilgard, 1969, p. 107).

Cautela and Upper (1978) designed a Behavioral Inventory Battery comprising several different scales to assess behavior, ranging from general behavior concerning the individual's life through to more specific questions relating to the individual's needs. Their aim was to attempt to determine more precisely both the nature of the problem and to select the most appropriate clinical techniques for dealing with the problem. With regard to memory assessment, several questionnaires, rating scales, and checklists have been developed. Questionnaires relating to memory failures include the Short Inventory of Memory Experiences (Herrmann & Neisser, 1978); the Subjective Memory Questionnaire (Bennett-Levy & Powell, 1980); the Cognitive Failures Questionnaire (Broadbent, Cooper, Fitzgerald, & Parks, 1982); and the questionnaire designed by Sunderland *et al.* (1983). All these tend to be fairly lengthy, and many patients become restless and reluctant to complete them. The same criticism applies to these measures as to behavioral interviews—namely, that completing the forms is a memory task in itself, and therefore is likely to be performed badly by memory-impaired people. Nevertheless, discrepancies between scores on such questionnaires and scores on more direct observations of memory may provide a useful measure of insight, or, more accurately, *lack* of insight. It is worth noting here that questionnaires can elicit useful information from relatives of a memory-impaired person, because relatives are sometimes able to provide information that has been forgotten by the patient. Questionnaires can also provide useful information on everyday problems.

Rating scales that have been employed to estimate memory problems include the one designed by Kapur and Pearson (1983). Their patients were asked to compare current performance on certain memory tasks (e.g., remembering which day of the week it was) with premorbid performance. Rating was on a 3-point scale: "unchanged," "slightly worse," and "a great deal worse." Often, memory-impaired people are unaware of the severity of their deficits, and markedly overestimate their ability to remember.

Checklists can provide additional or alternative information to that obtained from questionnaires and rating scales. The checklist designed by Sunderland, Harris, and Gleave (1984) has been modified for use at a rehabilitation center for brain-damaged adults, and has provided valuable information regarding the type and frequency of memory failures during physiotherapy and occupational therapy (Wilson, 1984b).

Self-Monitoring Techniques. Kanfer (1970) reported the finding that observing one's own behavior can lead to increases or decreases in aspects of that behavior. With behaviors like overeating or smoking, it is possible that recording each mouthful eaten or each cigarette smoked may be punishing, and a consequence of this might be a decrease in the undesirable behavior. At the same time, behaviors regarded as desirable (e.g., refusing a cigarette) may increase, particularly if these are being monitored too.

Lick and Katkin (1978) point out that one advantage of self-monitoring over questionnaires is that clients are more likely to report reactions immediately after they have occurred during the former. Emmelcamp (1974) believes that self-monitoring of anxiety may have a therapeutic effect that leads to a reduction in anxiety. However, it is also possible that self-monitoring can act as a reinforcer for certain behaviors, and thus can lead to an increase in *undesirable* behaviors. Furthermore, some behaviors are likely to be more reliably recorded than others. This will depend, in part, on the frequency of the behavior. Thus, infrequent visits to the local movie theater may be more accurately monitored than the number of times one makes eye contact with a colleague.

One major advantage of self-monitoring over other assessment techniques is that it provides access to information that would otherwise be unobtainable (Kazdin, 1974), such as personal attitudes, beliefs, and perceptions. Another advantage is that there is often a closer relationship between the target behaviors themselves and the assessment of change (Eisler, 1978). In other words, if one is trying to change the amount of social interaction, then the same measures used in the baseline (e.g., number of times one speaks to another person) are used in the treatment stage. In more global self-report techniques, such as filling in a questionnaire, the "Yes–No" answers may miss gradations of change. Eisler (1978) also comments on the reliability of self-monitoring. It has been observed that monitoring one's own behavior may cause changes in that behavior and thus cause a degree of unreliability; yet it is just such a change in behavior that is desirable in a self-monitoring procedure. As Eisler concludes, it would not be wise to rely solely on self-monitoring, and other methods should be employed to provide as full a picture as possible. A self-monitoring procedure in a memory-impaired patient is described by Brooks and Lincoln (1984). In this case, the patient was asked to keep a diary for a week, in which she entered all the occasions when she was aware of forgetting things or when other people told her of things she had forgotten. Although several memory failures were recorded, it was not possible to determine how many went unrecorded. Brooks and Lincoln point out the desirability of employing other supportive procedures, such as independent observation.

Behavioral Observation Procedures

Behavioral observation procedures may be classified into naturalistic and simulated observations.

Naturalistic Observations. Because behavioral treatments seek to change behaviors in the natural environment, it is often important to assess the problem in those environments. Haynes (1978) gives three reasons why natural observations are important. First, they often reveal behavior that is not reported in interviews, questionnaires, checklists, or tests. Second, they avoid the inference inherent in many of the assessment procedures. Third, they may be less subject to biasing effects. Kern (1984) looked at correlations between laboratory observations and unobtrusive observations in the natural environment of rat-phobic students. He found that for untreated subjects, there was a close agreement between their approach behavior in the laboratory and in the natural environment. For treated subjects, the relationship was lower. It was also noted that, for treated subjects, self-report measures were better than laboratory observation for predicting approach behaviors in the natural environment. This suggests that natural observations may be more important following treatment, and less important prior to treatment, when analogue or simulated situations may suffice.

There are several reasons why observations in the natural environment are carried out. Often it is important to determine what events or situations precede or follow the problem behavior. For example, O. E., a head-injured patient (discussed in Chapter 6), frequently repeated one particular phrase in reply to a specific question. If asked, "Are you ready, O.?" he always replied, "Ready, willing, and disabled!" Although mildly amusing on the first two or three occasions, this phrase became irritating to the staff working with O. E. The solution was to avoid asking that question and replace it with something like "We are going to start now."

Another reason for direct observation in the natural environment is to determine what is reinforcing or motivating for the individual patient. Although this is frequently ascertained by asking the person involved—for example, L. T. (the young woman described in Chapter 8) was in no doubt that visiting horses was her favorite reward for learning letters of the alphabet—there are occasions when observation is more profitable. Ayllon and Azrin (1965) observed psychiatric patients in a large hospital to see how they spent their time. This was done in order to implement the "Premack principle" (Premack, 1959), in which a preferred activity is used to reinforce a nonpreferred activity. It can be a useful principle in rehabilitation. If a patient likes reading motorcycle magazines or playing cards, or even sitting doing nothing, these activities can all be used to encourage efforts in physiotherapy, speech therapy, or cognitive remediation programs. For instance, 5 minutes of walking practice may be followed by 5 minutes of sitting staring into space. It is not always the case that frequently observed behavior is *preferred* behavior; such behavior may be used in order to avoid an unpleasant task. One Rivermead patient, for example, spent long periods asking questions of the staff working with him. It appeared that he did this in order to postpone the difficult memory therapy program designed for him.

Another reason for direct observation is to observe the success or failure of an intervention program. Thus, if it has been established that a patient can learn the names of unknown people in photographs by means of visual imagery, it may be desirable to determine whether or not the patient uses the procedure to learn the names of colleagues at work.

The observers themselves may come from a variety of sources. Specially trained observers may be used—as they were, for instance, in a study of stutterers, carried out by Adams and Hotchkiss (1973). The observers measured the frequency of stuttering and the length of silences before a sound was emitted. Other studies have used teachers (Frederikson & Frederikson, 1975) and parents (Iwata & Lorentzson, 1976). The behavior being observed will also differ. It has been suggested (G. R. Patterson, Weiss & Hops, 1976) that it is impractical to observe infrequent behaviors in the natural environment unless participant observers are involved, such as the individual being assessed or somebody else closely involved. Certain other behaviors are not amenable to direct observation because they typically occur in private, or because the presence of an observer inhibits the behavior. A variation on this was noted with L. R. (described in Chapter 9). He frequently made childish comments, such as "Am I being a good boy?" or "Look at the little piggie-wiggie!" This patient was a 26-year-old professional worker. Whenever an attempt was made to tape-record these comments, L. R. ceased making them. The tape recorder then became part of his treatment program; it was switched on during mealtimes and on the ward, when his comments had been particularly annoying.

Other behaviors may be difficult to observe in the natural environment. For example, difficulty in learning any new skills may prevent a successful return to work, yet the opportunities to observe this directly may be few in a nonwork environment. In such a case, a simulated observation may be more helpful.

Simulated Observations. Simulated observations are usually less time-consuming than naturalistic observations, particularly when infrequent behaviors are involved, or when the patient can only be seen in a limited range of situations. They may also avoid some of the changes in behavior that can result from natural observations. Thus, L. R., who stopped making childish comments when the tape recorder was on, was quite happy to role-play a situation in which he was asked to explain to another patient what he did in the clinical psychology department. If simulated and naturalistic observations provide the same information, then the former is usually more efficient. We have seen that Kern (1984) found that a laboratory-based rat-avoidance test with undergraduates correlated well with naturalistic observations of untreated subjects but less well with those of treated subjects, so we cannot assume that simulated and naturalistic methods will give the same results. It is necessary, therefore, when designing analogue test situations, to attempt to determine the relationship with real-life situations. This theme is considered in more detail in Chapter 5.

There are a number of ways in which environments can be structured or simulated. Sometimes a special room or situation is constructed—for example, a playroom in a child guidance clinic, or a typist's office in an occupational therapy department. Sometimes the individual patient may be asked to remain in a particular area while the observations are carried out. Patients may be asked to take part in role playing so that a certain aspect of their behavior can be considered. This technique is widely used in social skills training (e.g., Marzillier & Winter, 1978). Analogue situations are also frequently used, particularly in work with phobic patients when tests of behavioral avoidance are in operation. The analogue situation is potentially useful in cognitive rehabilitation. For instance, it may be difficult to observe the ability to learn a new skill in a natural setting, whereas it would be more amenable to simulated behavioral observation. An activity such as an assembly task or a new game can be devised and administered to a patient. Initially, it will be necessary to establish whether or not the task is valid—that is, whether it is measuring ability to learn a new skill, rather than simply tapping immediate memory span or perceptual abilities. If it proves to be valid, then a simple assessment tool will be available to predict skill-learning behavior in the natural environment. This analogue approach is the basis of the Rivermead Behavioural Memory Test, to be described in Chapter 5.

BEHAVIORAL TREATMENT STRATEGIES

There is a great diversity of treatment techniques used in behavior therapy or behavior modification. (The terms are used synonymously here, because of a lack of agreement as to how to separate the two.) Methods have been developed to increase and to decrease behavior. Systematic desensitization, flooding, modeling, shaping, and chaining are some of the methods that have been used to increase participation in feared situations or to teach new skills. Positive and negative reinforcement, time out, extinction, response cost, overcorrection, and aversive conditioning have all been used to reduce or eliminate undesirable activities. (See Rimm & Masters, 1979, and Yule & Carr, 1980, for fuller descriptions of these techniques.) The number of situations and client groups subjected to behavioral treatment is also diverse, having moved on from the initial interest in patients with psychiatric problems (H. J. Eysenck, 1960; Wolpe, 1958) to include groups such as the mentally handicapped (Yule & Carr, 1980); children with epilepsy (Lavender, 1981); drug addicts (Sobell & Sobell, 1978); sexual offenders (Quinsey & Chaplin, 1984); patients being treated for gynecological or obstetric problems (Broome, 1980); diabetics (Longwill, 1980); heart patients (Wallace, 1982); and the neurologically impaired (E. Miller, 1980). Behavior therapists work in homes, schools, clinics, factories, hospitals, and prisons.

The theoretical approaches underlying behavior therapy are also diverse. It draws upon a number of fields within psychology, such as learning theory, information processing, linguistics, developmental psychology, social learning theory, and other connected disciplines. Because of this considerable range, there is no generally agreed-upon definition of behavior therapy (Kazdin, 1979; Powell, 1981). Kazdin points out that features seen by some authors as essential are regarded by others as features that have become outmoded. H. J. Eysenck (1959), for example, sees behavior therapy as relying heavily upon experimental psychology, whereas Lazarus (1971) argues that behavior therapy should draw upon *any* discipline that proves to be helpful, regardless of its particular theoretical orientation. Lazarus believes that adherence to one approach will limit the range of procedures available to a therapist. Furthermore, many problems faced by practicing therapists and their clients will be uninformed by research experience unless the therapists can draw from a wide range of disciplines.

While it is true that there are differences of opinion as to the nature of behavior therapy, it should also be recognized that its multifaceted constitution is its strength. The richness and complexity of behavioral approaches enables them to be applicable to many areas, not least in the field of cognitive rehabilitation. It should be noted here that cognitive rehabilitation and cognitive therapy (otherwise known as cognitive-behavior modification) have different meanings. "Cognitive rehabilitation" refers to the training, remediation, amelioration, or alleviation or cognitive deficits; "cognitive therapy" refers to those strategies used to change a person's attitudes, beliefs, self-perceptions, attributions, and expectations (Marzillier, 1980). Cognitive therapy may be useful in cognitive rehabilitation: For example, it can help to change the perceptions of patients with unilateral neglect who may believe they are going crazy because a page of print no longer makes sense. It can also be employed with memory-impaired patients who think they are stupid because they cannot remember important details. Moffat and I (Wilson & Moffat, 1984b) discuss the role of self-instruction techniques, adapted from Meichenbaum (1977), in the treatment of memory disorders. Hussian (1981) used a similar procedure with an elderly, forgetful woman; and so did Moffat (1984), when treating a young head-injured man. It would appear, however, that many cognitive therapy strategies are inappropriate for the severely memory-impaired, who are unable to remember the reasoning or thought processes that lead to statements of belief or the adoption of attitudes observed in therapy sessions. On the other hand, it may be possible to change attitudes and beliefs toward cognitive deficits in some patients. This could be particularly useful for those who do not believe there is much the matter with them.

In spite of the wide range of techniques and theoretical approaches, Powell (1981) believes that several features or principles are common. First, he argues that behavior therapy is an applied science. In treating the neurologically impaired, he suggests that psychology and neuropsychology should join forces. Furthermore, "all treatments must have a sound theoretical and scientific footing, and must not be pure whim on the part of the therapist" (1981, p. 17). It is also incumbent on the therapist to use a proper single-case design, and to carry out treatment in an experimental manner so that unambiguous, meaningful information can be obtained. This information will be used to evaluate the efficacy of treatment. The second principle identified by Powell is that behavior therapy should formulate targets at the beginning of treatment. This is in contrast to, say, interpretative psychotherapy, which arrives at specification of or insight into the problem at the *end* of therapy. In behavior therapy, there is a specific target to be aimed at. This should not be too broad or general, such as "improving memory" or "changing personality," but should be much more narrowly defined, such as "teaching the patient 10 names" or "enabling the patient to walk 5 yards in the physiotherapy gym without a stick." Third, Powell argues that behavior therapy should use measurement, because accurate observation and recording are essential features of an applied science. Measurement is important in order to avoid subjective or merely intuitive decisions about behavior change or treatment effectiveness.

Behavioral approaches have been used in rehabilitation for many years, but it is only recently that they have been more widely used for the amelioration of acquired cognitive impairment. Goodkin (1966), working with three stroke patients and one Parkinson patient, used operant conditioning to improve a number of skills, including wheelchair pushing, machine operating, and handwriting. Also in 1966, Edwards and Rosenberg published a paper describing how more than 200 mentally handicapped people were assessed and trained to make visual discriminations by means of positive and negative reinforcement. Ince (1969) used the Premack principle with two stroke patients who refused to go to speech and occupational therapy. Both regularly attended physiotherapy, so physiotherapy was used as reinforcement for attending the disliked therapy sessions. Taylor and Persons (1970) used principles of behavior modification in the ward management of three rehabilitation patients, and Booraem and Seacat (1972) used money to reinforce exercising in brain-damaged adults in a general hospital.

In 1976, Ince produced a book on behavior modification in rehabilitation. Most of the treatment examples provided by Ince concentrated on improving cooperation and decreasing disruptive behaviors in various departments, rather than specifically attempting to improve cognitive functioning. Nevertheless, some interesting and valuable suggestions regarding the application of behavioral principles to rehabilitation are discussed in this book. In a later publication edited by Ince (1980), one chapter is devoted to cognitive remediation. This is written by Diller, who, along with his colleagues (e.g., Weinberg *et al.*, 1979), have done much to stimulate treatment of hemi-inattention and unilateral spatial neglect. Some general principles of behavior modification in rehabilitation were described by Series and Lincoln (1978), and a review of the applications of biofeedback in rehabilitation was provided by Basmajian in 1981. Also in 1981, I (Wilson, 1981a) published a survey of behavioral treatments carried out at a rehabilitation center for stroke and head injuries. A number of different behavioral strategies were used during the 9-month period surveyed. These ranged from desensitization for fear of the hydrotherapy pool through to Portage treatment programs originally designed for preschool mentally handicapped children. (See Wilson, 1985, for a discussion of adapting Portage for neurological patients.) The survey also identified several patients referred for cognitive remediation programs, including those with memory impairment, aphasia, and visual object agnosia.

E. Miller (1980) produced an interesting paper that discussed the application of psychological management techniques to the management and rehabilitation of neuropsychological impairments. This paper was concerned entirely with cognitive impairments, and emphasized that treatment should be concentrated on amelioration of deficits rather that restitution of function. This idea has since been expanded by Miller (1984), who suggests that amelioration is concerned with assisting an individual to function as well as possible despite handicaps, whereas restitution implies the recovery or regaining of lost capacities. On the whole, Miller is likely to be correct, but there are occasions when restitution of function is feasible. A patient described by us (Wilson, White, & McGill, 1983) provides an example: He had received a gunshot wound some 5 years earlier, which rendered him totally alexic; and 3 years later he actively sought help to relearn to read. Several approaches were tried but only one led to any improvement—namely the phonetic approach. Within a few months, the man's reading level rose from being unmeasurable to the equivalent of a 9-year-old's. Each time this man has returned for assessment, his reading has continued to show improvement. In this case, restitution of function appears to be a reasonable goal.

In the majority of cases, however, it is more realistic to attempt amelioration than restoration. This is certainly true for the alternative-communication programs described for global aphasics (e.g., Wilson,

1981a). In this study, normal speech or comprehension was impossible for all the patients; of those who benefited from the alternative systems, only small improvements in communication occurred.

Elsewhere, I have stressed the value of behavioral techniques in the management of memory problems (Wilson, 1984). I have argued that behavioral approaches are profitable because (1) they are adaptable to a wide range of patients; (2) the goals are small and specific; (3) assessment and treatment are inseparable; (4) treatment can be continuously and easily evaluated; and (5) there is some evidence that these approaches are effective (see also Wilson, 1981a, 1982). In addition to these advantages, the behavioral methods provide a structure or procedure to follow in designing treatment. When a therapist is faced by a disturbed or severely handicapped person who has been referred for treatment, he or she may not be sure what to do or what steps to follow. Having a series of stages to complete within a designed treatment program reduces anxiety in the therapist, as well as being of possible benefit to the patient. These stages or steps are the same as those described in the section on behavioral assessment (it will be remembered that assessment and treatment in clinical practice are indistinguishable). However, at this point it is perhaps appropriate to describe how a behavior program for the treatment of a memory-impaired person should be organized:

1. *Specify the behavior to be changed.* "Inability to learn names" or "difficulty in remembering short routes" would be appropriate ways of describing such problems. Vague and general descriptions, such as "impaired concentration," would be unhelpful.

2. *State the goals or aims of treatment.* Again, these should be as specific and precise as possible. Appropriately expressed goals would read like the following: "To teach Mrs. A. the way from the ward to physiotherapy" and "To teach Mr. B. to check his notebook every half hour."

3. *Measure the deficit in order to obtain a satisfactory baseline.* This may be achieved in several ways. Examples of deficits to be measured might include "how often Mr. C. repeats the same question in a week" or "how many times Mrs. D. forgets to put her wheelchair brakes on before transferring."

All recording methods used in behavioral assessment and treatment are of potential use. It may also be necessary to carry out a more detailed analysis of factors affecting the memory failures. For example, does stress make the problem worse? Is relaxation training indicated? Does it help to pace information—that is, to present it at a slower rate?

Does extra rehearsal improve matters? What happens if the material is written down? What happens if another person presents the information?

4. *Decide on the most suitable treatment strategy for the particular individual.*

5. *Plan the treatment.* The following questions will provide guidance for the therapist through this stage, although it may not be necessary to go through *all* of these questions in each particular case:

a. What particular strategy should be used?
b. Who is to do the training?
c. When is the training to be carried out and where?
d. How is it to be conducted, and how often?
e. What happens if the patient succeeds in remembering the task?
f. Will such success be a sufficient reward in itself?
g. May some further reinforcement be required?
h. How is success to be measured?
i. What happens if the patient fails at the task?
j. In the event of such a failure, is the patient to be reminded?
k. Who will be responsible for keeping records? Will it be the therapist, the patient, the family, or an independent observer?

6. *Begin the treatment.*

7. *Monitor and evaluate progress according to the plan outlined in stage 5.*

8. *Change the procedure if necessary.*

Belief in the value of behavior therapy techniques in cognitive rehabilitation is an assumption underlying all the treatment studies to be described in this book.

SINGLE-CASE EXPERIMENTAL DESIGNS

Single-Case versus Group Designs: Comparative Merits

In evaluating the effectiveness of treatment for a particular individual, single-case designs are usually more informative than group designs. A typical group study would provide different treatments for two or more groups of people, although one group is sometimes subjected to two or more treatments. Usually, results are described in terms of the average or mean response of each group under each condition. Wide individual differences are common. Group studies rarely indicate how many people improve, how many remain unaffected, or how many are made worse by the treatment. The findings are often of little value in predicting whether or not a particular treatment is likely to be effective for a given individual. Because of their quantitative emphasis, group studies highlight statistical significance rather than clinical significance. To illustrate the difference between statistical and clinical significance, consider the following examples. In the field of biofeedback, it might be possible to demonstrate that training a particular muscle in the arm of a stroke patient leads to a statistically significant improvement in the control of that muscle. Clinically or functionally, however, the patient still cannot move the arm or make a cup of tea or get dressed without assistance. Conversely, it might be possible to demonstrate that group training for memory problems is statistically no better than a placebo treatment, but certain individuals within the group may benefit considerably, and their ability to cope with their memory problems may improve.

Single-case experimental designs avoid many of the problems inherent in group studies. The experimenter can tailor the treatment to the individual's particular needs and continuously evaluate his or her responses to the treatment or intervention strategies while controlling for the effects of spontaneous recovery or improvement over time.

Types of Single-Case Designs

The Reversal Design

The simplest single-case design is the reversal or ABAB design, where A equals baseline and B equals intervention. An example of this design is given by Zlutnick, Mayville, and Moffat (1975) in a program to reduce the number of motor seizures experienced by a 17-year-old mentally retarded girl. In the baseline period she was observed to have an average of 16 seizures per day. The seizures were noted to occur after a characteristic "chain" of behaviors, so treatment consisted of interrupting the beginning of the "chain." During the first treatment period, the seizures dropped to almost zero level. When baseline conditions were reinstated, however, the number rose again, although not to the same level as observed during the first baseline. Reinstatement of the second treatment phase resulted in almost complete elimination of the seizures. Variations on the ABAB design are frequently made. One might, for example, include a C stage in the program, where C equals an alternative treatment. The design would then become ABAC or ABABC. (For further discussion of these designs, see Hersen & Barlow, 1976; Kazdin, 1982; and Kratochwill, 1978.)

Although the reversal design has the benefit of being simple, its application to treatment programs is limited, for three main reasons. First, it is often impossible to revert to baseline conditions; if a person has been taught to remember the way from the ward to the occupational therapy department, for example, the person cannot "unlearn" this. Second, there are occasions when such an approach is unethical and even dangerous. Suppose, for example, that an amnesic patient has been taught to check whether he or she has left the stove on; then it would be hazardous to revert back to a time when the stove was not checked! Third, it is often impracticable to revert to baseline conditions. For instance, when treatment has been successful in preventing a patient from constantly repeating a particular question, then staff and relatives will not welcome a return to the previous state of affairs. Despite these limitations, the reversal design is worth having in one's repertoire of evaluation techniques.

Multiple-Baseline Designs

Multiple-baseline designs are probably more useful as evaluative procedures, at least as far as cognitive remediation is concerned. There are three main kinds of multiple-baseline designs, and each is described in turn.

Multiple-Baseline-Across-Behaviors Design. In the multiple-baseline-across-behaviors design, several different behaviors or problems are selected for treatment. Baselines are taken on all the behaviors, but only one is treated at a time. Again, this allows the therapist to separate out the effects of general improvement. An illustration of this design is provided by the case of a 22-year-old head-injured girl who was treated for fear of physiotherapy (Wilson & Powell, in press). She was physically very disabled, and the physiotherapy exercises were difficult for her. Also, in the past, she had received some harsh treatment at another center shortly after recovering consciousness from the head injury. All these factors would appear to have contributed to her fear. Baselines were taken of the amount of time spent in each of five exercises. One exercise, "head balancing," she actually enjoyed doing—no doubt because it was easy for her. Of the others, three were particularly disliked, and she spent less than 2 minutes on each of these before complaining. A multiple-baseline procedure was used, in which one of the three most disliked exercises was treated each week. The first week after baselines, the patient was (1) asked to try to increase the amount of time spent on that exercise; (2) given verbal feedback on her performance; (3) given visual feedback by means of a graph; and (4) allowed to spend several minutes on the head-balancing exercises if she reached her target (the Premack principle). For the remaining disliked exercises, baselines were still taken, but no encouragement was given. The following week, another disliked exercise was included in the treatment, and in the third week the final exercise was added. Improvement in the amount of time spent on each exercise only occured after treatment for that exercise was initiated. Thus, the patient's improvement could not be explained by spontaneous recovery or gradual change over time. If this were the case, then all behaviors should have improved at the same time and at the same rate.

Multiple-Baseline-Across-Settings Design. In the multiple-baseline-across-settings design, only one problem or behavior is tackled, but the effects of treatment are investigated in one setting at a time. This design is useful when situation-specific effects may occur. We (S. Carr & Wilson, 1983) used this procedure with a spinal patient who forgot (or refused) to lift himself from his wheelchair frequently enough to avoid pressure sores. The patient would not respond to the reasoning or cajoling of physiotherapists, nurses, or doctors. A machine was made that was attached to the wheelchair and recorded the number of lifts made. A lift was defined as the man's buttocks leaving the chair for at least 4 seconds, the patient having pushed himself up with his arms. At least one lift every 10 minutes was considered desirable. Following baselines in four different settings (the workshops, lunchtimes, coffee breaks, and the ward), the machine was fitted to his wheelchair in one setting only (the workshops). Here, the rate of lifting increased dramatically. The next stage was to introduce the machine during lunchtime, then during coffee breaks, and finally on the ward. In each situation, the patient lifted himself the required number of times only *after* the machine had been introduced.

Multiple-Baseline-Across-Subjects Design. Although the multiple-baseline-across-subjects design is not, strictly speaking, a *single*-case design, it is usually included in single-case methodology because the problems with very small groups of subjects are similar to those encountered when $N = 1$. We used this design (Wilson & Moffat, 1984) in a study that investigated the ability of four men to learn people's names, using a visual-imagery procedure. In the baseline period, patients were asked the names of people at the rehabilitation center where they were being treated. They were seen individually each day when all the names were tested. However, introduction of treatment was staggered for each individual. Again, improvements only occurred once the treatment procedure was introduced.

Other Single-Case Designs

The three multiple-baseline designs can be applied to a wide range of patients and problems; they are invaluable tools for monitoring intervention strategies. There are other single-case designs. For example, alternating treatments can be used where two or more treatment strategies are employed at the same time (Singh, Beale, & Dawson, 1981). Embedded designs are further variations of the single-case approach, where reversal and multiple-baseline procedures are used together (see, e.g., Wong & Liberman, 1981).

Use of Statistics

Statistics are less often employed in single-case designs than in group studies. There is controversy about their use in single-case studies, with some arguing that if statistics are needed to determine whether or not intervention is effective, then clinical significance is unlikely to have occurred. Others argue that there are occasions when statistics are useful. A supporting example for the latter argument would be the situation when one is faced by uncontrolled variability in the dependent variable. For further discussion of these arguments, and a description of the statistical techniques appropriate in single-case designs, the reader is referred to Hersen and Barlow (1976), Yule and Hemsley (1977), Edgington (1982), and Kazdin (1982).

CONCLUSIONS

In the three chapters of Secction II, I have discussed three major areas in psychology that contribute toward an understanding of the problems, assessment, and treatment of adults with acquired memory deficits. Neuropsychology helps us to understand the nature of memory impairment from different perspectives. One approach within this discipline is to identify the cerebral systems and structures involved in memory, and to ascertain whether or not these structures are intact in any given patient. This is important because rehabilitation frequently needs to establish which systems or skills are unimpaired, or relatively unimpaired, so that these can be utilized in order to bypass damaged systems. Another approach within neuropsychology is to investigate and specify the characteristics of particular etiologies, diagnostic categories, or syndromes, such as dementia, severe head injury, or Korsakoff syndrome. This, too, provides valuable information for therapists working with such patients—not only because it helps them predict what a patient's cognitive status is likely to be, but also because it helps with the general management of patients and their families. Neuropsychological assessment provides several techniques for identifying areas of strengths and weaknesses in patients referred for cognitive rehabilitation.

Cognitive psychology offers a theoretical framework for understanding the nature of memory deficits. Questions can be asked as to whether a disorder involves STM or LTM, visual or verbal memory, or semantic or episodic memory. As Baddeley (1984) suggests, a theory is like a map, in that it helps us find our way around. Cognitive psychology allows us to predict which areas are likely to respond to treatment. We know, for example, that procedural learning is easier than declarative learning for amnesic patients, and that some forms of paired-associate learning can be mastered with relative ease while other forms are virtually impossible for amnesics to learn.

Neither neuropsychology nor cognitive psychology plays a large role in establishing therapeutic procedures; for these, we must turn to behavioral psychology. From this field, we can utilize behavioral assessment procedures to specify and measure the nature of the practical, everyday problems faced by the memory-impaired. Behavioral psychology also provides a number of therapeutic strategies for changing behavior, as well as strategies for generalizing improvements across behaviors and settings. Finally, it has produced single-case experimental designs for evaluating the effectiveness of individual treatments.

None of the three fields is sufficiently informative that the cognitive remediator can afford to concentrate on one at the expense of the other two. Cognitive psychology has produced only very few useful assessment or treatment strategies, although as far as theory, description, and research are concerned, it has produced some sound building blocks. Neuropsychology has not been active in the management and treatment of cognitive deficit, although it has provided useful evidence regarding localization of function and cerebral asymmetry. Any intervention must take into account the neuropsychological status of the patient or client. Neuropsychology has also produced some valuable single-case studies (as opposed to single-case experimental designs). For example, Broca's study of his patient "Tan" (Broca, 1861) probably began the whole field of modern neuropsychology. To take a more recent example, Milner and colleagues' patient H. M., has almost certainly influenced he neuropsychological study of memory more than any other individual. Behavioral psychology applied to adults with acquired organic memory deficits will be limited if it does not take into account both the model of human memory established by cognitive psychologists and the characteristics of intellectual function established by neuropsychological investigation. On the other hand, when combined with these fields, behavioral psychology provides valuable tools for measuring everyday, practical problems resulting from memory impairment. It also enables us to implement strategies for reducing these problems, and for monitoring the rate and extent of any change.

It remains, at the end of this section dealing with theoretical frameworks, methodologies, and previous research findings, to remind the reader that the three disciplines described in these chapters have influenced the purpose, design, and procedure of each of the studies that are described in Section III. As noted in Chapter 5, for example, the development and piloting of a new memory test could not have progressed in the way it did without being influenced by concepts from all these disciplines discussed in these three chapters.

·III·
MEMORY REHABILITATION STUDIES

·5·

ASSESSMENT FOR REHABILITATION: THE RIVERMEAD BEHAVIOURAL MEMORY TEST

INTRODUCTION

This chapter is concerned with the identification of everyday memory problems. It has been placed first of all the studies in Section III because it deals with assessment and therefore represents our initial concern in rehabilitation. Although memory tests exist to measure acquisition and retention of experimental material (see Erickson & Scott, 1977, for a description of some of these), little is known about performance on these tests and its relationship (if any) with performance in everyday life. Erickson, Poon, and Walsh-Sweeney (1980) argue that the major justification of a memory test or battery "lies in the instrument's ability to contribute to the understanding and remediation of behavioral deficits. The instrument should be composed of tasks with clear behavioral analogues that can be validated in terms of everyday behavior and translated into meaningful intervention strategies" (pp. 380–381). However, none of the existing memory batteries attempt to identify the occurrence of everyday memory problems; furthermore, results from some tests can be misleading. The frequently used Wechsler Memory Scale (Wechsler, 1945), for example, was administered to the densely amnesic patient described in Chapter 7. The MQ he obtained was 96, which is within the average range; it was not at all an accurate reflection of the severity of his handicap for nomal living.

Other measures, such as the Recognition Memory Test from the National Hospital of Great Britain (Warrington, 1984), provide useful

Further research has been carried out on this test, and some modifications have followed. The four parallel versions are available from Thames Valley Test Co., 22 Bulmershe Road, Reading, Berkshire, RGI 5RJ, England.

information, but the basic inadequacies of standardized tests in relation to their application to the identification of everyday memory problems remain. They are unable to specify *which* particular everyday problems are likely to be experienced by the memory-impaired, and they cannot quantify the frequency or severity of such problems.

Memory questionnaires have been used in an attempt to overcome some of these shortcomings. Sunderland *et al.* (1983), for example, examined head-injured patients and found that memory failures reported on questionnaires related to test performance for patients who had been injured some length of time previous to the examination, but not for those who had been recently injured (the group most likely to be undergoing therapy). In addition, the current test batteries and questionnaires have not addressed themselves to the remediation of any of the deficits they have identified.

The Rivermead Behavioural Memory Test (RBMT) was developed in order to detect impairment of everyday memory functioning and to monitor change following treatment for memory difficulties. The test attempts to bridge the gap between laboratory-based and naturalistic measures of memory. Thus, although it is administered and scored in a standardized way, the subtests aim to provide an analogue of a range of everyday memory situations that appear to be troublesome for certain patients with acquired brain damage. The subtests were chosen (1) on the basis of the memory difficulties reported by patients in a study of memory problems in head-injured patients (Sunderland *et al.* 1983), and (2) through observations of patients at Rivermead. The items require either remembering to carry out some everyday task or retaining the type of information needed for adequate everyday functioning. The subtests are combined with some conventional memory measures. There are four alternative versions of the RBMT, so that practice effects through repeated testing can be reduced.

As the study is presented, the influence of the major theoretical disciplines discussed in Section II can be identified. The influence of neuropsychology and cerebral organization is present in the selection of some of the items of the test. Verbal items, on the whole, tap left-hemisphere skills, while visual and spatial items tap right-hemisphere skills.

The interest shown by cognitive psychologists in the assessment of everyday memory problems is reflected in a recent publication by Harris and Morris (1984), although Neisser was already arguing for a move in this direction in 1978. The areas in which cognitive psychologists are currently showing interest include memory for people (Bahrick, 1984), cognitive failures in everyday life (Broadbent et al., 1982), and remembering to do things (Harris, 1984). All these topics are included in the RBMT, which as noted, was greatly influenced by the work of Sunderland et al., (1983) on everyday memory problems following head injury. The RBMT also reflects cognitive psychologists' interest in the structure of human memory, with its emphasis on both immediate and delayed tasks, together with verbal, visual, and spatial tasks.

Behavioral psychology has also influenced the structure of the RBMT. A series of tasks analogous to everyday situations was designed in order to measure success or failure in memory performance. This approach is in the tradition of the behavioral assessment procedures that use simulated conditions to make observations. It has been pointed out in Chapter 4 that observations from simulated conditions are usually less time-consuming than naturalistic observations, and this is an important consideration in assessment.

THE RIVERMEAD BEHAVIOURAL MEMORY TEST

Description of the RBMT Items

1. *Remembering a name.* The subject is shown a photograph and told the person's first name and surname. Both names are tested after a delay, during which other items are presented.

2. *Remembering a hidden belonging.* A possession belonging to the subject is borrowed and secreted (e.g., in a drawer or cupboard). The subject is requested to ask for the belonging at the end of the session and to remember where it has been hidden. The possession should not be valuable. For inpatients at Rivermead, we ask for their rehabilitation timetable, which is printed on a small card. For others, we usually select a comb, pencil, or handkerchief.

3. *Remembering an appointment.* The subject is told to ask a particular question relating to the near future when he or she hears the alarm. The alarm is set to ring in 20 minutes.

4. *Picture recognition.* Line drawings of 10 common objects are shown one at a time for 5 seconds each. The subject is required to

name each picture and, after a filled delay, to select the original 10 from a set of 20. (These pictures are taken from Snodgrass & Vanderwart, 1980.)

5. *Prose recall.* (This subtest is included in the RBMT with permission from Alan Sunderland.) The subject is read a short passage of prose and is asked to relate as much of it as he or she can remember, both immediately and after a delay. This offers a test of episodic memory for meaningful material, and proved to be the best predictor of everyday memory problems in the study by Sunderland *et al.* (1983).

6. *Remembering a short route.* The tester traces a short route within the room. The route consists of five sections. The subject is required to reproduce the route immediately and after a delay.

7. *Remembering an errand.* While demonstrating the route, the tester leaves an envelope at a specified location. The subject is required to leave the envelope in the same location.

8. *Orientation.* The subject is asked for the year, month, day of the week, and place and city of location. He or she is also asked selected "Personal and Current Information" items from the Wechsler Memory Scale (Wechsler, 1945).

9. *Date.* The subject is asked for the date, which is scored separately, because the pilot study (to be described later in this chapter) did not suggest a high correlation between this and the other orientation questions.

10. *Face recognition.* The subject is shown photographs of five faces, one at a time. For each photograph, the subject is required to say whether the person depicted is a male or female, and whether the person is over 40 years of age. It is explained that this is to help concentration. The subject is subsequently required to select the original five faces from a set of 10 after a filled delay.

11. *Learning a new skill.* The subject is required to learn the six steps involved in putting a given message into the memory of a calculator. Three trials are allowed.

Conventional Memory Tests Accompanying the RBMT

The following tests are administered immediately after the RBMT items:

1. *Paired-associate learning.* Six paired associates from the Randt, Brown, and Osborne (1980) test are presented verbally, and are subse-

quently tested for a total of three trials. This provides a test of long-term verbal learning.

2. *WAIS Digit Span.* In this standard STM, a subtest of the WAIS (Wechsler, 1955), the subject is required to repeat back sequences of digits until a point is reached at which he or she consistently makes errors.

Instructions and Sequence for Giving the RBMT

1a. *Remembering a name.* "What I want you to do is to remember this person's name." (The tester shows a photograph.) "Her name is Catherine Taylor. Can you repeat the name? Later on I am going to ask you what her name is." (The photograph is then placed face downward on the table.)

2a. *Remembering a hidden belonging.* "What I am going to do now is to put something of yours away, and see if you can remember to ask me for it when I have finished this series of tests. I also want you to remember where I put it." (Some item is then selected that belongs to the patient. As noted earlier, the item should be personal, but not too valuable.)

3a. *Remembering an appointment.* "I am going to set this alarm to go off in 20 minutes." (The tester demonstrates the alarm, and sets it.) "When it sounds, I want you to ask me about your next appointment. Say something like 'Can you tell me when I have to see you again?' or words to that effect."

4a. *Picture recognition.* "Now I am going to show you a series of pictures. Look at each one carefully and tell me what object is pictured. Later, I am going to show you some pictures and I want you to pick out the ones I have just shown you. With each picture, I shall leave it there for 5 seconds to give you a chance to memorize it." (Ten pictures are then shown, each for 5 seconds.)

5a. *Prose recall.* "Next I am going to read you a passage of about five or six lines. Listen carefully, and when I have finished, tell me back as much as you can remember. Ready?"

Mr. Brian / Kelly, / a Security Express employee, / was shot dead / on Monday / during a bank raid / in Brighton. / The four raiders / all wore masks, / and one carried / a sawn-off / shotgun. / Police detectives / were sifting through / eyewitness accounts / last night. / A police spokesman said, / "He was a very brave man. / He went for / the armed raider / and put up a hell of a fight." /

"Now tell me back as much of that story as you can."

4b. *Picture recognition.* "Now we are going back to those pictures I showed you earlier. For each picture, I want you to tell me whether you saw it before or not." (The tester then presents 20 pictures—the 10 seen before, and 10 new ones—in random order. Presentation is unpaced, but the subject is encouraged to guess if unsure.)

6a. *Remembering a short route.* "What I am going to do now is to trace a short path around this room. I want you to watch what I do, and when I have finished, do the same thing. I am going to start from this chair, and take this envelope with me." (The patient is shown the envelope.) "From here, I am going over to the door, and from the door to the window, and from the window to the desk." (The tester walks through the route as he or she speaks.) "I am going to leave this envelope on the desk, and from here, I am going back to my chair." (The tester returns to the chair, and then fetches the envelope back and places it on the desk in front of the patient.) "Now what I would like you to do is to start where I started and follow the same path."

7. *Remembering an errand.* (The tester simply records whether or not the patient leaves the envelope in the correct place.)

8. and 9. *Orientation and Date.* "Now I would like to ask you a few questions. Ready?"

   a. "What year is it now?"
   b. "What month is it?"
   c. "What day of the week is it?"
   d. "What date is it?"
   e. "What place are we in now?"
   f. "What city are we in?"
   g. "How old are you now?"
   h. "What year were you born?"
   i. "What is the name of the present Prime Minister?" (for a British patient)
   j. "Who is the current President of the United States?" (for British and American patients; American patients also are asked to identify their state governor)

10a. *Face recognition.* "This time I am going to show you some faces. I want you to look at each one carefully, and tell me whether it is male or female, and whether the person is under or over 40 years old. This is just to help you concentrate, since you will have to remember them later." (The tester then shows five faces one at a time for 5 seconds each.)

11. *Leaning a new skill.* (The tester should first check whether the alarm [see item 3a] is about to sound shortly. If it is, he or she should engage the subject in conversation until it does, rather than risk having this task disrupted.) "What I am going to do now is to try to teach you to set the date and the time on this machine." (The tester shows the calculator.) "There are six steps involved; I want you to watch me do it first, and then see if you can do it. Watch what I do.

"The first step is to put this button over to SET." (For this and each succeeding step, the tester demonstrates the action required.) "The second step is to put in the month. For example, it's the third month now, so we put in 03. Then we put in the date. For example, it's the 16th, so we put in 16. Now we have to tell the machine that that is the date. So we press the DATE button, which is this one here. Now we have to put in the time, which is 1:54. So we press 1-5-4. Now we have to tell the machine that that is the time. So we press the TIME button, which is this one here. And that's it." (The tester then sets the top button to normal and wipes off previous input by pressing the RESET button at the back of the machine.)

"Now I'd like you to try this. What did I do first?" (After each step, any errors are corrected, so that each trial eventually succeeds in putting in the appropriate date and time. Subjects are allowed up to three attempts. If all six steps are correct on any one trial, the test stops at that point.)

10b. *Face recognition.* The tester presents 10 faces, five of which are new and five previously presented, one at a time. The patient is required to say in each case whether or not he or she has been shown the particular face before. Order of new and old faces is random, presentation is unpaced, and subjects are encouraged to guess if necessary.)

3b. *Remembering an appointment.* (When the alarm sounds, if the patient asks the tester spontaneously when the next appointment is to be, the tester scores 1 point. If not, the tester asks, "What were you going to do when the alarm sounded?" and records the answer.)

5b. *Prose recall (delayed).* "Do you remember that story I read to you earlier? I want you to see how much of it you can remember now. Tell me as much as you can." (If the patient cannot remember anything about it, the tester should provide a cue: "It started off like this: 'Mr. Brian Kelly, a Security Express employee' . . . If the patient needs the cue, this is to be noted.)

6b. *Remembering a short route (delayed recall).* "Do you remember the path I took around the room earlier? I want to see if you can still remember it. So could you start where I started and take the same route?" (If the patient does not spontaneously pick up the envelope the tester should stop him or her and say, "I took something with me. Do you remember what it was?" If not, the tester should say, "It was this envelope; do what I did with it.")

1b. *Remembering a name.* (The tester shows the photograph.) "Do you remember what this person's name was?" (If not, then the tester should give the first letter of the first name and see if the correct response is forthcoming. Then the tester should wait to see if the surname is recalled spontaneously; if not, the tester should give the first letter of the surname. If the subject gives an *incorrect* name that begins with the correct letter—e.g., "Turner" for "Taylor"—the tester should say, "No, but it did begin with a T.")

2b. *Remembering a hidden belonging.* "We have now finished this series of tests." (The tester then pauses for 5 seconds to see whether the patient spontaneously asks for the belonging. If not, the tester should say, "You were going to remind me to give you something of yours. Can you remember what it was, and can you remember where I put it?")

The paired associates from the Randt *et al.* (1980) test, and the WAIS Digit Span subtest, are then administered.

PILOT STUDY OF THE RBMT

Norms

The RBMT was given to 25 brain-damaged patients described by the occupational therapy department at Rivermead as having everyday memory problems, and to 16 brain-damaged patients described by the

Table 5-1. Characteristics of Patients in the Pilot Study

Characteristic	Memory-impaired ($n = 25$)	Non-memory-impaired ($n = 16$)
Diagnosis		
Head injury	16	8
CVA	5	7
Other[a]	4	1
Sex		
Male	15	10
Female	10	6
Age		
$\bar{x}$	31	36
SD	14	15
Range	13-62	17-57

[a]Encephalitis, tumor, and gas poisoning.

same department as not having everyday memory problems. The characteristics of the patients are given in Table 5-1.

The scoring used for the pilot study was pass–fail, with 1 or 0 being given for each item (see Appendix A for details of the procedure). A control group of 20 non-brain-damaged patients aged 17 to 60 years (all living at home) scored 100%. All patients in the memory-impaired group, however, failed at least three items. The mean number of items passed was 3.76, with a range of 0–9, and a standard deviation of 2.84. The results can be seen in Table 5-2. In contrast, those categorized by the occupational therapists as not having memory problems achieved a mean score of 10.12, with a range of 9–12, and a standard deviation of 1.16.

A comparison of the two brain-damaged groups on the individual items can be seen in Table 5-3. The five items that appeared to be most difficult for the memory-impaired group were these: remembering the two names[1]; remembering a hidden belonging; remembering an appointment; and face recognition. On the whole, these caused relatively little difficulty for the non-memory-impaired group, although 6 of the 16 people failed on face recognition. This could have been due to perceptual rather than memory problems. Of the 16 non-memory-

1. The item described earlier in this chapter as "remembering a name" was scored as two items in the pilot study: "remembering a first name" and "remembering a surname."

Table 5-2. Performance on the RBMT of the 25 Memory-Impaired Patients

Patient	1	2	3	4	5	6	7	8	9	10	11	12	Totals
1					*	*	*						3
2					*	*		*		*			4
3											*		1
4			*		*	*	*	*			*	*	7
5	*	*			*	*	*	*	*	*		*	9
6													0
7													0
8				*	*	*	*	*	*	*	*		8
9					*	*	*		*	*			5
10													0
11													0
12					*	*			*				3
13	*		*		*		*						4
14	*	*						*	*	*		*	6
15		*			*	*	*		*		*		6
16					*	*	*		*				4
17					*		*		*			*	4
18			*	*	*	*	*		*	*		*	8
19													0
20				*			*	*	*	*		*	6
21	*	*		*	*	*	*		*				0
22													0
23					*		*		*	*			4
24					*								1
25						*	*	*		*			4
Totals	4	4	3	4	15	12	14	7	12	9	4	6	

Items[a]

Note. An asterisk signifies that an item was successfully completed.

[a]Items corresponding to numbers: 1, remembering a first name; 2, remembering a surname; 3, remembering a hidden belonging; 4, remembering an appointment; 5, immediate remembering of a short route; 6, delayed remembering of a short route; 7, remembering an errand; 8, learning a new skill; 9, orientation; 10, date; 11, face recognition; 12, picture recognition. Note that prose recall was not included as an item in this pilot study, and that the items described earlier in this chapter as "remembering a name" and "remembering a short route" were each treated in the pilot study as two separate items (1-2 and 5-6, respectively).

Table 5-3. A Comparison of Memory-Impaired ($n = 25$) and
Non-Memory-Impaired ($n = 16$) Patients on Individual Items of
the RBMT

Item[a]	Memory-impaired (percentage succeeding)	Non-memory-impaired (percentage succeeding)
1	16	87.5
2	16	75
3	12	93.75
4	16	68.75
5	60	100
6	48	100
7	52	87.5
8	28	93.75
9	48	81.25
10	36	75
11	16	62.5
12	24	87.5

[a]For items corresponding to numbers, see footnote a to
Table 5-2.

impaired subjects, 5 also failed on remembering an appointment.
However, the most frequently failed item in the memory-impaired-
group—remembering a hidden belonging—was failed by only 1 of the
non-memory-impaired group. Remembering a short route, both immediate and delayed,[2] was passed by everyone in the non-memory-
impaired group. Immediate remembering of the route was also passed
by a majority of the memory-impaired. The test would thus certainly
seem sensitive to memory impairment, but can it really be seen as a
valid measure of everyday memory problems?

Judgments by Occupational Therapists

The RBMT scores of those patients judged by the occupational therapists treating them as having everyday memory problems were compared with scores of the group judged as not having such problems. A

2. The item described earlier in this chapter as "remembering a short route" was
scored as two items in the pilot study: "immediate" and "delayed" remembering of a
short route.

Mann–Whitney test was applied to see whether the two sets of scores were significantly different from each other. The results indicated such a difference ($U = 3.5$, $p < .001$).

Validity

Validity was assessed in two ways. First, results on the RBMT were correlated with scores on several standardized tests; second, scores were correlated with therapists' observations of memory failures during treatment.

Correlations with Standardized Tests

The majority of the 41 patients in the pilot study were also assessed on the WAIS, the Logical Memory passages from the Wechsler Memory Scale, and the Randt et al. (1980) paired-associate learning test. A smaller number were also assessed on the Forced-Choice Words and Forced-Choice Faces subtests of the Warrington Recognition Memory Test (Warrington, 1984). The results are shown in Table 5-4.

Table 5-4. Correlations between the RBMT and Standardized Tests

Test	n	r
Full-scale IQ (WAIS)	35	.18
Verbal IQ (WAIS)	37	.14
Performance IQ (WAIS)	35	.23
Immediate Logical Memory (Wechsler Memory Scale)	38	.47**
Delayed Logical Memory (Wechsler Memory Scale)	38	.72***
Delayed Logical Memory as percentage of immediate Logical Memory	38	.81***
Forced-Choice Words (Warrington Recognition Memory Test)	22	.56**
Forced-Choice Faces (Warrington Recognition Memory Test)	22	.53*
Paired associates (Randt et al., 1980)	39	.61***

*$p = .02$.
**$p = .01$.
***$p = .001$.

From Table 5-4, it can be seen that the RBMT did not correlate with tests of intelligence. As Erickson and Scott (1977) have pointed out, tests of memory should *not* correlate highly with tests of intelligence, and those that do are redundant. However, the RBMT did correlate with all other memory tests investigated. This certainly suggests that it is a genuine test of memory. Furthermore, the RBMT, unlike the standardized tests, investigates performances analogous to real-life situations; it should, therefore, provide more practical information to patients, to their relatives, and to the staff treating them. The RBMT also has face validity, so it may well avoid problems with poor motivation (e.g., those seen in paired-associate learning tasks).

Therapists' Observations

Therapists' observations probably constituted the most powerful investigation of validity. All patients at Rivermead spend four sessions a day in rehabilitation. Therapists treating a group of 20 patients completed a checklist for each individual member of the group at the end of each session. This procedure continued for a period of 2 weeks. The checklist asked whether or not a memory failure had occured in each of 19 areas (see Appendix B for a copy of the list); it was adapted from one designed by Sunderland, Harris, and Baddeley (1984). The correlation between therapists' observations and subjects' scores on the RBMT was .70 ($p < .001$).

Thus, on both validity measures, the RBMT proved to be a valid assessment tool.

Reliability

Three measures of reliability were completed. Interrater reliability was established by two judges independently scoring 11 patients who had been randomly selected from the 25 memory-impaired patients in the pilot study. The interrater reliability was 100%. This is hardly surprising, as there is little subjectivity involved in the scoring; subjects either pass or fail each item.

As Anastasi (1982) points out, the most obvious method for finding the reliability of test scores is to administer the same test on two separate occasions. However, certain difficulties are inherent in such a test for reliability: Not only are the results affected by testing conditions such as patient fatigue and environmental distractions, but also the subjects will have had previous experience of taking the test and might thereby benefit from practice. This may be more likely with a simple test such as the RBMT than with a more complex test like the WAIS. If the test–retest interval is increased to maximize forgetting, then a further complication arises in the case of patients undergoing rehabilitation: They may be responding to treatment in a positive way, so that they become more proficient in the very skills that are being measured in the tests. This, in turn, will reduce reliability. Nevertheless, retesting was carried out with a small group of four subjects, all of whom were severely amnesic (subjects 3, 6, 7, and 10 from Table 5-2) and thus unlikely to remember the previous assessment. Each patient was reassessed on form 1 of the RBMT 1 week after the first testing. The agreement on the two occasions was 96% (Only one patient obtained a different score on the two occasions, and this was for only 1 of the 12 items.)

The most important measure of reliability in this study was parallel-form reliability. Four different versions of the test are available in order to allow for repeated assessments to monitor change after treatment and/or over time. Parallel-form reliability was investigated by administering all four tests to a group of 12 subjects (none of whom were included in the earlier investigations). The patients in this group had varying degrees of memory deficit (the number of items successfully completed on the RBMT ranged from 0 to 10). The four tests were administered in a counterbalanced order at intervals ranging from 2 days to 1 week. The correlations between the forms are shown in Table 5-5.

Table 5-5. Correlations (Product–Moment) between the Four Parallel Versions of the RBMT

	A	B	C	D
A	—	.83***	.85***	.65*
B		—	.73**	.72**
C			—	.78**
D				—

$*p < .05.$
$**p < .01.$
$***p < .001.$

Table 5-6. Analysis of Variance to Determine Whether or Not There Was a Significant Difference between Scores on Four Parallel Versions of the RBMT

Source of variation	Sum of squares	df	Mean squares	F
Between people	388.65	11		
Within people	65.75	36		
Treatments	0.40	3	0.13	0.06
Residual	65.36	33	1.98	
Total	454.40	47		

From Table 5-5, it will seen that all correlations were significant, and that those between A and B and A and C were particularly high. Although the correlation between A and D was lower than the others, a one-way analysis of variance (see Table 5-6) showed that there was no significant difference between the forms ($F = 0.06$, $df = 3,33$). This means that no one form appears to be easier than any other form.

CONCLUSIONS

The RBMT was developed in order to predict which brain-damaged people are likely to experience everyday memory problems. Therapists treating patients with and without obvious memory impairments were asked to record patients' everyday memory failures for a period of 2 weeks, and scores obtained by the therapists correlated significantly with scores on the RBMT. This strongly suggests that the RBMT does indeed detect everyday memory problems. The RBMT also correlated with standardized memory tests, and, in particular, with delayed recall of the Logical Memory passages from the Wechsler Memory Scale. Again, this provides evidence that the RBMT is a test of memory. However, it is suggested that the RBMT provides more information than the standardized tests, as it assesses skills necessary for adequate functioning in normal life, rather than performance on experimental material.

The RBMT is also a *reliable* procedure, with very high interrater reliability and good alternate-form reliability. The test, therefore, allows for repeated assessments to monitor stability, improvement, or deterioration over time. Because of this, it is potentially useful for other groups of patients (not included in the present studies) who may be in the process of changing. Such groups include patients with recent head injuries; patients with dementia, multiple sclerosis, or depression; alcoholics; and children being treated for leukemia.

Finally, the RBMT fulfills the practical requirements of a psychological test: It is short; it is easy to understand, to use, and to interpret; and it is applicable to a wide range of environmental settings.

Although severely amnesic patients will probably fail all parts of the test, it is possible with less impaired patients to see various patterns emerging that may in time prove to correlate with various neuropsychological dysfunctions. One use of the RBMT is to measure changes over time (Wilson, Cooper, & Kennerley, 1983), and the four parallel versions are available for this purpose. This means that the test could prove to be particularly useful in measuring either improvement (e.g., after head injury) or deterioration (e.g., in patients with Alzheimer disease). There is a need for a simple test to be widely available in neuropsychology to measure the severity of memory deficit over a broad range of conditions. The RBMT may prove to be a suitable test for this purpose.

The findings reported in this Chapter are now part of a 3-year research project funded by the Medical Research Council of Great Britain. Therapists at Rivermead filled out checklists for 80 patients on when memory failures occurred in therapy sessions. They were the same checklists used to establish validity during the pilot study. What remains to be determined through analysis of the checklist findings, however, is whether the individual items on the RBMT correlate with particular kinds of memory failure. For example, does the patient who fails delayed remembering of a short route also get lost going from one part of the rehabilitation center to another?

There is also a need to see how other groups of people perform on the RBMT. Professor Zimmerman and his colleagues in Germany are collecting data on demented patients, Dr. Poon in the United States is working with Alzheimer and with elderly depressed patients, and Janet Cockburn in Oxford is carrying out a similar investigation with an elderly control group. Norms from children will also be available soon.

·6·

VISUAL IMAGERY
FOR LEARNING PEOPLE'S NAMES

INTRODUCTION

The pilot study described in Chapter 5 indicated that difficulty in remembering people's names often constitutes a major memory problem in the everyday lives of those who have suffered brain damage, causing bewilderment and embarrassment to the memory-impaired persons, and sometimes irritation to those whose names have been forgotten. However, it is usually possible to teach one or two names to even the most severe amnesic, and the success that can be gained from learning names may encourage patients to apply particular strategies to other problem areas.

Several approaches can be adopted to help people who have difficulty in remembering names. All persons coming into contact with a memory-impaired individual could be asked to wear name badges, thus reducing the load on that individual's memory (although he or she would still have to remember to *look* at the badges). Such badges may be regarded as external aids, many of which are used by people with normal memory (Harris, 1980a). Another external aid would be a notebook in which the memory-impaired person could keep photographs and names of certain people likely to be contacted during the day or week. There are several different kinds of external aids, each with their own particular strengths and weaknesses as far as their operation in daily life is concerned (e.g., the notebook would involve some delay while the memory-impaired person took time to look up the required photograph and name). Advantages and disadvantages of

A version of the report of Experiment 1 appeared as "Teaching a Man to Remember People's Names after Removal of a Temporal Lobe Tumour" by B. A. Wilson, 1981, *Behavioural Psychotherapy*, 9, 338–344. Adapted by permission of the British Association of Behavioural Psychotherapy.

different external aids are discussed elsewhere (Wilson & Moffat, 1984).

Therapists who are actually engaged in teaching new names to their patients have several approaches available to them. Rote learning may be attempted, although this is unlikely to be effective for severe amnesics. If practice/rehearsal is employed, then the therapist can benefit from the suggestions supplied by Landauer and Bjork (1978). This method involves presenting the new name, testing after a short delay, and gradually increasing the interval as learning proceeds. The principle here is to combine success and reinforcement with a slowly increasing distribution of practice.

There are two main groups of internal strategies or "mnemonics"; these are verbal and visual techniques, each of which can be further divided. Verbal methods include alphabetical searching and first-letter cueing. In attempting to retrieve a particular name, it is sometimes possible to work through the alphabet, asking whether the name begins with A or B or C and so on, until the correct letter is recognized. This in turn may act as a retrieval cue for the full name. This approach is likely to be erratic, and there does not appear to be any published investigation into its effectiveness with brain-damaged people. First-letter cueing, on the other hand, has been studied. Jaffe and Katz (1975), for example, taught a Korsakoff patient, who had not learned a single person's name after 5 years in a hospital, the names of two members of the hospital staff by this method. The patient was told, "This person's name is Paul Doty. Try to remember the initials P. D." The next time the two met, Paul Doty was introduced as Paul D. The patient was required to complete the name. The verbal cues were gradually reduced, and two names were learned in this manner over a period of 2 weeks. Moffat (1984) describes how this method has been used with head-injured patients.

Visual-imagery techniques may hold the greatest promise for enabling the memory-impaired to learn new names. "Visual imagery" can be defined as "remembering by pictures." These may be mental images or actual drawings. Some visual-imagery techniques will be less appropriate for the learning of names than others. The method of loci and the visual-peg system (to be described in Chapters 10 and 11), for example, are probably of less value for learning people's names than for remembering things to do and shopping lists. The visual-imagery procedure designed specifically for learning names is the face–name association method. The finding from cognitive psychology, reported in Chapter 3, that amnesic patients can learn some paired associations more easily than others influenced the choice of a variant of this method of treatment for the subjects to be described in this chapter. Face-name learning is a paired-associate task, and amnesic patients can learn paired associates if they are based on some logical association—for example, rhymes or phonetic similarity. Therefore, in order to teach amnesic patients people's names, a logical association has to be sought. The method chosen for doing this in the present studies was to combine phonemic similarity with a simple visual image of the transformed name.

Face-name association, as originally devised, involves four stages in which the subject is asked (1) to select a distinctive feature from the face of the person whose name is to be remembered (e.g., bushy eyebrows); (2) to transform the person's name into one or two common nouns (e.g., to change "Barbara" into "barber"); (3) to link the distinctive feature and the transformed name in some way (e.g., to imagine a barber trimming the bushy eyebrows); and (4) on meeting the person whose name is to be remembered, to select the distinctive feature, retrieve the image, and recall the name. McCarty (1980) found that undergraduate subjects who followed all stages of the procedure did better in a face-name learning task than those who only selected the distinctive feature or only transformed the noun. However, these subjects were not brain-damaged. Glasgow, Zeiss, Barrera, and Lewinsohn (1977) used the method with a head-injured student and found it to be an impractical approach. We (Wilson & Moffat, 1984) have described a mildly aphasic man who did equally well with rehearsal and with the face-name method when required to learn names. In this case, however, the failure to show any difference appeared to be due to the man's spontaneous use of imagery for recall of those names for which no image was explicitly provided. To prevent this happening, a slightly different procedure was used with a Korsakoff patient (Loftus & Wilson, 1984). Following a baseline period of several weeks, during which no learning of names of people in photographs occurred, extra rehearsal was allowed for each name. Learning still failed to occur. Half the names were then assigned to the face-name association method and half to more rehearsal. Only those names subjected to the face-name association procedure were learned successfully. However, reports of this method with brain-damaged people are sparse, and more research is needed to compare this approach with the simpler procedure employed in the studies to be described in this chapter.

This simpler method involves turning the name to be remembered into a picture, which is drawn on a card. Mental imagery is not required, and distinctive features do not play an explicit part in the learning procedure. Five experiments investigating the effectiveness of this method with a small number of brain-damaged people are reported below. From published reports, it would appear that visual imagery is one of the most promising procedures (Crovitz, 1979; Crovitz, Harvey, & Horn, 1979; Glasgow *et al.*, 1977; Jones, 1974; Patten, 1972). With the exception of Glasgow *et al.*, however, these investigators have found that the imagery has been of limited value in the patients' everyday lives. The present studies attempted to teach patients the names of people they came into contact with regularly in their daily social intercourse.

EXPERIMENT 1

A multiple-baseline-across-behaviors design was used to teach 10 names to a man following removal of a left temporal lobe tumor. Each stage of treatment (i.e., each new name) was introduced separately. The teaching strategy was based on two assumptions: first, that visual imagery enhances learning; and, second, that a complex task is often learned best when it is taught one step at a time (e.g., P. Moore & Carr, 1976; Wilson & Moore, 1979).

Case History

C. M. was a 42-year-old, well-educated man who had been previously employed as an assistant bank manager. Some 2½ years prior to the experiment, he had received radiotherapy for a large left parieto-temporal astrocytoma, which was malignant and extending forward into the frontal lobe. It was also an infiltrating tumor, and its exact size could not be determined. He was no longer able to work, although the tumor was successfully treated, and to date has shown no evidence of recurring. He attended a rehabilitation center for 2 days each week, where he spent most of his time in the metalwork shop. When referred to me for his impaired memory, he complained about several practical problems. For example, he was unable to remember where he was to go or what he had to do without making extensive use of his diary; he was unable to remember the beginning of a television program shortly after it began; he spent much of his time worrying that he might forget something important; and he also became exasperated because he could not remember people's names. The only names available to him were those of his wife, children, and other family members. C. M. and I decided to tackle the problem of names because it seemed the most specific of his problems to treat, and because C. M.'s natural good manners caused him to be embarrassed at not being able to address people by name.

Pretreatment Assessment

Before beginning treatment, C. M. was given a psychological assessment to determine his general ability, the extent of his memory problems, and whether or not he could make use of visual imagery to remember words. On the WAIS, Raven's Standard Progressive Matrices (Raven, 1960), and other tests of "general" intelligence, he consistently scored in the bright–average range. His immediate recall of prose (Logical Memory Subtest from the Wechsler Memory Scale; Wechsler, 1945) and of designs (Benton Visual Retention Test; Benton, 1974) was only slightly below average, but his delayed recall of verbal and nonverbal material was markedly impaired.

The Recognition Memory Test (Warrington, 1984) was given to assess recognition memory. In these tests, the subject is given 50 words to read, or 50 faces to look at—one every 3 seconds. The subject is then shown 50 pairs of words or faces, one of which he or she has just seen and one he or she has not. The task is to identify the word or face previously seen. Here, C. M. achieved a scaled score of 0 for words and 3 for faces. (A scaled score of 10 represents the average.) His raw scores were 30/50 and 36/50, respectively. He remembered faces better than words, but was not good at either. In another of Warrington's tests (personal communication), 12 famous faces are presented for the subject to identify. C. M. named only 2 of the 12, although he could give other information about each of the famous people (e.g., their work and the country of origin); this showed that he recognized them, but could not supply their names. He was then given a paired-associate learning task based on the procedure used by Jones (1974). This involves three paired-associate learning lists, each of which is presented three times. The subject is asked to recall the first 10-pair list without any instructions on using visual imagery. The same list is given a second and third time. Next, the subject is given the second 10-pair list after the experimenter has previously drawn a picture linking each pair (e.g., if the pair is "elephant-bouquet," the drawing shows an elephant holding a bouquet of flowers). After three presentations of the second list, the subject is given the third list and asked to create his or her own visual image for each pair. Two hours later, each list is recalled once again. C. M.'s performance improved with visual imagery, although it was still below normal. In the delayed-recall condition he remembered no words from the first list, four words from the second list, and five words from the third list.

Treatment

After assessment, C. M. and I decided on 10 names he would like to learn (all were members of the staff at the rehabilitation center, except for one friend). It was explained that if the procedure was successful, we could extend the method to the names of neighbors and other friends. Two baselines were then taken. C. M. was asked, "What is the name of the social worker?" (or "canteen lady," or "doctor," etc.). He scored 0/10 on both occasions.

Treatment consisted of teaching one name at a time, using both rehearsal and visual imagery. A photograph of the first person on the list was obtained and mounted on a white card, and the name was printed underneath (only the name, *not* the person's role or position). This was shown to C. M., who made a conscious effort to remember the name before placing the card in his diary. As he resorted to his diary several times a day in order to find out what he had to do next, he could not help seeing the photograph. He was asked to rehearse the name each time he saw the photograph by looking at it, saying the name to himself, then closing the diary and testing himself on the name while trying to visualize the face. This happened at least three times a day, as he always referred to the diary at mealtimes. He also rehearsed the other names at these times, as he was anxious to learn all 10 names as quickly as possible. C. M. was seen twice weekly for 45 minutes each time. He was tested on all 10 names (in random order) at the beginning and end of each session. For the remainder of the session, he did unrelated psychological tests, which he enjoyed and regarded as good for making him think.

When he had learned the first name (i.e., recalled it within 30 seconds when asked; see Figure 6-1), the second name was introduced with the procedure as before. He was thus rehearsing two names. This strategy was used until six names had been introduced and "learned." He still needed to rehearse regularly, although he himself adapted the rehearsal procedure early in treatment by testing himself *before* looking at the photographs and only referring to them when his memory failed.

At this point, several members of staff had failed to bring photographs of themselves, and so we decided to draw visual images. "Dr. Hunt," for example, was illustrated by a felt-tip drawing of a hunt scene. Several weeks after beginning treatment, C. M. had learned nine names through the combination of visual imagery and rehearsal. At this point he had to return to a hospital to check that his tumor had not recurred. He was there for 2 weeks, but was unable to return to Rivermead for another 6 weeks, as his medication had to be adjusted and he was in a state of toxic confusion. On his return, he recalled 8 of the 10 names with no help, despite several weeks of feeling unwell and (he claimed) of not rehearsing. He had apparently retained the information without treatment and despite potentially interfering procedures. The remaining names of the original 10 were then introduced. Over the following six treatments, all 10 names were remembered on each occasion, and C. M. began learning his neighbors' names.

It can be seen in Figure 6-1 that C. M. occasionally forgot a name after having apparently learned it thoroughly; conversely, he remembered names at times before a photograph/image was given. This may have been due to constant repetition, but was also due (in at least one case) to other associations being available to him (e.g., one name was the same as a town where he had lived for some years, and this almost certainly helped him to remember). It is suggested that the procedure was successful because (1) it made greater use of his less damaged right cerebral hemisphere in learning the associations (i.e., using pictorial rather than verbal associations); (2) the images provided a retrieval cue for the name, and it has been established that amnesic patients are helped considerably by such retrieval cues (Warrington & Weiskrantz, 1970); and (3) restricting the amount to be learned helped C. M. to retain the names. This is supported by the findings of Milner *et al.*

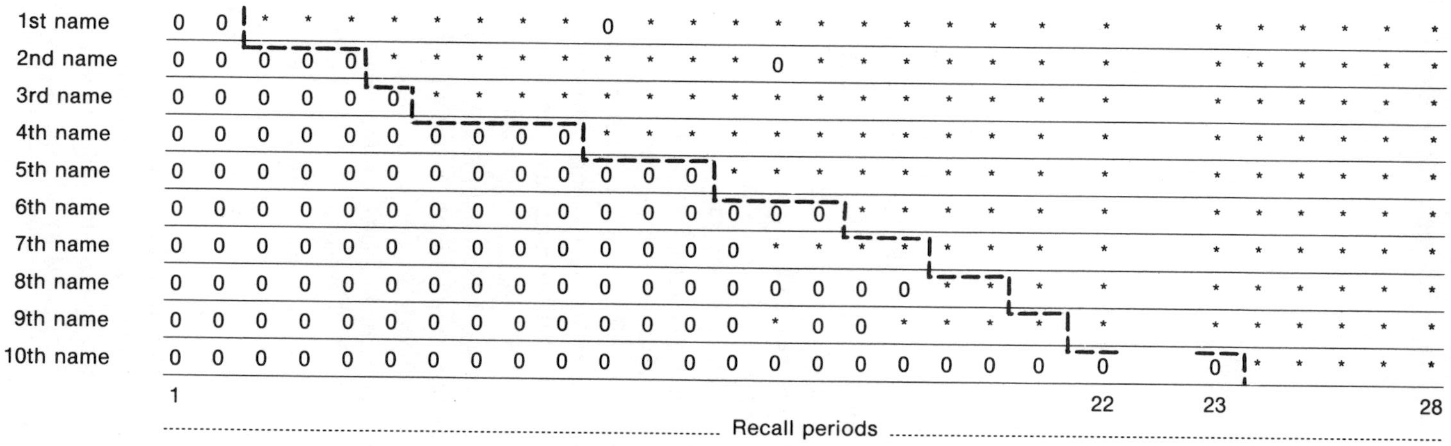

1st name
2nd name
3rd name
4th name
5th name
6th name
7th name
8th name
9th name
10th name

1   22   23   28

.... Recall periods ....

Figure 6-1. A multiple-baseline-across behaviors design to examine the effectiveness of teaching name recall to a man following removal of a left temporal lobe tumor. Symbols: 0, name not recalled; *, name recalled; dashed line, next stage of treatment introduced here. Between recall periods 22 and 23, there was an 8-week no-treatment period.

(1968) that H. M.'s maze learning was aided by teaching him very short sequences of the maze at any one time.

EXPERIMENT 2

Although Experiment 1 demonstrated that a step-by-step approach can lead to successful learning, it can be argued that visual imagery was not an influential part of the treatment and that all of the names could have been learned without visual imagery, provided that each name was introduced separately. In order to compare rehearsal with visual imagery, two multiple-baseline designs were used with a young head-injured man to see whether or not visual imagery was more effective than rehearsal when names were introduced in a step-by-step manner in *both* conditions.

Case History

F. E. was a 21-year-old man who had received a severe head injury in a motorcycle accident some 10 months before treatment began. He sustained a fracture of the right parietal bone and was unconscious for 4–5 weeks. He was referred to Rivermead Rehabilitation Centre for memory therapy; several problems were identified for treatment, including difficulty in remembering people's names. He was much less worried about his problems than was C. M. despite the fact that his amnesia was more global than C. M.'s. F. E. had left school at 16 years of age with five Ordinary Level passes in Great Britain's General Certificate Examinations. He was an apprentice in an electronics firm at the time of his accident.

Pretreatment Assessment

F. E. was assessed prior to treatment, and the following results were obtained: On the WAIS, his verbal IQ was in the bright–average range; his performance IQ was in the average range (the verbal–performance discrepancy was due, in part, to physical problems). His immediate memory was good, but his delayed memory for all kinds of material was poor. On the Warrington Forced-Choice Words, he obtained a scaled score of 1, while on the Forced-Choice Faces his scaled score was 0.

Treatment

Following the assessment, F. E. was seen daily in clinical psychology for memory therapy. In addition to investigating his ability to learn names, an attempt was made to improve his retention of prose passages (see Chapter 7). In order to determine whether or not visual imagery led to better learning of names than rehearsal, I selected 18 names of people working at the rehabilitation unit, all of whom came into contact with F. E. regularly. Their photographs were obtained and shown to F. E. once each day for 4 consecutive days. He was asked, "What is this person's name?" and given up to 30 seconds to provide a correct answer for each photograph. If he gave the wrong answer or said he did not know the person's name, that particular name was provided for him. He was able to name two of the people in the photographs on two of the baseline occasions. These two were removed from the set, leaving 16 photographs of people he had not, on any occasion, been able to name correctly during the baseline period. These 16 were randomly assigned to one of two conditions: namely, visual imagery or rehearsal. After the fourth baseline, one name was selected from each condition for treatment.

In the visual-imagery condition, F. E. and I discussed how the name could be turned into a picture, and this picture was drawn on a card by the therapist. For example, "Laurette" was drawn as a launderette (a row of washing machines). The drawing was shown to F. E.; he was reminded of the name; and the picture was placed next to the photographs for 5 seconds before being removed. In the rehearsal condition, he was shown the photograph, told the name, and asked to say it six times and to try to remember it. Exposure time for each name was roughly equivalent. Recall was tested after 2 minutes, 30 minutes, and 24 hours. At each test of recall, the 16 photographs were placed one at a time in front of F. E., and he was asked, "What is this person's name?" Any mistakes were corrected but were scored as errors. Two new names (one from each condition) were added every 1 or 2 days thereafter, with the order of presentation alternating on each occasion.

The results can be seen in Figure 6-2. A Wilcoxon matched-pairs signed-ranks test (Siegel, 1956) was applied to the data. A nonparametric test was used because such tests do not require normal distribution. The Wilcoxon procedure was used because the pairs of names were matched, in view of the fact that (1) none were recalled correctly in the baseline period and (2) they were introduced for treatment at the same time. Comparisons were made on the basis of the number of occasions each name was successfully recalled. The Wilcoxon test indicated a significant difference in favor of the visual-imagery condition ($T = 2$, $p < .01$).

EXPERIMENT 3

A multiple-baseline-across-subjects design was used here to see whether four patients would be able to benefit from the visual-imagery procedure. All four patients had difficulty learning names, and all four received the same treatment. However, they followed different baseline periods. Thus treatment was staggered in order to determine whether improvement was directly related to treatment (i.e., to the visual imagery procedure) or whether it was due to some other factor, such as natural recovery or practice effects.

Case Histories

T. J. was a 61-year-old man who had had a left-hemisphere stroke some 6 months before arriving at Rivermead. He was mildly aphasic when treatment began and had been assessed on the Boston Diagnostic Aphasia Examination by a speech therapist. He was the ony patient in this study who did not undergo a formal psychological assessment.

O. J. was a 32-year-old man who had suffered a left CVA some 6 months earlier. This left him with mild dysphasia.

V. I. was a 43-year-old man who was also dysphasic following a stroke in the left hemisphere.

F. D. was a 51-year-old man who had had a bilateral stroke affecting both temporal lobes. F. D. is described more fully in Chapter 7. He was the only one of the four subjects with the classic amnesic syndrome.

All subjects had difficulty in remembering names.

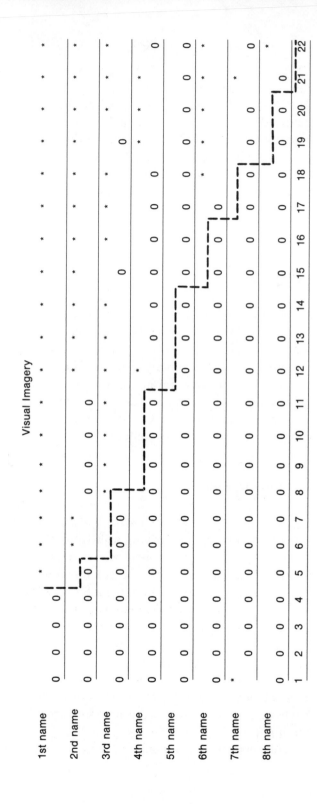

Visual Imagery

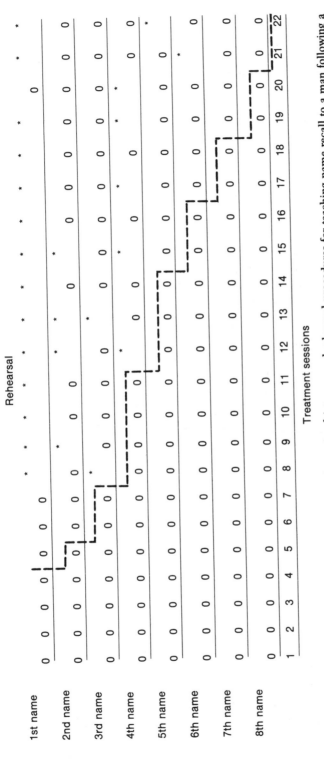

Figure 6-2. Two multiple-baseline designs to investigate visual-imagery and rehearsal procedures for teaching name recall to a man following a severe head injury. Symbols as in Figure 6-1.

Pretreatment Assessment

All subjects except T. J. received psychological assessment prior to treatment. (See Table 6-1 for a summary of the test results for these subjects and all other subjects referred to in this chapter.)

Treatment

Ten names to be learned were selected for each subject. All were names of staff members or patients at Rivermead. Each subject selected the names he particularly wanted to learn. The procedure followed was similar to that described in Experiment 1. Thus, in the baseline period, subjects were asked, "What is my name? What is the name of your speech therapist? Physiotherapist?" and so on. The name was supplied following an incorrect response. None of the subjects recalled any of the names correctly during the baseline period. Following baselines of two, four, six, and eight test sessions, respectively, each subject was told, "I am going to see if you can remember Alison's name [for example] more easily if you turn it into a picture. Think of the word 'Alison' . . . how could we make a picture of that? It makes me think of an alley and a sun. Let's try drawing that." I then drew a picture of an alley and a sun on a white card using a felt-tip pen. This was shown to the subject, who was then asked, "Try to fix this picture in your mind. Next time I ask you the name of the speech therapist, try to see this picture, and it should help you recall her name." No more than one visual image was introduced during any one session. The results can be seen in Figure 6-3. All four patients were able to learn some names following treatment, although none were able to do so during the baseline period.

EXPERIMENT 4

There is considerable evidence that amnesic patients can learn some tasks with little difficulty (e.g., Brooks & Baddeley, 1976; Corkin, 1968). These are the procedural-learning tasks described in Chapter 3. Some procedural-learning tasks involve motor memory (e.g., pursuit-rotor and mirror-writing tasks), and intact motor memory in amnesia has led to speculation about the effectiveness of motor movements as a

Table 6-1. Test Results of Patients in Experiments 1-5

Test	C. M. (age 42)	F. E. (age 21)	O. J. (age 32)	V. I. (age 43)	F. D. (age 51)	O. E. (age 27)	M. L. (age 59)
Verbal IQ (WAIS)	119	117	86	77	133	96	133
Performance IQ (WAIS)	103	93	93	87	121	56	131
Full-scale IQ (WAIS)	113	107	88	80	130	78	134
Raven's Standard Progressive Matrices	117	126	115	—	>126	<80	>126
Immediate Logical Memory (Wechsler Memory Scale)	8.5	8	6	2	9.5	3.5	12
Delayed Logical Memory (Wechsler Memory Scale)	2	0	7	1	0	0	0
Rey-Osterreith complex figure	9	6	23	18	2	0	0
RBMT	6	0	—	—	0	0	0
Forced-Choice Words (Warrington Recognition Memory Test)[a]	0	1	—	5	8	0	5
Forced-Choice Faces (Warrington Recognition Memory Test)[a]	3	0	—	3	7	0	6
Benton Visual Retention Test (correct)	7	7	8	5	6	2	—
Benton Visual Retention Test (errors)	4	5	2	9	6	11	—

[a]Scaled score.

119

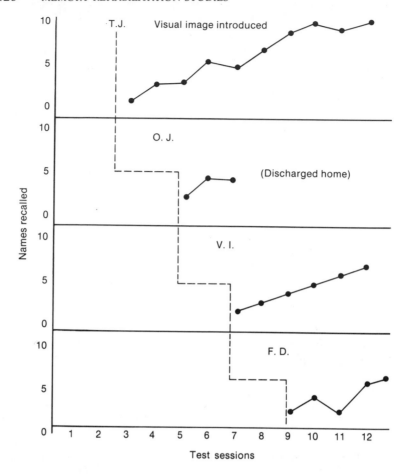

Figure 6-3. A multiple-baseline-across-subjects design to demonstrate the effectiveness of visual imagery in teaching name recall.

memory aid. Powell (1981) has suggested that certain names may be learned by a pattern of movements. He gives the examples of "Mr. Potter," "Mr. Crow," and "Mr. Hatter." Moffat (1984) describes an experiment with an amnesic head-injured patient whereby two lists of words were taught, one using movement (e.g., the word "baby" was represented by an arm-rocking action) and the other using rehearsal. The mean number of words recalled following the movement condition was 7.58, while the rehearsal led to a mean recall of 3.17 words.

No formal studies have been reported using motor movement as a rehabilitation procedure, in spite of the fact that it would appear to be well worth investigating, given the procedural-learning evidence mentioned above. The experiment reported below was carried out in order to see whether a head-injured man was more successful in learning names paired with motor movements or paired with visual images.

Case History

O. E. was a 27-year-old man who had received a severe head injury 2½ years prior to the experiment. He had suffered a depressed fracture of the right temporo-parietal bone, necessitating removal of part of the bone. He had had a bone flap inserted, but this became infected and was removed. Besides an extremely dense amnesia, O. E. had perceptual problems, including difficulties with face-matching tasks and some degree of unilateral neglect. There was no language disorder, however. He indicated that photographs of faces were confusing to him; they were simply pictures that did not convey any meaning.

Pretreatment Assessment

The psychological assessment showed O. E. to have a verbal IQ in the average range of ability, with a performance IQ in the retarded range. His predicted premorbid IQ on the basis of the National Adult Reading Test was in the bright–average range. In addition to physical problems he had severe memory difficulties, with the exception of immediate memory span for digits. In recalling two prose passages, he confused the two and confabulated. He also had severe perceptual problems, including unilateral neglect, inability to match faces, and some problems identifying photographs of objects.

Treatment

After 2 years of rehabilitation, O. E. was able to recall the names of three therapists who regularly worked with him *only* if the initial letter of each name was given. A fourth therapist called Anita told him that he could remember her name because she had "*a neater* way" of arranging her hair, whereupon she shook her hair. From then on O. E. reliably recalled her name, provided she shook her hair first. Trouble was caused, because any woman who shook her hair in front of him was called Anita! However, O. E.'s success here led to a systematic investigation of his ability to learn names using movements. Twenty names were selected; all were names of staff members or patients who knew O. E. well. It was difficult to say whether or not he knew them because of his face-perception difficulties and his memory problems. Half the names were randomly allocated to the motor-movement condition, and the remainder to the visual-imagery condition.

In the first session, O. E. was shown a photograph of one of the people on the list. He was told, "This is a photograph of your physiotherapist. What is her name?" He failed to give the correct answer and was then told, "We are going to think of a sign to help you remember her. Her name is Sue. What sign could we have to remember Sue?" O. E. replied, "Eating soup," and he mimed the action of eating soup with a spoon. A photograph of the second person on the list was then presented, and O. E. was told, "This is the nurse on your ward. What is his name?" Again, he failed to give the correct answer and was told, "His name is Mike. We are going to draw a picture to help remember his name. What picture could we draw for Mike?" O. E. selected a microphone, and a picture of a man holding a microphone was drawn for him on a white card. This procedure was followed for the first eight names on the list, four from each condition.

After each name, O. E. was tested on all the ones we had covered. Thus, following the first name, he was shown the sign for Sue and was asked, "Who is this?" After the second name, he was shown the picture of the microphone and asked, "Who is this?" He was then shown the sign for Sue again. After the third name, all three were tested in random order, and so forth. The following day began with a 24-hour recall, with signs and pictures being shown to O. E. one at a time. He had to supply the correct name. Two new names were then added. The results can be seen in Table 6-2.

A sign test (comparing the number of names successfully recalled in each condition on the 11 test occasions) was applied to the results. On 10 of the 11 occasions, more names were recalled under the motor-movement condition than under the visual-imagery condition ($p = .01$). However, although this meant that O. E. could produce the correct name significantly more often when he was shown a motor

Table 6-2. Number of Names Successfully Recalled by O. E. after a Delay of 24 Hours

Date	Motor movements	Images
11-25-82	4/4	4/4
11-26-82	5/5	1/5
11-29-82	5/6	4/6
11-30-82	7/10	5/10
12- 1-82	8/10	5/10
12- 3-82	10/10	7/10
12- 6-82	10/10	7/10
12- 8-82	10/10	4/10
12- 9-82	9/10	4/10
12-13-82	10/10	9/10
12-14-82	9/10	4/10

movement than when he was shown a drawing, in practice it did not help a great deal, as he never learned to match the appropriate movement to each face.

A shaping procedure was adopted in an attempt to overcome this problem. The first photograph (Sue) was shown, the correct movement was made in front of O. E., and he said, "Sue." The photograph was removed for 3 seconds, and he was still able to retain the information. Two photographs (Mike and Sue) were then shown, and the same procedure was followed. A third photograph was then shown alongside the other two. O. E. immediately made errors. However, after 17 trials he made three consecutive correct responses (i.e., he pointed to each of the three photographs and said, "Sue, Mike, and Anne"). Following each trial, the photographs were removed for several seconds and then replaced on the table in a different order. After a 15-second delay, O. E. never managed to supply the correct name on four consecutive occasions. The face-recognition problem was such that O. E. did not recognize the photograph of me that was placed in front of him, even though I was the person testing him. When this was pointed out to him he said, "So it is." He said this each time I told him, "That's a photograph of me." After 85 trials, attempts to match names to faces were abandoned.

EXPERIMENT 5

The final experiment to be reported in this chapter aimed to discover whether the results obtained with O. E. in Experiment 4 would hold for another memory-impaired person, M. L. Two questions were asked: (1) Would M. L. also find names easier to learn with motor movements than with visual images; and (2) given that he did not have a face-recognition problem, would M. L. be able to match the right name to the right face once he had learned the paired associates? The same procedure was followed here as in Experiment 4, with the exception that fewer names were selected for treatment. The reason for this was that M. L. had been at Rivermead for a relatively short time (2 weeks), and during that time he had come into regular contact with few of the staff members.

Case History

M. L. was a 59-year-old man who had developed meningitis and encephalitis 18 months previously. Initially he was ataxic and dysphasic, but he recovered physically, and immediately prior to treatment showed no sign of a language disorder. His problem was that he suffered from a severe global amnesia. He repeated information and questions he had previously volunteered; did not know what month or day it was; and, if not at home, did not know where he was. He could not find his way from one place to another unless it was a very familiar route. His memory for events in the past was more reliable than for those that had recently occurred. He had a reasonable understanding of his problems and realistic expectations of what memory therapy could offer.

Pretreatment Assessment

M. L.'s IQ on both verbal and performance scales was assessed as being in the superior range of ability. His immediate recall of a prose passage was good, but he retained nothing after a delay. There was no evidence of any physical, language, or preceptual problems. M. L. showed the classic amnesic syndrome.

Table 6-3. Number of Names Successfully Recalled by M. L. after a Delay of at Least 24 Hours

Date	Motor movements	Images
12-17-82	6/6	5/6
1-10-83	4/6	6/6
1-11-83	6/6	6/6
1-12-83	6/6	6/6

Treatment

The names of 12 members of the staff were selected, and two baselines were taken by showing M. L. a photograph of each one of the 12 and asking for each person's name. The correct name was supplied if M. L. made an error. On the first occasion M. L. scored 0; on the second occasion he scored 2/12; and on the third he scored 1/12. Following this, he was given motor movements for half of the names (e.g., "Mick" was represented by a movement for mixing or stirring a pot and "Dr. Rushworth" as a rushing-along movement, arms working like pistons). The other group of names were drawn, in this case by M. L. himself (e.g., "Carrie" was drawn as a woman carrying a basket). M. L. quicky learned all the names from both groups (see Table 6-3).

There was obviously no difference between the two conditions in this first stage, probably because of a ceiling effect. However, there was no ceiling effect in the next stage, matching the right name to the right face. In this stage, after testing names by presenting images and movements, M. L. was shown the photographs one at a time and was asked for each name. The correct answer was supplied if M. L. failed to give it. Results are shown in Table 6-4. It can be seen that although M. L. did not reach 100% success, he certainly improved. There was no apparent difference between the two conditions.

DISCUSSION

The studies described in this chapter have shown that visual imagery can be used to teach people's names to memory-impaired adults. Previous research into the ability of amnesic people to benefit from

Table 6-4. Number of Faces Correctly Named by M. L. after He Learned to Pair the Names with the Movements or Images

Test session	Motor movements	Images
1	0/6	2/6
2	0/6	4/6
3	5/6	4/6
4	5/6	4/6
5	4/6	4/6
6	3/6	5/6

imagery has provided conflicting findings. Baddeley and Warrington (1973), for example, found that non-brain-damaged subjects benefited considerably from using imagery to remember groups of words, but that amnesic subjects did not benefit. Jones (1974) demonstrated that patients who had undergone a left temporal lobectomy were able to improve their recall of paired associates. Two globally amnesic patients, on the other hand, were not helped at all by the procedure. Cermak (1975) found that Korsakoff patients performed better under imagery than no-imagery conditions. All of the patients in the present study improved, so they would appear to have reacted more like Cermak's Korsakoff patients than like those of Baddeley and Warrington (1973) or the global amnesics studied by Jones (1974). However, differences among subjects are unlikely to provide the explanation for the discrepancy between these studies and the two that found imagery ineffective.

Although four of the subjects in the present study had primarily verbal-memory deficits (C. M., O. J., T. J., and V. I.), and may, therefore, be seen as comparable with Jones's left temporal lobectomy group, there were also two pure global amnesics in the investigations (F. D. and M. L.). In addition, two subjects (O. E. and F. E.) showed an equally severe amnesia together with other cognitive deficits. Thus, these last four subjects were more similar to the amnesic patients of Baddeley and Warrington, and of Jones, for whom imagery was unsuccessful. Why, then, should there be these differences between the findings of the studies? There are, perhaps, several factors, which might include a number from the following list.

1. *The nature of the task.* Baddeley and Warrington (1973) used groups of four words (e.g., "boy," "short," "jump," and "clock"). Jones used paired-associate words. All the experiments reported in this chapter used the names of real people. On the whole, these were single words (e.g., "Barbara" and "Carrie") although sometimes two words were used (e.g., "Mary Thorne"), and sometimes a title was included (e.g., "Sister Vaughan.") Furthermore, each image had a logical association with the name to be recalled, in that it depicted the name itself. As we know that amnesics learn logical or easy associations but not difficult ones (Warrington & Weiskrantz, 1982), this would also appear to have made learning easier. Another important difference is that Jones, and Baddeley and Warrington, required patients to create mental images, whereas all of the patients in the present study had the images drawn for them (or, in the case of M. L. used images drawn by the subject himself). This may have led to more discriminable or memorable pictures.

2. *Motivation.* Presumably, the subjects of Jones and of Baddeley and Warrington did not particularly *want* to learn lists of words or of paired associates in the same way as subjects in the present studies wanted to learn the names of people working with them. Indeed, the patients in the present studies showed concern and sometimes distress at their inability to remember the names of people with whom they came into regular contact.

3. *The teaching method.* In the present studies, the names to be learned were introduced to subjects in step-by-step sequences, so that patients were not expected to learn too much at any one time. Given that shaping and chaining procedures are known to be effective teaching techniques for the mentally handicapped (Yule & Carr, 1980), it is perhaps sensible to incorporate such procedures into cognitive rehabilitation. The earlier studies from the 1970s used several lists or paired associates in each trial. A corollary of this is that much more time was allowed for learning each name in the present studies, and this may indeed have been the crucial factor.

Although visual imagery was successful in these studies, it cannot be claimed that the results reported here represent dramatic improvements in general memory functioning among the subjects. Neither can I claim that name learning in particular is better in the patients who have undergone this treatment. Thus, few if any of them will spontaneously use visual imagery or motor movements to remember names of new people they meet. It might therefore be argued that the techniques employed have failed to improve the learning abilities of the patients. Ideally, of course, it would be hoped that each patient would adopt strategies and apply them to new situations. In the absence of attainment of such a goal, it is worth pointing out that for people with severe cognitive impairment, *any* improvement is welcome. Furthermore, relatives can be taught the strategies in order to encourage the learning of other names. The emphasis in memory therapy, and particularly for those with severe impairment, is not on restoring lost functioning. As E. Miller (1978) points out, it is almost certainly impossible to restore memory to its premorbid level in patients with amnesia. Instead, the emphasis must be on ameliorating the problems caused by the memory deficit, and such amelioration will include establishing ways of learning new information that are appropriate to the needs and learning behavior of each individual.

CONCLUSIONS

Five studies have been reported here in which attempts were made to teach brain-damaged people to remember names of staff and patients at Rivermead Rehabilitation Centre. The methodologies of the studies were heavily influenced by the principles and practices developed within the field of behavioral psychology. For example, the assessment procedure involved the use of analogue situations, when testing for memory of staff members' names was performed by presenting a series of photographs of the staffers. Behavior modification techniques such as chaining and shaping also influenced the teaching techniques used in these experiments, whereby material to be learned was broken down into a series of small units and tackled one at a time, rather than as a total block. It is worth asking at this point whether in fact many of the failures reported in the memory therapy literature were due to inappropriate teaching that did *not* break down the material or behaviors to be learned into small components. Finally, I must of course reiterate that the multiple-baseline designs for the experiments owe their origin to methodologies developed within the behavioral sciences.

The first study presented in this chapter involved a man with verbal-memory problems that followed removal of a left temporal lobe tumor. A multiple-baseline design using visual imagery, rehearsal, and a step-by-step approach was employed to teach him the names of

10 people. The subject's successful learning helped him to overcome his embarrassment at not being able to address people by name. It also demonstrated that a step-by-step, structured program can help alleviate even very marked memory impairment, and it is postulated that this approach might be valuable in teaching other skills to people with neurological damage.

The second study used two multiple-baseline designs to compare visual imagery with rehearsal in helping a yound head-injured man learn the names of his therapists. Visual imagery appeared to be significantly superior to rehearsal.

The third study used a multiple-baseline-across-subjects design with four stroke patients (three had sustained left-hemisphere stokes, while the fourth had sustained a bilateral stroke). All four benefited from visual imagery, having failed to improve at all during differing baseline periods.

The fourth study compared motor movements with visual imagery as ways of learning names. The patient in this study was a head-injured man with considerable perceptual and physical problems in addition to severe amnesia. His ability to produce the correct name was significantly better following motor movements than following visual images. However, he could not learn to pair names with faces. This was probably due to his marked difficulty in face perception.

In order to compare motor movements with visual imagery in someone without face-perception problems, the experiment was repeated in the fifth study with a man demonstrating the classic amnesic syndrome. He learned the names easily whether they were paired with motor movements or images. Furthermore, he showed some ability to learn which name belonged to which face. However, there was no evidence of any superiority in either method.

An intact right hemisphere would not appear to be necessary for successful use of visual imagery, given the conditions described in the above experiments. Although C. M., O. J., and T. G. had unimpaired (or relatively unimpaired) right hemispheres, the remaining patients all showed evidence of bilateral damage. Only O. E. had marked perceptual deficits, and he was the only subject who was totally unable to learn to identify any of the staff members working with him, either from their photographs or in person.

The reasons why visual imagery worked for most of the patients described here when earlier researchers failed to demonstrate improvement with visual-imagery techniques probably include one or more of the following: (1) the nature of the task; (2) motivation of the subjects; (3) the practical value of the material to be learned; and (4) the teaching method.

Finally, to reflect again on the influence of another of the major theoretical disciplines, it can be seen that O. E. provides an example of the necessity to take neuropsychological functioning into account when designing a treatment. His severe face-perception problems prevented any face–name learning, although he could learn other paired associates, such as pairings of motor movements and names. On the other hand, C. M., who had a specific verbal-memory deficit, learned the face–name associations with little trouble. His right cerebral hemisphere was, of course, intact (or at least much less damaged than his left). It should not be assumed, however, that right-hemisphere damage prevents successful use of visual imagery. Several of the patients described in this chapter had bilateral damage, yet were able to learn the associations. Only O. E. had severe perceptual problems, so this may be the important consideration when choosing a visual-imagery procedure. No patients with unilateral right-hemisphere damage were included, because it is our experience at Rivermead that these patients do not appear to have difficulty in the learning of names.

·7·

SUCCESS AND FAILURE IN MEMORY TRAINING FOLLOWING A CVA

INTRODUCTION

Several procedures have been used to improve memory performance in brain-damaged adults. Jones (1974), for example, used a visual-imagery procedure to help temporal lobectomy patients recall lists of paired-associate words. Crovitz (1979) used an elaborate coding procedure with brain-damaged people to aid retrieval of a list of words. Glasgow *et al.* (1977) used a PQRST rehearsal strategy with a young woman who had been involved in a road accident. Gianutsos and Gianutsos (1979) taught their patients to make up a story using words they were asked to remember; and I (Wilson, 1981b) have used a visual-imagery and step-by-step approach to teach people's names to a man after removal of a left temporal lobe tumor (see Chapter 6, Experiment 1). None of these studies, however, required one individual to use different strategies for different memory problems. Yet memory is not a unitary concept: as noted in Chapter 3, we refer to verbal and nonverbal memory, visual and auditory memory, STM and LTM, and episodic and semantic memory. Furthermore, it has been established that after brain damage some memory functions may be less impaired than others (Brooks & Baddeley, 1976), so it may be that certain strategies are more beneficial for some memory problems than for others. In addition, the ability of a brain-damaged individual to benefit from any particular treatment will depend, among other things, on cause and site of the brain damage, plus the individual's personal style and preferences. The study reported in this chapter was undertaken in order to investigate which mnemonic strategies would help which particular problems faced by one amnesic patient. Over and above this, it was hoped that something could be done to improve his

An earlier version of this chapter appeared as "Success and Failure in Memory Training Following a Cerebral Vascular Accident" by B. A. Wilson, 1982, *Cortex, 18*, 581–594. Adapted by permission.

memory generally. Milner *et al.* (1968), in a follow-up study of H. M., found "profound amnesia for most ongoing events" (p. 215), and there is little evidence that practice alone will significantly reduce a brain-damaged person's memory deficit. Nevertheless, it was decided to see whether or not this was true for this particular patient. A final consideration was to see whether this person's response to treatment could throw further light on the nature of human memory.

CASE HISTORY

F. D. was a 51-year-old right-handed man who had a CVA in April 1980. He was reported to have complained of tinnitus for about 9 months before his CVA, and of forgetfulness and irritability for 3 months. Two days before admission to a hospital, he collapsed at home and was unconscious for about 5 minutes. He went to work the following day but in the evening complained of poor vision and vomited. Next day he was confused and complained of an odd sensation in his left face, arm, and leg. On admission to the hospital, he was reported to have a gross memory defect and impairment of visual acuity on the left side. A left upper quadrantic hemianopia was noted and has remained with him ever since. The patient himself complained of blurred vision and some problems in distinguishing colors. He made very few mistakes, however, on color-matching tasks, and his complaints of blurring diminished during his stay at Rivermead Rehabilitation Centre. He recovered physically, but severe memory problems remained.

A computed tomography (CT) scan demonstrated a softening in the territory of both posterior cerebral arteries. The report stated that there was better-defined atrophy on the left side, suggesting a more long-standing lesion.

In September 1980, assessment of F. D. revealed that his full-scale IQ on the WAIS was in the very superior range, and he scored at the 98th percentile on Raven's Standard Progressive Matrices (Raven, 1960). There was no evidence of dysphasia, dyslexia, or dysgraphia. Two memory batteries were administered—the Wechsler Memory Scale (Wechsler, 1945) and the Warrington Memory Battery (Warrington, 1974; Warrington & Weiskrantz, 1968; Weiskrantz & Warrington, 1979). His MQ on the Wechsler was 96 and on the Warrington was 79 (the batteries measure different aspects of memory). The picture of F. D.'s memory that emerged was as follows: (1) Immediate recall of verbal material was normal: (2) immediate recall of nonverbal material was low–average: (3) delayed recall of both verbal and nonverbal material was severely impaired. (See Table 7-2, below, for a summary of the pretreatment test results.) However, the test results did not convey the extent of F. D.'s handicap in everyday life. For example, he did not remember the ages of his two children, or which of them was the elder. He did not know the current year or his own age. His wife reported that at home he sometimes wanted to go to the house they had lived in several years previously. Observation showed that he had great difficulty finding his way around the rehabilitation center. He kept a notebook in which he had written details of his stroke and previous hospitalization, his daily timetable, and how to find various departments in the center. He never once lost the notebook while in the center, and spent most of his spare time reading it. Prior to his stroke he had been self-employed and financially successful, although he was described as secretive and friendless. He had been a talented musician who played in professional orchestras.

In short, F. D. was a highly intelligent man with no physical or intellectual problems apart from a severe memory deficit. As a result of a 2-week initial assessment period, F. D. was offered 6 weeks of memory therapy. It was explained to him and his wife that this might result in little, if any, noticeable improvement. They were both happy to accept treatment on these terms.

MATERIALS AND METHOD

General Memory Training

A timetable was devised for F. D. so that he spent 4 days a week for 6 weeks practicing memory tasks. Table 7-1 provides a description of this timetable.

Specific Problems

The specific problems treated were (1) remembering the daily timetable; (2) remembering people's names; (3) remembering a shopping list; and (4) remembering short routes. A multiple-baseline procedure

Table 7-1. F. D.'s Daily Timetable

Time	Department	Tasks
9:00–10:30 A.M.	Occupational therapy	Write autobiography.
10:30–10:45 A.M.	Canteen	Coffee break.
10:45–12 noon	Occupational therapy	Verbal-memory tasks. Examples: Find day, date, etc., and write down; read newspaper articles using PQRST strategy (Glasgow *et al.*, 1977); listen to tapes of stories, articles, etc.; answer questions set by occupational therapist.
12 noon–1:30 P.M.	Ward	Lunch break.
1:30–2:20 P.M.	Clinical psychology	Nonverbal-memory tasks. Examples: Benton visual Retention test; Rey–Osterreith figure; Rey–Davis nonverbal learning; pursuit rotor; finger mazes.
2:20–3:15 P.M.	Clinical psychology memory group	Work with other memory-impaired people: Memory games; mnemonics; practice with notice boards, timers, and diaries.
3:15–3:30 P.M.	Canteen	Tea break.
3:30–4:45 P.M.	Clinical psychology	Work on specific problem areas (see text).
4:45 P.M.	Ward	

was used. Baselines were taken on all these areas once a day for 4 days. This was achieved for the timetable by asking, "Where do you go first session in the morning?" The answer was recorded, and F. D. was corrected if wrong. He was then asked, "What happens next?" As the day was broken down into eight periods and eight start–finish times, he was scored on the number correct out of a total of 16. With names, he was asked, "What is my name?" "What is the name of your occupational therapist?" (or "social worker," "doctor," etc.). He was told the correct name if he gave an incorrect answer, or failed to reply. There were 12 names in all. For the shopping list, 10 items were read to him (the same every day), and he was asked to recall them immediately in any order. The ones he missed were then read to him again. Finally, he was asked to follow eight short routes (e.g., "Can you show me the way to the canteen?"). There were signs outside each department, and these were covered up prior to his session each day. F. D. could obviously read the signs, and this was how he usually managed to find his way. It was considered desirable, however, to see whether or not he could remember a route without relying on the signs. The order for the baselines was changed each day.

> Remembering Timetable, Names, and
> Shopping List: Procedures

At the end of the first baseline period, all baselines were stable with the exception of the timetable. This appeared to be improving with re-hearsal alone, so baselines were continued for a further 4 days. Im-provement on the timetable continued, so rehearsal alone was chosen as the treatment for learning this information.

The second task, learning names, was introduced next by a visual-imagery procedure much like the one described in Chapter 6: Each name was illustrated. For example, "Barbara" was represented by a drawing of a barber holding a letter "A" ("Barber-a"); "Stephanie" was drawn as a "Step" and "knee"; and "Dr. Crossley" was a "cross" and "leaf" with the "F" crossed out. On the first visual-imagery day, three images were introduced and explained to F. D. One or two more names were added each day thereafter.

The third problem was the shopping list. F. D. invariably recalled either four or five items whenever the list was presented for immediate recall. Despite the fact that the same list was presented day after day, he failed to report more than five items (these were not always the same). A visual-peg method (the "one is a bun" method described by Lorayne, 1979) had already been tried in the memory group; however, he found this strategy extremely difficult, even when the images were drawn for him or by him, and he performed worse than in free recall. A first-letter mnemonic system was therefore introduced and explained to F. D. The first letters of the items on the list could be arranged to spell the words "Go shopping." This was written down for F. D. as is shown below.

He understood the procedure and liked the method. After this mnemonic device had been introduced, he was asked to recall the items without the list being read to him first. For 2 days he required reminding of the cue words "Go shopping," but after that he provided the words himself.

G = Grapes
O = Oranges
S = Sugar
H = Ham
O = Olives
P = Paper
P = Pears
I = Ink
N = Nails
G = Grass seed

Learning Routes: Procedures

For learning routes, the last of the problem areas, several methods were tried; each one is described below.

Extra Rehearsal: F. D. had, of course, been rehearsing all eight routes every day as part of the multiple-baseline procedure. He showed no improvement, however, so during the treatment stage one route only was tackled (from the clinical psychology department to the social work department). This was considered an easy route and one that was used frequently by F. D. During the last session each day, F. D. and I went to and from the social work department six times. F. D. was asked to lead the way, and each time he deviated from the correct path his error was pointed out to him. At no time did he remember the route without faltering, either within a session or between sessions. After a week, the procedure was abandoned and another was tried.

A Fading Procedure: A chalk line was drawn from my room to the social work office. The plan was for F. D. to follow the line, and for a few inches of this line to be rubbed out each day. However, F. D. usually forgot to look at the line, and when he did, he forgot the reason why it was there. When he was asked to lead the way, he strode off purposefully as if he knew exactly where he was going. He made use of what cues were available (e.g., he looked at me to see if I was glancing in the right direction). However, he was not able to make use of the cue that was specially provided—the chalk line. After a few days, the third strategy was introduced.

A Letter-Sequencing Cue: As F. D. did not look at the ground, and as his verbal skills seemed to be more intact than his nonverbal ones, a series of letters was tried. A large capital "A" was chalked on the corner of the psychology building, a "B" on the adjoining corner, a "C" at the end of the wall, and a "D" at the door of the social work department. Again, F. D. usually forgot to look at the cues, and when he did remember to do this he forgot how he was supposed to react. This method was therefore also abandoned, and the fourth and final method was applied.

A Letter–Word Mnemonic Strategy: Because of the success of a first-letter mnemonic strategy in teaching the shopping list, this technique was adapted for teaching the route to social work. The words chosen, and the highlighted letters (in italic capitals) were "*ReaL* Emergency." The "R" meant "Turn right on leaving clinical psychology"; the "L" meant "Turn left at the corner of the building"; and the "E" meant "Look for the door with the 'Emergency Exit' on it" (this being one of the doors into the social work department and not one that was covered up each day prior to each session). This method also failed because, although F. D. remembered what the mnemonic was when reminded of "*ReaL* Emergency," he could not remember exactly where he had to turn right or left. As the 6-week treatment period was then at an end, the teaching of routes was stopped.

RESULTS

General Memory Training

Retesting on most memory tests showed no significant improvements. The exceptions were the pursuit-rotor and finger-maze tasks. These are the tasks amnesics typically find easiest to learn (e.g., Brooks & Baddeley, 1976; Milner *et al.*, 1968). See Table 7-2 for a summary of the results.

Findings of particular interest were these: First, F. D. became very proficient at the PQRST strategy. He remembered both what the letters stood for and between 80–100% of the information for up to half an hour. When tested 24 hours later, he remembered between 20% and 50% of the original questions. His nonverbal memory, however, showed very little improvement. On the Benton Visual Retention Test

Table 7-2. A Summary of F. D.'s Test Scores

Test	September 1980	October 1980
WAIS		
Verbal IQ	133	—
Performance IQ	121	—
Full-scale IQ	130	—
Wechsler Memory Scale		
MQ	96	101
Personal and Current	2/6	3/6
Orientation	3/5	5/5
Mental Control	9/9	9/9
Logical Memory		
Immediate (Form 1)	9.5/23	15/23
1-Hour Delay (Form 1)	0/23	0/23
Immediate (Form 2)	—	9/23
1-Hour Delay (Form 2)	—	0/23
Digits	13/15	15/15
Visual reprod.	10/14	11/14
Associate Learning	4/21	5.5/21
Warrington Memory Tests		
MQ	79	71
Scaled score		
Forced-Choice Words	8	3
Forced-Choice Faces	7	9
Incomplete Pictures	4	4
Incomplete Words	8	10
Prompt	9	8
Recognition	6	3
Rey–Osterreith complex figure		
Copy (1)	34/36	35/36
Immediate recall	—	13/36
40-minute delay	0	5/36
Copy (2)	—	33/36
40-minute delay	—	5/36[a]
Benton Visual Retention Test		
Form C (Admin. A)		
Correct	6	7
Errors	6	4
Form D (Admin. A)		
Correct	—	7
Errors	—	3

[a] He actually recalled Form 1 (i.e., the form presented 24 times during treatment) and not Form 2. However, he scored 5 points because certain features occur in both forms.

Table 7-2 (*Continued*)

Test	September 1980	October 1980
Rey–Davis pegboard		
Errors	14/16	10/16
Pursuit rotor		
% time on target at 1 revolution per second	9	54
Finger maze		
Time (seconds)	19	5
Errors	2	0
Raven's Standard Progressive Matrices		
Raw score	53	—
Percentile	98	—

(Benton, 1974), for example, his baseline score was 6 correct and 6 errors. He was given the same version of this test once each day for 6 weeks. At the end of training his score was 7 correct and 4 errors; this represented very little change from baseline. With the Rey–Osterreith complex figure, he was asked to copy Form 1 each day during training and reproduce it immediately. His baseline (immediate recall) score was 6/36, and at the end of 6 weeks it was 13/36. He had therefore improved, but, given that the recall was immediate and the same figure had been copied 24 times, performance was still very poor. The Rey–Davis pegboard was never mastered within five trials, despite being given three times a week for 6 weeks.

Specific Problem Areas

See Figure 7-1 for a summary of results in the specific problem areas.

1. *Remembering daily timetable*: F. D. was able to learn most of his timetable, but never reached 100% success. Over the last 3 weeks, all the mistakes were time errors. For example, he said that the morning coffee break was at 10:20 A.M. instead of 10:30 A.M., and that the afternoon session began at 1:00 P.M. instead of 1:30 P.M.

2. *Remembering people's names*: The visual-imagery procedure for names enabled F. D. to reach 100% success with 12 names 12 days after treatment began, and he maintained this success.

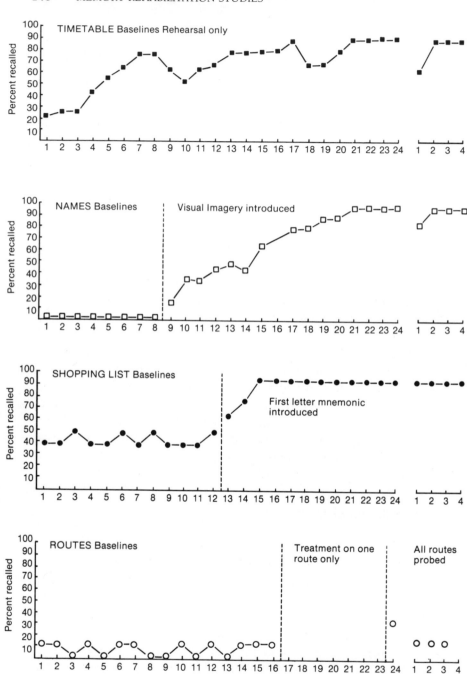

3. *Remembering the shopping list:* The first-letter mnemonic system was a favorite for F. D. and he rapidly reached 100% success using this method.

4. *Remembering routes:* F. D. failed to learn the particular route introduced during the treatment stage. When the other routes were probed, however, immediately before his departure from the unit, he successfully led the way to three of the eight destinations. He did not "remember" the way, but he did make use of external cues. For example, one of the places he succeeded in reaching was the "White House" (a day center within the grounds). Although the sign saying "White House" had been covered up, it was the only building in the grounds painted white. F. D. looked all around him until he saw the white building and then moved toward it. Similarly, he was able to find the way to the front gate by listening to traffic noises and heading in that direction. He also found his way to the river by first looking around to see where the trees were thickest and then making his way toward them. He was never able to go straight to any destination without reading signs, responding to cues, or looking in his notebook for directions.

Reassessment

After 3 months, F. D. came back for reassessment. He was retested on the four specific problem areas. He remembered 75% of his original timetable on the first retest and 92% thereafter. He remembered 83% of the names on first retesting; the rest he remembered with a prompt (e.g., "There was a picture with horses" for "Dr. Hunt"). Thereafter, his recall of names was 100%. With routes he found two of the eight places (25%). One was the "White House" and the other the ward where he slept (although he had not remembered the way to the ward during his first admission).

Figure 7-1. A multiple-baseline design to treat four of F. D.'s specific memory problems, together with follow-up after a 3-month delay. (From "Success and Failure in Memory Training Following a Cerebral Vascular Accident" by B. A. Wilson, 1982, *Cortex, 18,* 581–594. Adapted by permission.)

DISCUSSION

Effectiveness of Treatment

It cannot be said that the intensive memory training improved F. D.'s memory to any extent. However, it was possible to teach him some types of new information. Two strategies led to 100% success—visual imagery for names, and a first-letter mnemonic for items in a shopping list. Possibly the problems presented by the timetable and routes could have been solved by other strategies and/or more time. However, F. D.'s own method for the routes was probably the best one for him to use; this was to read the signs on the buildings, to use any other cues available, and, if these failed, to write the directions down and read them.

It may be thought that F. D.'s particularly severe route-finding problem resulted from a difficulty with spatial relationships rather than, or in addition to, a memory problem. This did not appear to be so, however, for the following reasons: (1) He could follow a map. (2) Immediate memory for spatial tasks was adequate. In the memory group, for example, one of the tasks was for the therapist to walk between a series of lettered or numbered circles on the floor and for one member of the group to follow the sequence; F. D. was invariably the best one in the group at this task. (3) He could perform any of the maze tasks set him with little trouble. (4) His Rey–Osterreith copy was good.

One question frequently asked by the staff and others who knew about F. D.'s treatment program was "How does he put the strategies into practice in his everyday life?" The answer would have to remain "Very little at present," although suggestions as to how to learn various kinds of new material were sent home for him and his wife. For one thing, visual imagery could be used for introducing other names such as those of public figures, and for helping him to reorient himself in time. For example, when asked the name of the British Prime Minister, F. D. invariably replied "Harold Wilson." During his final 2 weeks at Rivermead, a drawing was given him of a woman thatching the roof of 10 Downing Street, and after that he successfully recalled "Margaret Thatcher." Similarly, when asked the name of the President of the United States, F. D. always gave the response "Carter," so a drawing was shown of a man holding a ray gun, and he was then able to recall "Reagan." He did not recall them before the images were introduced, even though he was told their names for 3 consecutive days in the memory group.

F. D. was able to use the first-letter mnemonic system in other situations. For example, he was asked at the beginning of one session to remember to take his glasses, watch, notebook, memory aid, and pen when he was due to leave an hour later. He was also asked to think of a way to remember what the items were. He wrote down the five items, looked at the initial letters, and said, "Go With No Memory Problems." At the end of the session, it was necessary to remind him not to forget some items; he then recalled the sentence plus the items. The following day, he was reminded about some items he should not leave behind. He remembered neither items nor mnemonic, but after he was told, "Go With No Memory Problems," the five items were promptly recalled.

A first-letter mnemonic was also used in an attempt to teach F. D. the Rey–Davis nonverbal-learning task (described by Williams, 1968). It will be remembered that F. D. was unable to learn this task, despite being presented with it several times a week for 6 weeks. On his return it was readministered, and he made 10 out of a possible 16 errors (a typical score for him). At that point, the sequence was written down as follows:

Board 1—Top Center
Board 2—Top Left
Board 3—Dead Center
Board 4—Bottom Left

When F. D. was asked to think up a sentence beginning with the Letters "T-C-T-L-D-C-B-L," he produced "Try Cautiously and Think Long but Don't Come with a Bad Lady." He repeated it to himself, returned to the pegboards, and successfully completed the task. On the following day, when he first attempted the task, he failed. He was then asked to recall the sentence, but he could not do this. Next he was told the sentence and asked to try the task again. This time he succeeded. On the 4 following days, he remembered more of the cue sentence himself, but he departed before he had time to complete all of it. It must be admitted that the sentence was unusual and complicated! However, he was able to apply a verbal mnemonic to some degree in order to solve a task involving nonverbal learning.

In many ways F. D.'s life, and that of his family, remained unchanged by the treatment he received. Ways of teaching him new information were found, but he had to spend considerable amounts of time learning very small pieces of information. The strategies themselves were ineffective in dealing with constantly changing information. For example, F. D. returned for 2 weeks in February, and twice every day he was asked, "What month is it now?" His answer was always "April" (the month before his stroke). It might have been possible to teach him that the month was February, either by a visual image of by a first-letter mnemonic procedure; however this would not help F. D. a great deal, because he would find it extremely difficult to switch from one month to the next as time passed.

One of the most irritating problems for the relatives, friends, and therapists of many memory-impaired patients is their constant repetition of a story, anecdote, or piece of information. F. D. was no exception. During each session he produced the same information, with the same intonation and the same mistakes. When asked to repeat the shopping list, for example, he always said, "N for 'nectarines,' but you changed it from 'nectarines' and now it's N for 'nails' " (N had *never* been "nectarines"). He always said each day, "I'm not usually as stupid as this; it must be because I am tired." When he was informed of his difficulty in finding his way around the unit, he always denied it. If I asked him to wait outside the office for a few minutes until I had finished therapy with another patient, he forgot why he was waiting outside, came back in, and repeated the conversation of 2 or 3 minutes before. Every day he went into the speech therapy room instead of the clinical psychology room and had to be shown to the right room by the speech therapist. Each day he went to occupational therapy he forgot where to sit, although he always sat in the same chair in the same part of the office. Unfortunately, these kinds of problems were not helped by memory training.

Nature of the Lesion

For the following reasons, F. D.'s performance would appear to reflect greater damage to the right hemisphere than to the left:
1. He was generally better at verbal than nonverbal tasks.
2. He had particularly severe route-finding problems.
3. He had difficulty with visual-imagery procedures, being unable to use the visual-peg method to learn the shopping list. He remem-

bered the rhymes very easily (e.g., "one is a bun; two is a shoe," etc.) but could not recall any images paired with the pegs. He was quite unlike C. M., a man with a left temporal lobe tumor (see Chapter 6), who was unable to remember the rhymes accurately but was very good at recalling the images. On the "airplane list" (Crovitz, 1979), F. D. recalled only one or two of the images. It is suggested that with the visual images for names he was incorporating a verbal-mediation strategy: The names he recalled quickest were those with a "wordy" description, such as "*Rush* all you're *worth*" for "Dr. Rushworth" (represented by a person rushing along) and "Step" and "Knee" for "Stephanie." The names that took longest for him to retrieve from his memory were the short (and, one would think, relatively easy) ones, like "Dr. Hunt" (a drawing of a hunting scene) and "Mrs. Long" (a drawing of a long, thin woman). Again, this behavior was quite unlike that of C. M., who did best with the drawings most representative of names (such as "Hunt").

4. F. D. preferred the first-letter mnemonic strategy. This, presumably, was the easiest of the systems for him to use, giving further support for the diagnosis of a more intact left hemisphere.

5. He was able to learn the daily timetable by verbal rehearsal, but was unable to learn nonverbal tasks such as the Rey–Osterreith and Rey–Davis, with a similar amount of rehearsal time.

6. He benefited from verbal retrieval cues, but not from nonverbal retrieval cues (this is further discussed in the next section). The behavior of C. M. was, again, quite the reverse. It is a possibility that F. D. may have always had poor right-hemisphere skills, although his premorbid musical skills did not indicate this.

Theoretical Implications

How does the case of F. D. contribute to our understanding of the nature of human memory and forgetting? Warrington and Weiskrantz (1970) suggest that amnesia is primarily a problem of retrieval rather than consolidation. Milner (1968) takes a rather different view, suggesting that amnesia is failure to store information. As F. D. would appear to have a relatively pure amnesic syndrome uncontaminated by other handicaps, can he provide evidence for either the storage-deficit or retrieval-deficit hypothesis? Warrington and Weiskrantz showed that amnesics' recall could be improved by presenting retrieval cues— for example, an incomplete drawing or the first few letters of a word. If a person is to benefit from retrieval cues, the information must, of necessity, be stored or consolidated. If retrieval cues do not help, then it is possible that the material has never entered the memory store. F. D. did benefit from retrieval cues. The first-letter mnemonic is a retrieval cue, and we know that he liked this technique and was able to use it. Further evidence comes from his performance on the Warrington Memory Battery. Three of the six subtests here provide retrieval cues, and on two of them—both involving printed words—F. D.'s score was in the average range. He was not helped, however, by retrieval cues on Incomplete Pictures, a picture-memory subtest. Thus some retrieval cues worked, but not all of them. This discrepancy between good response to verbal retrieval cues and poor response to nonverbal cues is consistent with poorer right-hemisphere skills.

F. D., then, supports Warrington and Weiskrantz's view that amnesia is a deficit of retrieval rather than consolidation—but only as far as his verbal memory goes. The position is much less clear with regard to his nonverbal memory. He never remembered his seat in occupational therapy, even after being out of the room for only 5 minutes. It can be argued that his seat and its position in the room constituted a retrieval cue for where he should sit. He was unable to benefit from this retrieval cue, however. Indeed, the room appeared unfamiliar to him; he was never sure if he was in the correct room or not unless he read the sign on the door. Similarly, he often sat down in the speech therapy room instead of the clinical psychology room, thinking he was in the correct place. The two rooms are the same size but differently furnished. F. D.'s inability to learn the routes may have been because of a failure of consolidation rather than retrieval. The "ReaL Emergency" mnemonic, for example, was a retrieval cue that failed to work for him, although he understood the mnemonic. F. D. may, therefore, provide evidence both for Milner and for Warrington and Weiskrantz. His verbal deficits were due to retrieval problems and his nonverbal deficits to consolidation ones. Meudell, Northen, Snowden, and Neary (1980) also failed to prove strong evidence for a retrieval deficit in Korsakoff patients. In other words, perhaps both storage and retrieval deficits can be found in the amnesic syndrome.

At another level, we may address the issue of theory and its relation to research, assessing again how the major theoretical disciplines have informed this research. Neuropsychological assessment proved to be important. F. D.'s cognitive functioning has been delineated, and it is clear that his was purely a memory disorder. No other deficits were identified. His reasoning, language, and perceptual skills were good. Indeed, his high IQ meant he was able to implement some of the strategies taught to him in a complex and sophisticated way. His use of first-letter cueing to solve the Rey–Davis nonverbal-learning task was an example of this.

Cognitive psychology has offered descriptions of the classic amnesic syndrome that proved to be of assistance in formulating the diagnosis for F. D. In order to analyze the nature of his deficits, two different theories have been invoked. The "failure-to-consolidate" theory of amnesia would appear to explain F. D.'s nonverbal deficits. On the other hand, his verbal memory did respond to retrieval cues (initial letters). This ability to benefit from retrieval cues would seem to support the proposal that amnesia is due to a retrieval deficit. F. D.'s case also provides support for the view that amnesics do not demonstrate abnormal forgetting; he retained a considerable amount of the information taught to him when retested 3 months after the close of treatment.

Behavioral assessment was incorporated into the identification and monitoring of F. D.'s therapy but, despite considerable efforts and some ingenuity, behavioral treatments failed to teach F. D. even one of the eight routes included in the program. This, perhaps, was a case in which environmental cues and external aids turned out to be the most ameliorative devices in the learning process. F. D. discovered these and implemented them himself. He used signposts, written directions, and environmental cues such as traffic noises to help him find his way around the center. A lesson is contained in this case for perhaps most therapists, and that is not to underestimate the patient's capacity to solve his or her own problems.

·8·

RELEARNING LETTERS OF THE ALPHABET IN A CASE OF ACQUIRED DYSLEXIA

INTRODUCTION

Although the treatment described in the bulk of this chapter was for a reading disorder, the patient had to relearn, and therefore had to remember anew, letters of the alphabet. In addition to her reading problems, the patient suffered from many other cognitive deficits, including a severe AA, which adversely affected relearning. For these reasons, the description of her treatment is considered to be as suited to the field of memory therapy as it is to remediation of dyslexia.

If a person with normal reading ability develops reading difficulties following a stroke or head injury, or some other kind of brain disorder, then he or she is said to have "acquired dyslexia." Several syndromes of acquired dyslexia have been described (see, e.g., Newcombe & Marshall, 1981, and K. E. Patterson, 1981). The four major types of acquired dyslexia are "deep dyslexia," "phonological dyslexia," "surface dyslexia," and "letter-by-letter reading." It would appear from an examination of published material that deep dyslexia has been studied in greatest detail (Coltheart, Patterson, & Marshall, 1980). Patients with this syndrome can read some words reasonably well. Typically, they are better at reading nouns than verbs, and find prepositions particularly difficult. Nonwords that might be used in a test situation (e.g., "spug") are usually impossible for these patients to read, although they can repeat such words, thus indicating that the problem is not one of articulation. The most interesting feature of deep dyslexia is the tendency for patients to make semantic errors. An example of this would be responding to the word "angel" by reading out "mermaid," or reading "barrister" for the word "judicature." Other reading

Much of the material reported in this chapter is to appear in "Single Case Methodology and the Remediation of Dyslexia" by B. A. Wilson and A. D. Baddeley, in G. Pavlides and D. Fisher (Eds.), *Dyslexia: Neuropsychology and Treatment*, in press, London: Wiley. Adapted by permission.

errors that are frequently observed include visual mistakes, such as reading "bussing" for "busy"; derivational errors, such as "posting" for "postage"; and a combination of visual and semantic errors, leading to a mistake such as "really old" for "generosity" ("geriatric").

Phonological dyslexia is much less often reported (Ellis, 1984), perhaps because it is rarely investigated. The main deficit in this syndrome is the inability to read nonwords. For case descriptions of phonological dyslexia, see Beauvois and Dérouesné (1979) and Shallice and Warrington (1980).

The main characteristic of the third major syndrome, surface dyslexia, is the inability to read irregular words. ("Irregular" words are ones that would be mispronounced if the normal grapheme–phoneme conversion rules were applied.) Thus a surface dyslexic may be able to read the regular word "mint" but not the irregular word "pint." Non-words are typically read reasonably well by the surface dyslexic, as the normal rules of reading apply to such words. It is not possible to be a surface dyslexic in languages such as Finnish or Italian, where there are no irregular words.

In the fourth major dyslexic syndrome, letter-by-letter reading, the reader appears to be unable to read a word as a whole unit and can only tell what the word is by identifying each separate letter in turn. The letters may be spoken, but frequently they are named subvocally or covertly. K. E. Patterson (1982) states that a letter-identification deficit is usually, but not invariably, present; that is, some letters will be misidentified.

K. E. Patterson (1981) provides a useful table to show how each of the four main syndromes are influenced by word dimensions. Table 8-1 has been adapted from this source.

Other varieties of acquired dyslexia have been described, of which two are relevant to this chapter. The first is "attentional dyslexia," described by Shallice and Warrington (1977), in which the patient typically makes errors when shown groups of letters. An example of this would be reading "metal" as "meal." Attentional dyslexics can name letters correctly when presented one at a time, but have difficulty naming strings of letters. The second type is rather similar to this and is known as "visual dyslexia" (Marshall & Newcombe, 1973). Examples of errors caused by visual dyslexia would be reading "hob" for "hope" and "men" for "mean." Coltheart (1981) describes this as "approximate visual access." Newcombe and Marshall (1981) suggest that impaired visual analysis cannot explain this disorder, because one of their

Table 8-1. The Main Influences of Word Dimensions on the Ability to Read Aloud in Four Syndromes of Acquired Dyslexia

Dimension	Dyslexia Syndrome			
	Deep	Phonological	Surface	Letter-by-letter
Words vs. nonwords	Yes	Yes	No	No
Content words v. function words	Yes	Yes	No	No
Imageability, concreteness	Yes	No	No	No
Word length	No	No	Yes	Yes
Regularity of spelling	No	No	Yes	No

Note. Adapted from "Neuropsychological Approaches to the Study of Reading" by K. E. Patterson, 1981, *British Journal of Psychology, 72,* 151–174. "Yes" in the table means that the dimension influences reading ability; "No" means that it does not.

patients usually named all the letters in words, yet still went on to misidentify the words themselves. Newcombe and Marshall believe that these errors are similar to those made by children learning to read, and by children with developmental dyslexia. Such errors can also be elicited from normal adult readers with tachistoscopic stimuli.

Several models have been produced to attempt explanations of the nature of the deficit in acquired dyslexia (e.g., Coltheart, 1985; Morton & Patterson, 1980; Newcombe & Marshall, 1981). The model presented in Figure 8-1 is a simple dual-route model of reading (see Coltheart, 1985, for a discussion of the dual-route models). It suggests that reading aloud can be achieved by two routes, a lexical and a nonlexical route (see Figure 8-1).

An illustration of this model can be provided if we consider the word "pint," which, as noted above, would be mispronounced if the normal grapheme–phoneme conversion rules were applied. Readers know how to pronounce this word correctly because it is in their lexicon. They have met the word many times before and have "pint" represented as a whole word. The nonword "fint," on the other hand, will not be in the lexicon, as it is very unlikely that the reader will have come across this word previously. In order to read "fint," the nonlexical or phonological route is necessary. (Marcel, 1980, argues that even nonwords are read via the lexical route; however, see Coltheart, 1985, for a refutation of this argument.) A regularly spelled English word such as "mint" can be read by either the lexical or nonlexical route. If the

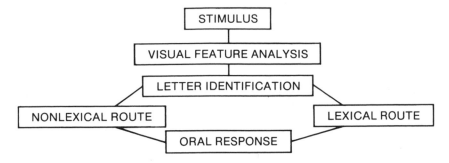

Figure 8-1. A simple dual-route model of reading.

model presented here is sound, then it should be possible to find people with selective impairment of the lexical route but normal functioning of the nonlexical route, and other people for whom the reverse is true. Such double dissociation is necessary in order to demonstrate separate processes (Baddeley, 1982b; Coltheart, 1985). People with these impairments do, of course, exist.

Phonological dyslexia is an example of a nonfunctioning (or at least severely impaired) nonlexical route that can account for the inability to read nonwords. The converse impairment is surface dyslexia. In this syndrome, the nonlexical route is functioning (surface dyslexics can, on the whole, read nonwords and regular words), but the lexical (or whole-word) route is almost nonexistent. This accounts for the severe deficit in reading words that are exceptions to rules. Even though some whole-word reading may be retained, the fact that surface dyslexics frequently misidentify homophones (e.g., reading "brews" aloud correctly but defining the word as if it were "bruise") suggests that whole-word recognition is through an auditory route rather than a visual-representation route.

It is less clear how deep dyslexics and letter-by-letter readers fit into the model. In the case of deep dyslexia, it is clear that the nonlexical route is nonfunctional because people with this disorder cannot read nonwords. The lexical route, however, is also imperfect, because semantic, visual, and derivational errors all occur. Additionally, abstract and function words are much harder to read than concrete and imageable words. Morton and Patterson (1980) believe that this is evidence for deep dyslexia's being due to the fact that several components of the reading system are damaged. Coltheart (1980,

1982) has argued that the characteristics of deep dyslexia reflect right-cerebral-hemisphere reading. The parts-of-speech effect and the semantic errors can readily be explained by the hypothesis of right-hemisphere reading.

An explanation for the letter-by-letter reader is perhaps more difficult to obtain by reference to the dual-route model. The whole-word route is clearly not functioning adequately in letter-by-letter readers, as they need to name each letter before identifying the word. The phonological route is also inadequate for providing an explanation of this phenomenon. Although letter-by letter readers can read non-words reasonably well, they still need to name each letter first, and do not appear to "blend" the letters together in the way a normal reader— or even a surface dyslexic—would. Shallice and Warrington (1980) believe that reading in such patients is mediated by an intact spelling system. It is possible that the visual dyslexic described by Marshall and Newcombe (1973) was like a letter-by letter reader with additional damage to the spelling system. However, if we assume for the sake of argument that such patients have a deficit in the visual-analysis system, then the model would provide an adequate explanation for letter-by-letter reading.

It is possible that lexical and nonlexical routes are both intact in letter-by-letter readers (after all, nonwords *can* be read, albeit slowly), but that *access* to these routes is impeded. It will be remembered that K. E. Patterson (1982) found that most letter-by-letter readers in her investigations were not 100% perfect at letter identification. Such a finding supports a deficient-visual-analysis hypothesis. It could also be argued that this syndrome is the linguistic equivalent of simultanagnosia. This perceptual disorder has been described by Luria (1959), Kinsbourne and Warrington (1962), and others. Such patients are unable to recognize or identify the whole of a picture or series of pictures, although they are able to perceive individual parts correctly.

Benton (1979) also describes problems of visual synthesis and analysis in the field of perception research. Letter-by-letter readers would appear to have deficits in visual analysis and synthesis with letters rather than pictures. Attentional dyslexia may also be due to deficits in the visual-analysis system. As such patients make errors with strings of letters and groups of words, despite correct identification of individual letters, it is arguable that this could be caused by a disorder of visual synthesis.

PREVIOUS ATTEMPTS TO IMPROVE READING
IN ACQUIRED DYSLEXIA

Little attention has been given to the remediation of acquired dyslexia. F. Benson and Geschwind (1969), for example, devoted one page of a 30-page book chapter, "The Alexias," to treatment. They were not optimistic about attempts to improve reading. However, when one considers that moderately mentally handicapped children (i.e., those with an IQ between 50 and 70) have been taught some reading skills, then it could be argued that Benson and Geschwind were unduly pessimistic. In the field of mental handicap, B. F. Walsh and Lamberts (1979) describe the use of errorless discrimination and a picture-fading technique with moderately mentally handicapped children. In the former method, the learner is initially taught to respond to one word only; gradually other words are introduced. At first these are dissimilar in appearance from each other, but later they become more alike. In the picture-fading method, each word is at first accompanied by a pictorial representation, which is gradually faded out until the child is reading the word on its own. The range of words taught in this way is typically small, and some researchers argue that teaching useful everyday words (e.g., "danger," "stop," and "exit") should be aimed at, rather than teaching more advanced reading (see, e.g., Gunzburg, 1973).

Bradley (1981) has used an interesting method with backward readers in normal schools. She has employed a tactile approach using plastic letters. The reading problems described by Bradley are similar to those demonstrated by some acquired dyslexics. For example, one boy confused "d" with "b" and "s" with "c." He also wrote "rag" as "rak" and "slip" as "sip." Bradley believes that plastic letters are an aid to reading because (1) they facilitate the learning of generalization (e.g., "ound" can be made into "round," "sound," "found," etc., simply by adding one of the letters by hand); (2) backward readers are more confident using plastic letters than writing, because the latter increases uncertainty as to what letters or how many letters actually to commit to paper; and (3) children with visual–perceptual problems find it easier to discriminate letters with a tactile image, rather than written or printed letters. Perhaps the teaching procedure used by Bradley may prove to be of benefit to some acquired dyslexics, given the fact that some neurological patients can "read" if they trace the letters with their fingers (M. L. Albert, 1979). There are, of course, several other strategies for improving the reading skills of developmental dyslexics (see, e.g., McGinnis & Smith, 1982) However, their usefulness as aids to improving the reading skills of adult neurological patients remains underinvestigated.

A paper by Moyer (1979) describes the treatment given to a 30-year-old man following an embolic stroke. Early treatment included improving his letter discrimination by encouraging him to trace sandpaper letters. He was also required to respond as quickly as possible to words printed on flash cards, and was given paragraphs to read for homework. The main teaching technique was practice in reading paragraphs, for which the patient was timed. The patient increased the speed with which he read new material from an average of 66 syllables per minute to 94 per minute some 3 months later. At the end of the treatment, the patient reported that for the first time since his surgery he was able to enjoy reading the newspaper.

Byng and Rickard (personal communication) have achieved some success with a deep dyslexic patient. This man, who retained considerable information about orthography, was taught to use an alphabetic cueing device to obtain the initial sound of a word. When confronted with the word "dog" he would not know whether the correct answer was "cat," "dog," "pig," or the like. However, he was able to look at the first letter and say the alphabet until he arrived at "D," realize that this was the initial sound, and thus eliminate the other options from his response. Nevertheless, many semantic and derivational errors remained in evidence with infrequent words. (He was the man who gave the reply "barrister" to the word "judicature" and "really old" to "generosity.")

A patient of ours (Wilson, White, & McGill, 1983) is possibly the most dramatically successful treatment of acquired dyslexia so far reported. F. R. E. was a young man who was shot in the head in 1977, at the age of 23 years. The bullet entered the left occiput and lodged in the left temporal area. Following a difficult postoperative period, including four operations and persistent meningitis for several months, he was found to be severely intellectually impaired. When assessed, prior to treatment for alexia, he was found to have a full-scale IQ of 56 on the WAIS (Wechsler, 1955). He was unable to read any words, letters, or digits. He was unable to sort real words from nonsense words and could not write from dictation. He could sort digits from letters; recognize when letters were upside down or not; copy letters and printed words; and match pairs of printed words, provided they were written in the same case. He could spell a few three-letter words orally, but made frequent errors. His speech was fluent and grammatical, but some word-finding problems and perseverations were evident. His performances on both the Peabody Picture Vocabulary Test (Dunn & Dunn, 1965) and the Token Test (De Renzi & Vignolo, 1962) were normal. He could not name colors or point to the correct color named by the examiner. He was, however, able to match colors. Although no formal record of his premorbid reading ability could be traced, he had passed examinations to enter the Royal Air Force, and must therefore have been at least an average reader.

In October 1980, 3 years after the gunshot wound, an attempt was made to teach F. R. E. to read again. The first approach was a "look-and-say" or whole-word method. Six words ("ladies," "gentlemen," "exit," and his own three names) were selected. These were introduced one at a time. For the first 12 treatment sessions (each lasting 30 minutes), an attempt was made to teach the patient to read the words aloud. In the second 13 treatment sessions (also lasting 30 minutes), F. R. E. was encouraged to recognize the correct words by pointing to them. He failed to identify any of the six words above chance level.

At that time, all of us working with F. R. E. believed he would never read again. He refused to accept this, however, and persisted in asking for reading tuition. In October 1982, 5 years after his injury, a phonetic approach was tried by Sam White, a helper at the local adult training center. The procedure was as follows:

1. Sounds of the letters of the alphabet were taught one at a time from A to Z. Upper-case letters were taught before lower-case.
2. Letters were presented in random order, and F. R. E. was required to say the sounds.
3. F. R. E. was taught to select the vowels from an array of letters.
4. Two- and three-letter regular words were introduced.
5. Irregular words were introduced.

In December 1982, formal teaching ceased, and F. R. E. worked alone at his reading. In May 1983, his reading age was 9 years and 1 month (he had failed to score on the reading-age scale prior to treatment). He still read almost every word phonetically, remembering very few words as whole units. Almost all errors were made with irregular words, and he appeared to have changed from an alexic to a surface dyslexic. However, he used context to help him and often deciphered an irregular word in a page of text. If, after several attempts, he failed to make sense of a word, he would ask for help. His spelling was almost completely phonetic. As many young children read like surface dyslexics before going on to learn irregular words as whole units, it is possible that F. R. E. might follow this pattern and become a more "normal" reader in time.

AN ATTEMPT TO IMPROVE THE READING SKILLS OF A YOUNG WOMAN WHO SUSTAINED A SEVERE HEAD INJURY IN A HORSE-RIDING ACCIDENT

Preliminary Remarks

The case of L. T., to be described here, illustrates how reference to the major theoretical disciplines can direct research procedure. Neuropsychological assessment was used to specify the nature of L. T.'s impairments. She had a severe visual object agnosia in addition to an almost complete alexia. Her language skills were normal (except when asked to describe visually presented material which she could not identify). Her memory was also impaired, thus indicating that any learning would be slow. However, there was little evidence of marked frontal lobe damage, and L. T. was a determined, independent young woman who showed no sign of personality disorder, apathy, or indifference to her situation. So even though her cognitive deficits were far more severe than L. R. (described in Chapter 9), L. T. was in many ways less handicapped—probably because of her largely intact frontal lobes. The same can be said for F. R. E. just described. The neuropsychological assessments of both L. T. and F. R. E. might have been interpreted as evidence that treatment was *unlikely* to succeed in their cases, as both were so severely impaired. Indeed, a leading expert in neuropsychology once told F. R. E. and his father that F. R. E. would never learn to read again and he should give up hope of doing so!

An understanding of L. T.'s reading disability was aided by the dual-route model of reading described in the introduction. (The same model also allowed for an explanation of L. T.'s success at follow-up 1 year later). Furthermore, the pattern of L. T.'s success adds more support for the dual-route model, thus showing not only that theory can help therapy, but also that therapy can come up with evidence for the soundness or otherwise of particular theoretical models.

L. T.'s treatment is a good example of a thorough behavioral approach that specified appropriate goals, included extrinsic rewards, and proceeded patiently for several weeks despite lack of early success.

Case History

L. T. was a young woman who sustained a very severe head injury in a horse-riding accident some 9 months before being admitted to Rivermead Rehabilitation Centre. Following the head injury, she was unconscious for about 3 months. A CT scan in February 1983, when L. T. was 19 years and 1 month old, indicated marked dilation of the whole ventricular system, and especially the left occipital horn, which extended almost to the tip of the occipital lobe.

L. T. began speaking 2 to 3 weeks after regaining consciousness. On admission to Rivermead she was found to have a right hemiparesis, a divergent squint with some temporal-field loss for the right eye, cerebellar ataxia, and cerebellar dysarthria. Despite these impairments, her speech remained perfectly intelligible. She was first seen in the clinical psychology department 1 month after admission—that is, 10 months after her injury, at which time she was 18 years old. Prior to her accident, she had been studying four subjects for the General Certificate of Education (Ordinary Level), which suggests at least average premorbid intellectual ability. The results of L. T.'s assessment can be seen in Table 8-2.

L. T.'s severe perceptual problems could not be explained by impaired visual acuity, as she could copy adequately, she could correctly describe features of the objects in front of her, and she was able to solve high-contrast grating tasks (Davidoff & Wilson, 1985). Her visual fields were almost normal. Her problems could not be due to dysphasia, because she was in the normal range on all tests administered by the speech therapist, except when she had to respond to visually presented material. Her naming to description was good (e.g., when asked "What is the name of something farmers put up in fields to frighten birds away?" she responded correctly without delay).

Her reading difficulties were also severe. She could not read words on the Schonell Graded Word Reading Test (Schonell & Schonell, 1963). When these same words were printed in large letters, she could only manage to read two correctly ("tree" and "little"). She could read her own name, her brother's name, and "horse," "saddle," and "stirrup" in large print; she could also read one word, "debt," from the

Table 8-2. Results of L. T.'s Psychological Assessment

Test	Results
WAIS	
Verbal IQ	79 (borderline impairment)
Information	6
Comprehension	3
Arithmetic	5
Similarities	8
Digit Span	8
Vocabulary	11
Performance IQ	Unobtainable (unable to identify material)
Digit Symbol	0
Picture Completion	0
Block Design	5
Picture Arrangement	0
Object Assembly	2
Logical Memory (from Wechsler Memory Scale)	
Immediate	8
Delayed	0 (severely impaired)
Recognition of objects	
Visual condition	9/35
Rotating in visual condition	10/35
Tactile condition	0/35
Recognition of photographs (adapted from Warrington & Taylor, 1973)	
Unusual views	1/20
Usual views	1/20
Recognition of line drawings	
Oldfield–Wingfield test (Oldfield & Wingfield, 1965)	8/36
Graded Naming Test (McKenna & Warrington, 1983)	1/30
Face recognition	
Same–different faces (adapted from Whiteley & Warrington, 1977	13/20
Famous faces (adapted from Warrington & Sanders, 1971)	1/12
Recognition of model animals	3/14
Color recognition	
Naming colors	8/14
Matching colors	8/8
"What is the color of . . . ?" (from memory)	11/11

National Adult Reading Test (H. E. Nelson & O'Connell, 1978). She correctly identified fewer than 25% of the individual letters of the alphabet. She was much more proficient at pointing to letters named by the tester and at writing single letters to dictation achieving scores of 23/26 on both tasks. She found the writing of words much more difficult and only wrote 4 of 12 correctly: "tree," "little," "horse," and "bun." Examples of her errors were "plAine" for "playing," "BoorK" for "book," and "darehrra" for "Barbara." She scored 4/80 on the Vernon Spelling Test (Vernon, 1977).

As L. T.'s impaired reading of individual letters appeared to impede her reading of words, it was decided to reteach her the letters of the alphabet before starting a more ambitious reading program. An investigation of her ability to read letters of different sizes was conducted. Eight cards were made for each letter of the alphabet, four for upper-case letters and four for lower-case. The sizes of the letters were 7 mm, 5 mm, 3 mm, and 2 mm. L. T. was presented with the 208 letters in random order and asked to identify them.

L. T.'s mean overall performance as a function of letter size and case is shown in Figure 8-2, suggesting a tendency for greater ease in naming upper-case letters as opposed to lower-case, and larger letters

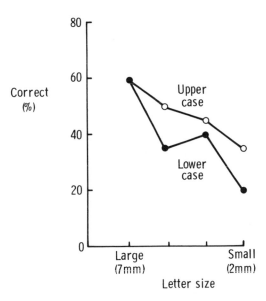

Figure 8-2. L. T.'s mean overall performance as a function of letter size and case.

rather than smaller. Of the 26 letters, 11 showed an advantage for the upper case and 4 for the lower. (This was a significant difference on the sign test, $p < .05$.) An indication of the size effect was obtained by comparing performance on the largest and smallest examples of the 26 upper- and lower-case letters: 32 showed equal performance for large and small letters, 18 showed an advantage to the largest size, and 2 showed an advantage to the smallest ($p < .01$, sign test).

Tables 8-3a and 8-3b show L. T.'s confusion matrices for upper- and lower-case letters. Examination of common confusions suggests a number of possibilites as to the nature of the underlying perceptual process. A number of errors seem to have occurred because the letters presented and the responses have broadly similar shapes. Examples of these are "D–O," "Q–O," and "V–W." In other examples, common features seem to be present, as, for example, with "B–E," "G–C," "J–T," "j–i," and "l–I." Finally, errors of orientation appear to have occurred including "d–p," "d–b," "u–n," and "M–W." While it would be unwise to draw strong conclusions from a small number of selected errors, they do suggest the possibility of a breakdown in different components of the process of perceiving and identifying letters.

Experiment 1

Method

The 10 letters selected for treatment in Experiment 1 were B, D, J, K, L, Q, R, V, Y, and Z. Sixteen letters were made for each letter, eight upper-case and eight lower-case. Each stimulus was a different size and shape (i.e., different typeface or style of handwriting) from any other. All stimuli were at least 7 mm high. Baselines were taken on two consecutive days, using the 7-mm upper- and lower-case letters from the test materials described above, to ensure that errors were made in the identification of each of the 10 selected letters. Following this, one letter was randomly selected for treatment. Letters were then intro-duced for treatment one or two at a time. However, baselines were taken on all letters during test sessions.

Teaching L. T. the letters consisted of the following:

1. Practice.
2. Feedback on whether or not she was correct.

Table 8-3a. Confusion Matrix for Upper-Case Letters

Response

Stimulus letter	A	B	C	D	E	F	G	H	I	J	K	L	M	N	O	P	Q	R	S	T	U	V	W	X	Y	Z
A	3																									
B	1	3																								
C			4																							
D			1		3										3											
E				1											1											
F					3		1							1	1								1			
G	2					1	1	2							1											
H	1							2						1												
I								4																		
J	1							1	1									1								
K									1	1															3	
L									1									2	1				2			
M						1							2	1									2			
N													1	1								1	1			
O															4											
P			1													2										
Q							1								3			1								
R	1					1			1					1												
S										3				1					4							
T																					4					
U																				1	1	1	1	1		
V																					1		4	1		
W														1												
X																						2	1	2	2	
Y																				2						
Z																		3								1

161

Table 8-3b. Confusion Matrix for Lower-Case Letters

Response

Stimulus letter	a	b	c	d	e	f	g	h	i	j	k	l	m	n	o	p	q	r	s	t	u	v	w	x	y	z	Other
a	2																										1 (4)
b		1												1	1												
c			2												1			1									
d			1												2	1											
e					2																		1				
f					1														2				1				
g			1		1													2									
h							4																1				
i									3																		
j									2																		
k							1	1															1				
l																		2								2	
m													4														
n				1									1	2													
o				1										2													
p	1			1									1	2													
q																2	1										
r														1		2		4									
s										3				1				1					1				
t														1							1		1				
u																					1	1	3				
v																						1	4				
w																							1	1			
x	1																		1						2		
y	1																		1			1				1	
z	1															2							1				

162

3. Description of the shape of the letter. (For example, when L. T. was asked, "What does the letter look like?" she replied, "An O with a tail." She was then informed, "An O with a tail is a Q.")
4. Any other associations we could think of. (For example, when learning the letter Y we sang, "*Why* are we waiting?" and chanted, "*Why* can't I remember Y?")
5. Rewards for 20 or 30 correct responses. Rewards consisted of a walk to the local fields to see the horses or being given a book about horses.

Results

The results are depicted in Figure 8-3. It can be seen that by the end of the treatment program L. T. had learned the 10 letters, although during the last month she still made occasional errors with X and Z. In

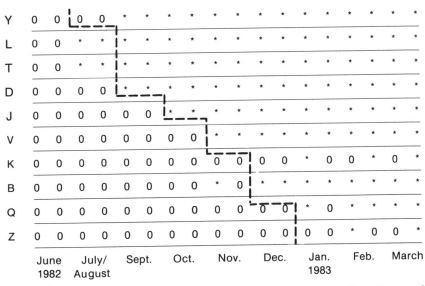

Figure 8-3. A multiple-baseline design to demonstrate L. T.'s relearning of letters of the alphabet. Symbols: 0, errors made in test session; *, no errors made in test session; dashed line, next stage of treatment introduced. (From "Single Case Methodology and the Remediation of Acquired Dyslexia" by B. A. Wilson and A. D. Baddeley. In G. Pavlides and D. Fisher [Eds.], *Dyslexia: Neuropsychology and Treatment*, in press, London: Wiley. Adapted by permission.)

July 1983, a posttreatment assessment with the original 208 letters revealed that she made only 7 errors on all 208 letters. The errors were on L (read as "J"), Z (read as "K"), q (read as "b"), Z (read as "x"), and j (read as "i" three times). Now that L. T. had successfully learned most of the letters of the alphabet in several different sizes, the program was extended to cover sound combinations.

Experiment 2

Method

Baselines were taken on L. T.'s ability to read and write sound combinations. Sounds such as "oi," "oa," "wr," "ph," and so on were given to her to read aloud. Thirty sound combinations were embedded in three words (e.g., "coin," "spoil," "hoist") and presented to her on three separate occasions, making 90 words in all. Her responses were recorded. She was also asked to write the words on three separate occasions. Order of reading and writing was randomized and no feedback was provided to L. T. as to whether or not her responses were correct. The 10 most difficult sound combinations were selected for treatment. She had failed to read or write any of these successfully on any of the baseline occasions.

It had been intended to use a multiple-baseline approach, as with the single letters. The first sound combination selected for treatment was "oa." Three treatment sesssions were spent practicing this sound. Lists of words containing the combination (e.g., "oak," "stoat," etc.) were given, and L. T. was required to find the combination in the word and then read the word aloud. Feedback was supplied as to whether or not she was correct. Any success was praised verbally. Unexpectedly, however, L. T. was discharged home and the program had to be abandoned. She returned for 1 month in July, prior to her summer holiday and admission to a further-education college for young handicapped adults. Given that a multiple-baseline design would take longer than 1 month, it was decided to teach L. T. all 10 sound combinations at once. A further baseline revealed that there had been no change in her ability to read or spell the 10 sound combinations during the intervening months. Encouragingly, though, she still succeeded with the "oa" combination, reading words like "boat" and "coat" successfully. Three times each week during that month, all 10 combinations were practiced. The method was that described above for "oa" words. Once a week, the practice sessions were preceded by a test of her knowledge of the sound combinations. The testing consisted of asking L. T. to read a list of words containing the combinations. These words had not been used in the practice sessions.

Results

The results of Experiment 2 are given in Table 8-4. These indicate that L. T. was able to learn to read sound combinations. Indeed, her learning ability appeared to have improved considerably since the reading program first began with the letter Y. That one letter took her 6 weeks to learn. In the following year she was learning eight or nine sound combinations within a month.

It would have been possible to carry out a nonparametric statistical test on L. T.'s results. A Wilcoxon matched-pairs signed-ranks test comparing pre- and posttreatment scores for the sound combinations would give a significant result. However, it is not necessary to employ statistics when the results are so obvious. As noted in Chapter 4, statistics are less often employed in single-case studies than in group designs; see that chapter for further discussion of the issue.

Table 8-4. Teaching Sound Combinations to L. T.

Sound combination	Baselines		Treatment			
	Baseline 1 (March)	Baseline 2 (July)	Week 1	Week 2	Week 3	Week 4
oa	0	*	*	*	*	*
ea	0	0	*	*	*	*
ur	0	0	0	0	0	*
ir	0	0	*	*	*	*
ai	0	0	*	*	*	*
aw	0	0	*	*	*	*
ie	0	0	0	0	*	0
igh	0	0	*	*	0	*
wr	0	0	*	*	0	*
Totals correct	0%	10%	80%	80%	70%	90%

Note. Symbols: 0, errors made during testing; *, no errors made during testing.

Discussion

There can be little doubt that L. T.'s ability to identify letters improved. She was unable to read any of the 10 letters selected for treatment in June 1982, and was making no errors at all in March 1983. Similarly, with the sound combinations, she was 80–90% better at follow-up than during the baseline sessions. However, the crucial question is whether or not improvement was due to the intervention strategy or to general recovery over time. Table 8-4 offers convincing evidence that the treatment itself was effective in teaching the letters, *not* natural recovery. Out of 10 letters, 8 of them were regularly misidentified until treatment procedures started. The remaining 2 letters were L. T.'s own initials. These were likely to have been more frequently seen and written by her than other letters selected for relearning. Inspection of the successes and failures depicted in Figure 8-3 shows that in the baseline periods only 6.9% of the data points indicated no errors for any given letter. In contrast, 88.8% of the data points taken after the introduction of treatment were free from errors. If improvement was due to recovery, then L. T. would have shown a reduction in errors unrelated to the staggered intervention of treatment.

Although treatment was not staggered in Experiment 2, the baseline readings showed that no improvement occurred over a 4-month interval; once the sound combinations were regularly practiced however, L. T. learned them. Again, this is evidence against natural recovery as an explanation for improvement. The change in ability was directly related to the introduction of the teaching technique.

Obviously, there are disadvantages in the multiple-baseline method as it was applied here. Taking 6 weeks to learn the letter Y and 9 months to learn the letters of the alphabet is, by any standard, a long period, and arguably not the best use of professional time. On the other hand, given that hardly any evidence exists to indicate whether or not alexia of this type is amenable to treatment, it seemed important to evaluate treatment thoroughly. The disadvantages connected with duration of treatment were offset by the fact that it was possible to provide evidence for the effectiveness of such treatment. In a more general program, such as working on all the letters together, or practice at general reading, progress *might* have been faster, but it would have been much more difficult to assess the relative influences of treatment and natural recovery. It should also be pointed out that L. T. might *not* have learned any faster in a more general program. Indeed, she might not have made any progress. It is worth considering the possibility that the slow start was imperative, given the severity of her difficulties. Had the technique used in Experiment 2 (working on 10 rules simultaneously) been implemented earlier, then L. T. might have found the tasks too demanding.

Another argument could be put forward with regard to L. T.'s treatment—namely, the question of whether or not it was worth putting in so much effort for a marginal and clinically nonsignificant improvement in her reading skills. This would be a fair question if all teaching/treatment had stopped when L. T. was discharged from rehabilitation. This did not happen, nor was it ever expected to happen. The *overall* goal of treatment was to improve L. T.'s reading skills. The first subgoal was to reteach her the letters of the alphabet as a stage in that process.

It is argued earlier in this chapter (and throughout this book) that a behavioral approach combined with adequate neuropsychological assessment and cognitive models gives the best chance of successful treatment. L. T.'s treatment followed this pattern. The neuropsychological assessment reported in Table 8-2 delineates her strengths and weaknesses. The model of reading described in the introduction to the chapter is considered below in relation to L. T.'s deficits before and after treatment.

The behavioral program designed for L. T. may be seen in Table 8-5. Following discharge from Rivermead, L. T. was admitted to a college of further education for disabled young people. In February and July of 1984, she returned to Rivermead for reassessment. In February her reading age on the Schonell Graded Word Reading Test was 8.0 years, and in July her reading age on the British Ability Scales List was 9.6 years. (The latter test was used in case L. T. had become too familiar with the Schonell Test through repeated testing.) Her reading thus seemed to be continuing to improve, and it can be argued that clinically significant gains were made. There is no reason to expect the improvement to stop.

Returning to the model of reading presented earlier in this chapter, we can ask whether it would account for L. T.'s deficits. Before treatment started, L. T. had great difficulty in identifying letters of the alphabet. In addition, she had equally severe problems with object recognition. There is little doubt, then, that she had a deficit in the visual-analysis component of the model. If attentional dyslexics and letter-by-letter readers also have deficits in the visual-analysis system

Table 8-5. Treatment Program for L. T.'s Reading Problems

Stage	Details
1. Define behavior.	Inability to read letters and words.
2. State goal.	Overall goal: To improve L. T.'s reading skills. First *subgoal*: To teach L. T. to identify letters of the alphabet correctly.
3. Obtain baseline.	(a) Size and letter effect obtained; (b) 10 most difficult letters selected (0/10 correct).
4. Decide on treatment strategies.	(a) Practice; (b) feedback; (c) description; (d) other associations; (e) rewards.
5. Begin treatment.	July 1982.
6. Monitor treatment.	10 letters learned over next 9 months.
7. Change procedure if necessary.	Program extended to cover sound combinations.

as postulated above, then it is clear that L. T.'s problems were more severe and perhaps occurred at an earlier stage of visual processing. Nevertheless, there were aspects of L. T.'s reading behavior prior to treatment that were reminiscent of visual dyslexia and letter-by-letter reading. For example, mistakes resembling the "approximate visual access" (Coltheart, 1981) of visual dyslexics were in evidence during L. T.'s pretreatment assessment. These included "arch" for "ache"; "work" for "walk"; and "wit" for "wait." Examples reminiscent of attentional dyslexia, where letters are correctly named but an incorrect word deduced, were also evident. Examples included "B-O-O-K" = "pork"; "U-N-C-L-E" = "eunuch"; and "O-U-T-S-E-T" = "oust." Finally, examples of letter-by-letter reading from L. T. included "D-E-B-T" = "debt"; "L-I-T-T-L-E" = "little"; and "T-R-E-E" = "tree." L. T.'s perceptual disorder has been well documented (Davidoff & Wilson, 1985), so it would appear that her acquired dyslexia was, to a large extent, perceptually rather than linguistically based.

We should also ask whether it is possible to fit L. T.'s follow-up level of reading ability into the model. By July 1983 (at the end of the treatment programs described in this chapter), there was probably no reason to suppose that her position in the model had changed at all. This was because her improvement was so marginal. However, by the time of the latest follow-up (July 1984), it was possible that the phonetic or nonlexical route was again open to L. T., leaving her with an impairment in the lexical or whole-word route. At this follow-up, L. T. appeared to be a surface dyslexic. Her reading errors included "sue" for "sew"; "comb" for "come"; and "burry" for "bury." However, many irregular words were read correctly (e.g., "guest," "building," and "dough"). This was probably because she was often able to make a reasonable guess when she produced a word that at first did not make sense.

Her spelling at this time was more typical of a surface dyslexic, or rather a surface dysgraphic, with errors such as "orlwase" for "always"; "aronious" for "erroneous"; and "giltee" for "guilty" (see Figure 8-4 for further examples). Finally, L. T. misidentified homophones, another characteristic of surface dyslexia. Examples here included "P-O-U-R," defined as "when you haven't got any money," and "U-S-E," defined as "The farmer worries when the ewes start lambing." Some perceptual problems remained, both with pictorial and linguistic stimuli. For example, L. T. still occasionally confused "p" and "g," and "g" and "q," when these letters were embedded in words. These errors are typically found in visual dyslexia. Other errors made by L. T. were characteristic of attentional dyslexia. For example, she read "dance" as "dank" and "aunt" as "gaunt." These perceptual problems at the July 1984 follow-up were not nearly as severe as they were in June 1982, however.

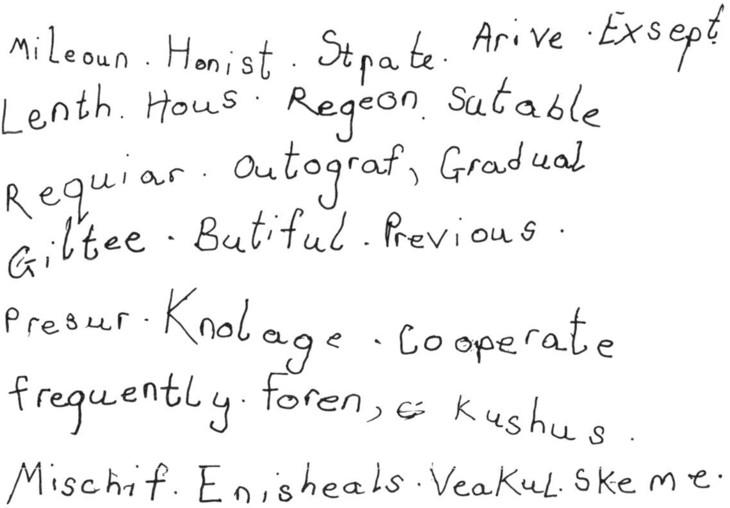

Figure 8-4. Examples of L. T.'s spelling at the July 1984 follow-up.

In short, it would appear that L. T. had residual deficits in the visual-analysis system at follow-up. The improvements in the functioning of the visual-analysis system appear to have increased access to the nonlexical/phonological route. Perhaps, like F. R. E. described earlier in this chapter, L. T. is on her way to becoming a normal reader with both routes available.

The most promising aspect of L. T.'s case as reported here is that success is possible even a long time after injury, and in someone with severe cognitive deficits who learns very slowly. L. T., like F. R. E., testifies to the fact that intensive, long-term rehabilitation or remedial teaching is not a waste of time. Both cases suggest that teaching reading via phonetics is likely to be more profitable than teaching by "whole-word" or "look-and-say" methods in cases where the dyslexia is perceptually based. More single-case studies with this particular type of acquired dyslexia are needed.

An important aspect of both L. T.'s and F. R. E.'s treatment was that in both these cases actual restitution of functioning would appear to have taken place. Both patients, as noted, seem to be moving closer to a normal reading pattern. All the other treatments described in this volume are examples of reducing the effects of cognitive deficit, often by tiny amounts in small stages. E. Miller (1978) has claimed that restitution of memory functioning is unrealistic and has argued that *amelioration* of memory problems should be the goal of therapy. On the whole, Miller is probably right, but not in every case—and certainly not in the two cases reported in this chapter.

·9·

INVESTIGATIONS OF THE PQRST STRATEGY FOR INCREASING RECALL OF PROSE PASSAGES

INTRODUCTION

Although, as we have seen in Chapter 6, visual imagery is one of the most promising procedures for improving recall in memory-impaired adults, verbal methods also have an important role. One such method is alphabetical searching. This involves working through the alphabet in the hope that a particular letter will act as a retrieval cue for an elusive word or name. It is probably helpful only when considerable information about the word is already available (e.g., when the number of syllables is known or when the searcher is aware that the word is either particularly common or, conversely, particularly unusual).

Another verbal method is first-letter cueing. This would appear to be fairly widely used by the general population (Harris, 1980a). Examples include remembering musical notes by the sentence "*Every Good Boy Deserves Fruit,*" representing the notes on the lines, and the word "FACE," representing the notes in the spaces. "*Richard Of York Gives Battle In Vain*" is another popular first-letter mnemonic for remembering the colors of the rainbow. However, Harris (1980b) claims that this method is likely to be used only when the material to be remembered is well known but difficult to recall in the correct order. It can also be used for learning *new* material, as observed in Chapter 7.

We (Wilson & Moffat, 1984) have suggested that first-letter cueing is successful because (1) "chunking" of information is in operation, and this process is known to increase recall of some material (G. A. Miller, 1956); and (2) it reduces the number of competing responses. Furthermore, as noted in Chapter 3, cueing by means of partial information is effective in improving the recall of amnesic subjects (Warrington & Weiskrantz, 1968). First-letter cueing, then, provides partial information and may enable people to establish their own retrieval cues.

Cermak (1975) showed that verbal-mediation strategies were helpful with a group of Korsakoff patients who were able to learn unrelated word pairs, such as "clock–glove," when either a verbal mediator (in this case, "hand") or a visual image (a glove on a clock) was used. Gasparrini and Satz (1979) compared visual-imagery and verbal-mediation strategies in a group of 30 left-hemisphere stroke patients. The verbal mediation here involved asking the subjects to make up a sentence containing two words in a paired-associate learning task. The visual-imagery condition involved imaging the two words interacting, and was adapted from the procedure used by Jones (1974; more fully described in the next chapter). Visual imagery was significantly superior to rote learning and to verbal mediation. However, all subjects had sustained left-hemisphere damage, so it might be expected that verbal strategies would be inferior to visual ones with them. This particular piece of investigation was also weakened by a flaw in the experimental design, whereby the visual-imagery condition was tested first, with half the subjects using imagery and half using rote learning. Thus, when all the subjects took part in the second experiment, involving a comparison of visual imagery with verbal mediation, half of the subjects were already familiar with visual-imagery techniques. Although the experimenters asked the subjects not to picture the words, there is no way of knowing whether or not those subjects who had already improved their scores by using imagery were prepared to abandon a successful procedure. Given these weaknesses in the design of the experiment, the findings should not be taken as a clear indication of the superiority of visual imagery over verbal mediation.

Elaboration, or making words into a story, is yet another method that has been used with both normal and brain-damaged subjects (Crovitz, 1979; Higbee, 1977). Gianutsos and Gianutsos (1979) used this method with four brain-damaged people, who were required to learn groups of three words by making them into a meaningful yet unusual story. The authors reported that all subjects showed gains, but that only in one case were the gains substantial. A multiple-baseline-across-subjects design was employed—one of the very few reported in the neurological literature. Unfortunately, this study, like the majority of others, used experimental material rather than real-life tasks. Crovitz (1979) describes the "airplane list," in which 10 words are embedded in a story with each word chained on to the next. The list/story begins: "The first word is AIRPLANE. Remember that however you like. The next word is GIRAFFE, because the airplane is filled with giraffes sitting in the seats . . ." (p. 131). Crovitz found that both a Korsakoff and a head-injured patient were able to retrieve many of the words in the list when cues were given by the examiner. The three patients described by Crovitz et al. (1979) would appear to have used both verbal and visual strategies to learn material similar to the "airplane list." Indeed, the fact that this method combines both visual and verbal elements may explain its success. This idea is considered further in Chapter 11.

Rhymes also serve as memory aids, as any one who has used the rhyme "Thirty days hath September . . ." will know. We have seen in Chapter 3 that amnesic patients can learn rhyming associations (Warrington & Weiskrantz, 1982), so, potentially, this would appear to be a valuable strategy to employ with the memory-impaired. Gardner (1977) describes how a severely amnesic man was able to learn important personal details by incorporating them into a song:

> Henry's my name
> Memory's the game
> I'm in the V.A.
> In Jamaica Plain.
> My bed's on 7D
> The year is '73
> Every day I make a little gain. (p. 199)

Moffat (1984) suggests that rhymes may be taught to the memory-impaired to enable them to select an appropriate strategy for a particular problem. For example:

> Pegs are the key to my memory
> Numbers make sounds and
> Names I can see.
> I can PQRST stories
> And say my ABC. (p. 81)

"PQRST" is an acronym for "Preview, Read, Question, State, and Test," which comes from the field of study techniques. Robinson (1970) was probably the first person to write about it. A similar method is known as "SQR3" (Rowntree, 1983). This acronym stands for "Survey, Question, Read, Recall, and Review." In practice, the stages followed are virtually identical. The procedure in PQRST is as follows:

1. Preview: Preview the material to be remembered; that is, skim through it briefly.
2. Question: Ask important questions about the text; for example, "What is the main point the author is trying to convey? In what country does the action take place? How many people were injured?"
3. Read: Read the material thoroughly in order to answer the questions.
4. State: State the answers. If the answers to the key questions are not clear, read through again until they are.
5. Test: Test at frequent intervals for the retention of the information.

Little has been published on the effectiveness of the PQRST method as a strategy for the brain-damaged. Glasgow *et al.* (1977) have given the most detailed description, and their work was particularly encouraging because they taught their patient to implement the procedure in a nonexperimental situation. A 22-year-old undergraduate had sustained a head injury in a road traffic accident some 3½ years prior to treatment. She complained of problems in remembering information from lectures and reading assignments. She was tested for recall of prose passages and showed good immediate recall, as 88% of information from the passages was reported. However, at the end of a session she reported only 54%, and after a week only 8%. If cues were provided in the form of multiple-choice questions, she was able to recall 60% of the main points after a week's delay. Thus she was diagnosed as having difficulty with long-term recall of verbal material. Recognition of this material was estimated to be moderately good.

Two treatment strategies were introduced following the assessment. The first was rehearsal, in which the patient simply stated aloud as much of the stimulus material as she could remember, both immediately after presentation and again 2 days later. The second strategy was PQRST, modified by Glasgow *et al.* in two ways. First, they combined the P and Q stages; second, they developed four standard questions, rather than requesting the patient to select her own ques-

tions. The PQRST, thus modified, resulted in higher scores than rehearsal, which, in turn, resulted in higher scores than the control
procedure (i.e., the procedure used in the baseline period).

Following this, the strategy was applied outside the clinic. The
student was asked to read articles from the newspaper. The PQRST was
reintroduced following 10 days of baselines on the newspaper articles.
The main measure here, however, was the patient's self-rating of her
recall. Her estimation of her ability rose following the use of PQRST.
Thus the method looked as if it were beneficial. However, as the
authors point out, the PQRST took about three times as long as the
control method, while the rehearsal method took about twice as long. It
is not clear, then, whether the superior performance under PQRST was
due to the extra time involved.

With the exception of the studies reported later in this chapter,
the only known published report of the PQRST method being used
with brain-damaged people is that by Grafman (1984). Lewinsohn,
Danaher, and Kikel (1977) have described a similar procedure for
improving recall of stories by teaching patients to break each story
down into the main ideas and to remember as many of these as they
can, but the approach adopted does not fit into the framework of
PQRST. Grafman's method involves an additional P (for "Probe") stage;
thus this modification of the procedure can be labeled "PQRSTP." The
last stage requires probing for information available in the passage but
not contained in the answers to the questions. No data are reported by
Grafman.

An unpublished study that employed the PQRST strategy as part
of a multiple-baseline-across-behaviors design has been carried out
(Loftus & Wilson, 1984). The subject was a 46-year-old Korsakoff
patient. The PQRST strategy was introduced after five baseline sessions
in which newspaper articles were read to him and he was asked for
immediate and delayed recall. The mean score for items recalled
immediately in the baseline condition was 46%. Under the PQRST
condition, the mean score for items recalled was 64%. In the delayed
condition (scoring delayed recall as a percentage of immediate recall),
the mean score for items recalled was 3% in the baseline and 20%
following PQRST.

The studies reported in the remainder of this chapter were undertaken in order to see whether or not the PQRST strategy would be of
benefit to a group of brain-damaged patients with mixed etiology.

EXPERIMENT 1

A 26-year-old man sustained a subarachnoid hemorrhage following a ruptured aneurysm on the anterior communicating artery. This left him with an amnesic syndrome, as a consequence of which he frequently repeated the same questions. An attempt was made to teach him the answers to these questions, in the expectation that the repetition would then stop.

Case History

L. R. was a professionally qualified man who had his CVA 5 months before being admitted to Rivermead Rehabilitation Centre for memory therapy. Shortly after the hemorrhage, a right frontal craniotomy was performed to clip the aneurysm. A few days later, L. R. became confused and disoriented and showed marked confabulation. This deterioration was thought to be due to spasm of the arteries in the area of the clipped aneurysm, resulting in insufficient blood supply to some parts of the brain. (See Gade, 1982, for a description of the mechanism by which this can occur.)

L. R. was seen individually for about an hour each day, 5 days a week for a period of 3 months. Several problems were selected for treatment, one of these being repetition of the same question. This is a common problem in amnesic people, and a particularly irritating one for those in frequent contact with them. In L. R.'s case, the repetition consisted mainly of two questions: "Will I always have memory problems?" and "Why have I got a memory problem? I know I had a hemorrhage, but why should that leave me with a duff memory?"

In addition to memory problems, L. R. exhibited childish behavior that was considered inappropriate for someone of his age and ability. For example, he often talked in a babyish voice, saying things like "It's Mr. Porky Pig and Mr. Bow-Wow," or "Please say I've been a good boy—*please*." On occasions he went even further, such as the time when a visiting psychologist was present and L. R. put a cardboard box on his head and played "peek-a-boo" behind the filing cabinet! He was also excluded from the hydrotherapy pool, because he pretended for several days to be a frog and disrupted the therapy of the other patients.

Pretreatment Assessment

L. R. was assessed prior to treatment. On the WAIS, his verbal IQ was in the superior range of ability, and his performance IQ in the bright-average range. His immediate Logical Memory score (on the Wechsler Memory Scale) was normal, but he was unable to recall anything of the passage after a delay of half an hour. His Rey–Osterreith figure copy was good, but he recalled only 29% after a 40-minute delay. On the Warrington Forced-Choice Words subtest, his scaled score was 3— that is, impaired. Although on the Forced-Choice Faces subtest he did a little better, with a scaled score of 7, this was still below average, and well below the level that might be expected on the basis of his IQ. A summary of his results, together with those of the other subjects in Experiments 1–4, can be seen in Table 9-1.

Treatment

Treatment followed L. R.'s assessment. He was encouraged to use external aids, including an electronic aid (see a description of his response to this in Wilson & Moffat, 1984), and was taught several mnemonics. In addition to his individual sessions, he attended a memory group each day with four other people, and he also received help with his memory in occupational therapy. Baselines were taken on the number of times he asked his two most frequent questions (quoted above). The first of these, "Will I always have a memory problem?", was asked at least once each session over a period of 30 sessions. The other question was asked two to three times each week during that period, making a total of 17 times in all. Sometimes L. R. received answers to his questions, and sometimes he was asked to find the answers by looking at his notebook. In addition, L. R. was asking his occupational therapist the same questions, but baselines were not taken.

After 6 weeks, an attempt was made to stop these questions by means of a PQRST strategy. L. R. knew the strategy, as he used it both in occupational therapy and in the memory group for remembering stories and newspaper articles. As a first step, L. R. was requested to write a summary of what happened to him, what was likely to happen in the future, and what factors other than memory and concentration

Table 9-1. Test Results of Patients in Experiments 1-4

	L. R.	M. L.	M. U.	C. D.
Age	26	59	28	45
Sex	M	M	M	M
Verbal IQ (WAIS)	125	133	93	108
Performance IQ (WAIS)	112	131	94	101
Full-scale IQ (WAIS)	118	134	93	105
Raven's Standard Progressive Matrices	125	126	<85	—
Immediate Logical Memory (Wechsler Memory Scale)	10	12	7	7
Delayed Logical Memory (Wechsler Memory Scale)	0	0	0	0
Percentage retained	0	0	0	0
Rey-Osterreith Figure	13	0	5	—
Rivermead Behavioural Memory Test	—	0	0	7
Forced-Choice Words (Warrington Memory Test[a]	3	5	5	4
Forced-Choice Faces (Warrington Memory Test[a]	7	6	0	8
Benton Visual Retention Test (correct)	6	—	4	—
Benton Visual Retention Test (errors)	8	—	11	—

[a]Scaled scores *quoted*.

were hindering his progress. Having written the summary, he was asked to follow the PQRST procedure. The questions and answers were as follows:

Questions	*Answers*
1. a. What happened to me?	a. I had a hemorrhage.
b. When?	b. April.
c. What was the result?	c. I was left with a poor memory and impaired concentration.
2. What is the prognosis?	I will probably always have a bad memory, but some improvement is likely.
3. What am I doing at Rivermead?	a. Exercising my memory.
	b. Learning to use external aids.
	c. Learning mnemonic strategies, such as PQRST, visual imagery, method of loci, and first-letter cueing.

Table 9-1. (*Continued*)

				Patients				
F. E.	V. U.	R. J.	R. D.	V. L.	V. J.	T. E.	C. Y.	I. C.
21	21	22	21	22	21	17	18	40
M	M	M	M	F	F	M	M	F
117	92	91	82	89	84	94	94	112
93	60	64	51	68	76	78	82	101
107	77	78	67	79	79	87	88	108
126	<85	<85	<85	87	—	87	99	—
8	3	4.5	3	4	4	4	6	2.5
0	1	2	1.5	2	1	2	1	1.5
0	33	46	50	50	30	33	40	37.5
6	—	4	0	0	2	11	5	8
0	1	5	1	2	2	7	5	7
1	0	0	—	0	—	—	0	3
0	4	0	—	3	—	—	10	0
7	—	2	—	4	4	—	—	5
5	—	17	—	11	11	—	—	7

4. What other things are hindering my progress?

5. What are the plans for the future?

a. Failure to initiate steps to bypass the memory problem—in particular, not using my book.
b. Childish behavior and tantrums. Remain an inpatient until the end of November./Then come as a day patient twice a week./ Come back in 6 months for reassessment.

The following day, L. R. was asked to read through his summary, after which the summary was removed and he was asked the questions he had selected the day before. This procedure was repeated the day after. From then on, L. R. was tested *without* reading the summary first. He did, however, read the summary at the end of each session to remind himself of the answers he had forgotten.

Table 9-2. Summary of L. R.'s PQRST Results

Questions	Nov. 4	Nov. 5	Nov. 9	Nov. 10	Nov. 11	Nov. 13	Dec. 7
1. a.	*	*	*	*	*	*	*
b.	*	*	*	*	*	*	*
c.	*	*	*	*	*	*	*
2.	*	*	*	*	*	*	*
3. a.	*	*	0	*	*	*	*
b.	0	0	*	*	0	0	0
c.	*	*	*	*	*	*	*
4. a.	*	*	0	0	0	X	0
b.	—	*	0	*	*	X	0
5	*	*	0	*	0	X	0

Note. Symbols: *, correct; 0, incorrect; X, refused to answer.

The results are contained in Table 9-2. It can be seen that L. R. was able to learn some of the information (on one occasion, 90% of the questions were answered correctly). Unfortunately, although L. R. learned most of the answers to the questions, he still repeated his original two questions as frequently as before the treatment. Thus, he appeared to be unable to *use* information he had learned. In this, he was similar to some other patients with frontal lobe damage and memory problems. The following quotation from Barbizet is an apt description of L. R.'s condition.

> The examiner can, by taking the place of the faulty frontal lobes of his patient, force him with constant repetition to learn a list of words or a short text, which he will retain quite well. The fact that the patient cannot do this for himself suggests a loss of the strategies of learning. At other times frontal patients act as though they have lost the strategies of recall which enable them to utilise information they have already stored. (quoted in K. Walsh, 1978, p. 319)

EXPERIMENT 2

As stated in the introduction to this chapter, the only reported study comparing PQRST with rehearsal (Glasgow *et al.*, 1977) failed to equate the amount of time spent in each condition. The present experiment was conducted with a severely amnesic man to see whether PQRST or rehearsal led to better retention of newspaper articles. The amount of time for both conditions was controlled.

Case History

The patient in this experiment was M. L., the 59-year-old postmeningitic and postencephalitic man whose case history and pretreatment assessment have been described in Chapter 6 (see Experiment 5).

Treatment

Each day for a period of 8 days, two short paragraphs from the daily newspaper were selected. One paragraph was allocated to the PQRST method, and one to the rehearsal or control method. The order of presentation was changed each day. Each PQRST paragraph was read to M. L. and each of the component stages were followed. This took a total of between 7 and 10 minutes. For the control paragraphs, each was read to him four times. After each reading, he recalled as much of the paragraph as possible. After the fourth reading, M. L. was asked questions about the paragraph. This process also took between 7 and 10 minutes in all. Thus, there were five stages in each condition, and the total amount of time spent on each paragraph was approximately equal. (See Appendices C and D for examples of the paragraphs and questions.) After 30 minutes, questions from both paragraphs were repeated.

M. L.'s results on both immediate and delayed recall can be seen in Table 9-3. A Wilcoxon matched-pairs signed-ranks test comparing

Table 9-3. Percentage of Questions Answered Correctly by M. L. after PQRST Method and Rehearsal Alone

Test Session	PQRST		Rehearsal	
	Immediate recall (%)	30-minute delayed recall (%)	Immediate recall (%)	30-minute delayed recall (%)
1	75	50	25	0
2	75	50	100	25
3	100	50	75	25
4	75	75	75	50
5	75	50	75	0
6	25	0	50	25
7	100	50	25	0
8	75	50	75	0
Mean	77.7	47.1	62.5	15.6

immediate recall in both conditions showed no significant difference ($T = 10$). However, in the delayed-recall condition there was a significant difference in the amount retained ($T = 2.5$, $p < .05$). Thus the PQRST procedure would appear to have aided recall of prose material. It should be noted, however, that M. L.'s recall was in response to direct questioning. He could usually remember 50% of the material from the PQRST paragraphs when he was asked the questions. In a free-recall condition, without the prompting provided by questions, he would usually remember nothing from either paragraph. It seems that the PQRST procedure provided better retrieval cues than rehearsal alone. This idea is expanded in the discussion at the end of this chapter.

EXPERIMENT 3

To test for the generality of the findings in Experiment 2, a small study was pursued with a group of three memory-impaired patients. A multiple-baseline-across-subjects design was not considered suitable in this case, because pilot work performed at Rivermead by David Thomas showed a strong interference effect. In the pilot study, all stories/articles were given under the rehearsal condition for four or five occasions before the introduction of PQRST. With each successive article there was a buildup of proactive inhibition, so that subjects were recalling stories presented on previous days rather than those presented 30 minutes earlier. As this was likely to mask any superiority of the PQRST procedure, both conditions were used on each occasion. This minimized (but did not eliminate) the problem. Nevertheless, it ensured that an equal amount of proactive inhibition was present in both conditions.

Case Histories

M. U. was a 28-year-old man who had received a severe head injury in a motorcycle accident four months earlier. A CT scan showed evidence of diffuse brain edema and a left frontal intracerebral hematoma. He was unconscious for 3 weeks.

C. D. was a 45-year-old man who 6 months earlier had been diagnosed as having Korsakoff syndrome. He was referred from a nearby psychiatric hospital and attended Rivermead as an outpatient 3 days a week for memory therapy.

F. E. was a 21-year-old head-injured man; he has been described in Chapter 6 (Experiment 2).

Pretreatment Assessment

All subjects received psychological assessment prior to treatment. A summary of their results is given in Table 9-1.

Treatment

The procedure followed was similar to that used for M. L. in Experiment 2. Passages were selected from the daily newspapers. At each treatment session, one passage was allocated to PQRST and one to rehearsal. For each subject, the order of presentation was changed on each occasion so that if PQRST was the first passage on one day, then rehearsal would be the first on the next day. As with M. L., the amount of time spent under each condition ranged from 7 to 10 minutes, with each condition split into five stages. M. U. received three treatment sessions, C. D. seven, and F. E. four.

The mean percentage of questions answered successfully by each subject can be seen in Table 9-4. It can be seen that PQRST resulted in

Table 9-4. Mean Percentage of Questions Answered by Subjects in Experiment 3 under PQRST and Rehearsal Conditions

Subject	Condition	
	PQRST	Rehearsal
M. U.		
Immediate	61	46
Delayed	53	30
C. D.		
Immediate	86	74
Delayed	82	47
F. E.		
Immediate	72	57
Delayed	64	52

superior performance for every subject. A sign test showed that the difference was significant ($L = 0$, $T = 6$, $p = .032$).

EXPERIMENT 4

Although PQRST was superior to rehearsal in the studies described thus far, several questions remain. The patients described so far had severe memory impairments. It is possible that a less severely amnesic group would produce different findings. Rehearsal could prove to be as effective as PQRST, in which case rehearsal would be the preferred method, because it is an easier method for patients (it involves one step only, which is then repeated several times, whereas PQRST involves *five* different steps). However, PQRST might prove even more effective with a less impaired group, in which case therapists would consider that the time and effort involved in teaching the five steps would be a worthwhile endeavor.

PQRST might also result in better free-recall scores for a group of people with less severe memory problems. The subjects in Experiments 2 and 3 showed no improvements in their free-recall scores, whichever method was used.

Another question arises with regard to the rehearsal conditions described above. It could be argued that performance was better in response to questions following PQRST simply because the questions themselves were part of the treatment, instead of being presented at the end of the training strategy as they were in rehearsal conditions. That is to say, the reason for the superiority of the PQRST procedure might have been due to the fact that subjects were *trained* in answering the questions. Was this the crucial factor, or was there something else about PQRST that was influential?

Rationale

Experiment 4 was undertaken to see (1) whether less severely impaired people would find PQRST superior to rehearsal, both for free recall and for answering questions; and (2) whether presenting questions early in the rehearsal condition would reduce or eliminate the difference between PQRST and rehearsal.

Patients

The criterion for inclusion in this experiment was impaired verbal memory. This was assessed by administering the Logical Memory passages from the Wechsler Memory Scale. Any subject whose 30-minute delayed recall score was less than 51% of the immediate score was considered to have impaired memory and was included in the study. Eight head-injured patients took part (five male, three female). Their main characteristics are presented in Table 9-5.

Method

Twelve stories were selected (see Appenidx E for an example). Two of these were from Form 2 of the Logical Memory Scale (chosen because they had not been previously administered); eight were obtained from Alan Sunderland at the Applied Psychology Unit, Cambridge, England; and two were written by David Thomas at Rivermead. Four questions were devised for each story. These were written on cards (one card for each set of questions).

Each subject was seen individually on six occasions. Two stories were presented each time, one using PQRST and one using rehearsal. The order of presentation was balanced across subjects and across sessions.

Under the PQRST condition, subjects were told that PQRST was to be used; reminded of the stages; shown the card containing the four

Table 9-5. Main Characteristics of Subjects in Experiment 4

Subject	Age	Sex	Time after head injury	Other salient information
V. U.	21	M	6 months	General intellectual deterioration.
R. J.	22	M	22 months	Visual object agnosia.
R. D.	21	M	8 months	Slight nominal aphasia.
V. L.	22	F	20 months	General intellectual deterioration.
V. J.	21	F	11 months	Cerebellar dysarthria.
T. E.	17	M	26 months	Impaired vision.
C. Y.	18	M	3 months	General intellectual deterioration (transient).
I. C.	40	F	58 months	Some anxiety, and behavior problems.

questions, which were then read to them; and told that they would be returning to these shortly. The PQRST procedure was then implemented for each subject in the following manner:

1. Preview: The tester read the passage to the subject.
2. Question: The subject was requested to look again at the questions on the card.
3. Read: The story was read again to the subject, who was asked to call out each time the tester read the answer to one of the questions.
4. State: The tester asked the subject to state the answers to the questions. Help was given at this stage if the subject experienced any difficulty.
5. Test: The questions were asked again, but this time the subject was not given any help. Responses were recorded.

In the rehearsal condition, subjects were told that rehearsal was to be used; reminded that each passage would be read to them four times, and that each time they were to recall as much as possible; shown the card containing the four questions, which were then read to them; and told that they would be expected to answer the questions later but could look at them in the meanwhile if that helped. The rehearsal procedure was implemented for each subject in the following manner:

1. First rehearsal: The tester read the passage to the subject, who was asked to repeat as much of the story as possible.
2. Second rehearsal: As above, except that the subject was also asked to include the things he or she had said before.
3. Third rehearsal: As item 2 above.
4. Fourth rehearsal: As item 2 above.
5. Questions: Questions were asked and responses recorded.

The time spent on each passage under both conditions was approximately 10 minutes. At the end of this time, subjects returned to occupational therapy or occupied themselves with a task of their own choice in an adjoining room. Thirty minutes later, each of them was seen individually for the testing of delayed recall.

The following measures were taken:

1. *Immediate questions.* For the PQRST stories, these were the responses obtained in the "Test" stage. For the rehearsal sto-

ries, these were the responses obtained following the fourth rehearsal.

2. *Immediate free recall.* For the PQRST stories, this was obtained immediately following the "Test" stage. Subjects were asked to repeat back as much as they could remember, regardless of whether or not the information had been given in answer to the questions. For the rehearsal stories, the responses obtained in the fourth rehearsal stage were scored.

3. *Delayed free recall.* For both conditions, the card containing the questions was placed in front of the subjects, and they were asked to remember as much of the story as possible. Responses were recorded.

4. *Delayed questions.* The questions on the card were asked again, and the subjects' responses were recorded.

Scoring for immediate and delayed free recall was similar to that described for the Logical Memory passages in the Wechsler Memory Scale. Thus, each story was divided into about 23 "ideas," with 1 point given for each idea recalled word-perfect, or for an exact synonym. Half a point was given for a partially correct idea or close synonym. For the delayed-recall score, 1 point was subtracted if the subject needed prompting with the first few words of the story. This was the method recommended by E. W. Russell (1975), who also suggested using a "delayed recall as percentage of immediate recall" score.

Scoring of questions was more complex than the method used in Experiments 2 and 3. The standard answers were also divided into "ideas." The number of ideas in any answer ranged from one to five, but each set of four questions contained 10 ideas. (See Appendix F for examples of questions, answers, and scoring.) Points were given for each idea in the same manner as they were given in immediate and delayed recall. Two raters independently scored all the responses of five subjects, with an agreement of 93%.

Results

A mean score was obtained for each subject for both PQRST and rehearsal under the following conditions:

1. Immediate free recall.
2. Delayed free recall.

3. Immediate questions.
4. Delayed questions.
5. Delayed recall as a percentage of immediate recall (percentage-retained score).

The results are shown in Table 9-6. A Wilcoxon matched-pairs signed-ranks test was used to compare subjects' scores on PQRST and rehearsal in each condition; the results of this test are shown in Table 9-7. It can be seen from these tables that, with the exception of immediate free recall (where there was a nonsignificant trend in favor of rehearsal), PQRST was the superior strategy. It resulted in significantly higher scores for delayed free recall, percentage retained, immediate questions, and delayed questions.

DISCUSSION

All the studies reported here show that memory-impaired patients can acquire some new information through means of the PQRST study technique. In some of the present cases, however, the clinical usefulness of this information was very limited. In Experiment 1, L. R. was able to learn some of the answers to his frequent questions, yet knowing these answers did not stop him from asking the questions. He appeared to be unwilling or unable to retrieve the information himself, in spite of giving adequate answers in response to direct questioning from somebody else. It might have been possible to deal with this problem directly by means of a behavior modification program.

M. L., the man in Experiment 2, was also only able to retrieve information in response to direct questioning. Although he correctly answered significantly more questions following PQRST than rehearsal (at least in the delayed-recall condition), he was unable to remember anything from either the PQRST or rehearsal passages when asked to recall as much as he could from the stories that were told to him earlier in the day.

The three patients in Experiment 3 responded much as M. L. did, although in this study PQRST was better than rehearsal for both immediate and delayed questions. However, none of the three subjects were able to score anything in delayed free recall.

In Experiment 4, the PQRST was again more effective than rehearsal for both immediate and delayed questions. Encouragingly,

Table 9-6. Mean Scores of Each Subject in Experiment 4

Subject	Immediate free recall		Delayed free recall		Percentage retained		Immediate questions		Delayed questions	
	PQRST	Rehearsal	PQRST	Rehearsal	PQRST	Rehearsal	PQRST	Rehearsal	PQRST	Rehearsal
V. U.	2.9	3.1	3.5	1.6	67.0	40.1	5.1	4.2	4.0	2.8
R. J.	6.8	6.6	4.9	4.0	69.1	64.8	5.7	4.3	4.9	3.4
R. D.	7.3	7.7	3.5	3.8	51.2	50.6	5.7	4.9	3.8	3.3
V. L.	5.8	6.8	5.3	3.7	90.6	53.5	6.8	3.9	5.3	3.3
V. J.	6.3	6.8	4.3	3.4	62.0	50.1	6.9	4.2	4.3	3.8
T. E.	6.7	7.0	4.0	3.3	60.5	47.5	6.2	4.4	3.8	4.1
C. Y.	5.8	5.1	2.9	2.6	50.3	44.3	6.3	3.4	3.8	2.9
I. C.	10.0	10.5	8.0	8.0	85.2	78.3	7.6	6.9	6.6	6.6

Table 9.7 Comparisons between PQRST and Rehearsal
Using Wilcoxon Matched-Pairs Signed-Ranks Tests

Comparison	T
Immediate free recall	8.5
Delayed free recall	2.5*
Percentage retained	0***
Immediate questions	0***
Delayed questions	1**

*$p = .05$.
**$p = .02$.
***$p = .01$.

though, the patients in this experiment showed a superior performance in delayed free recall on the PQRST passages. This was probably
due to the less severe memory deficits among this group, as treatment
procedures were similar throughout. All patients in Experiments 1, 2,
and 3 had a score of 0 on the delayed free recall of the Logical Memory
passages during pretreatment assessment. None of the eight subjects in
Experiment 4 had a pretreatment score of 0 for delayed free recall;
these scores ranged from 33% to 50% of their immediate-recall scores.
(The following chapter also discusses the effect of severity of impairment on ability to benefit from mnemonics.) For this group, then,
PQRST appeared to have greater clinical usefulness, because significantly more information was accessible (without direct questioning)
after a delay. The amount of time spent on the passages did not seem
to be the crucial factor. Instead, something about the PQRST technique
itself was responsible for its effectiveness.

One explanation for the success of PQRST might be that it
provides better retrieval cues than does rehearsal alone. It will be
remembered that, under some circumstances, amnesic patients can
learn relatively normally (see Chapter 3). For example, amnesics, who
are normally very poor at learning lists of words, improve considerably
when they are provided with the first few letters of the original words
in the recall condition. Items of partial information, such as the initial
letters of words or fragments of pictures seen earlier, act as important
and effective retrieval cues. Is the PQRST procedure functioning in the
same way? The questions themselves may be providing part of the
original information, and thereby may help to improve recall. This
would explain why L. R., M. L., M. U., C. D., and F. E. were all poor at

delayed free recall but reasonably good at delayed questions. However, it does not explain the fact that PQRST questions were answered better than rehearsal questions. If the questions themselves were effective retrieval cues, then one would expect no difference to occur.

Again, if we return to the theoretical studies of amnesia, there are at least two other findings which might help us understand the mechanism by which PQRST works. First, let us consider the idea of "encoding specificity" (see Chapter 3). Encoding specificity means that retrieval is enhanced when the original encoding situation is reinstated at the time of recall. In other words, if the recall or test situation is similar to the situation present during original learning, then more information will be retrieved. To translate this into the current findings, it would seem that more questions were answered following PQRST because the questions themselves were part of the original learning experience. In contrast, the questions in the rehearsal condition followed the original learning, rather then being part and parcel of it. Even when rehearsal questions were presented early in the rehearsal condition (as they were in Experiment 4), they were not an integral part of the strategy. So far, then, the principle of encoding specificity readily accounts for the effectiveness of the PQRST strategy when subjects were questioned on the information contained in the passages. (M. L.'s results were only significant in the delayed questioning, not in the immediate. However, he showed a tendency to answer immediate PQRST questions better. Also, M. L. had a very good immediate memory, which might explain why so much of the rehearsal material was available to him.)

The principle of encoding specificity does not, however, explain the superiority of PQRST for delayed free recall and percentage retained. For an explanation of these findings, we need to turn to the second of the theoretical positions referred to above—namely, the "levels-of-processing" model of Craik and Lockhart (1972). The assumption here is that deeper processing leads to better retention. PQRST appears to lead to deeper processing than rehearsal, because subjects have to think about what they are listening to in order to complete each of the PQRST stages. In rehearsal, on the other hand, less thought is needed, as subjects simply need to listen and repeat back. Further support for this idea comes from Craik and Tulving (1975), who describe a study in which subjects were shown lists of words and had to answer questions about each word. The questions varied in the level of processing required to answer them. Cued and noncued recall were compared, with the cue being the original question. It was found that cueing improved recall (similar to the current findings on questioning); perhaps even more to the point, the effect of the cueing was greater when semantic encoding—that is, the deepest level of processing—was required. Thus, in Experiment 4, the PQRST appears to have been superior to rehearsal in the delayed-free-recall condition because it led to deeper encoding than did the rehearsal strategy. This can also explain why less was forgotten between immediate and delayed free recall in PQRST than in rehearsal. That is to say, it accounts for the significantly higher percentage-retained scores.

There was no significant difference between PQRST and rehearsal for immediate free recall, although there was a tendency for rehearsal to be better here, possibly because of encoding specificity again—the test condition was similar to the learning condition. Despite this, there was a significant difference in favor of the PQRST in delayed free recall, indicating that, at least for this group of head-injured patients, the PQRST really was a robust and worthwhile technique.

Although the findings are encouraging, particularly in Experiment 4, one point should be borne in mind by those intending to use the PQRST procedure. Ideally, subjects should generate their own questions, as this is likely to lead to even better retention. For research purposes, however, it is difficult to allow subjects to do this, because it is necessary to keep factors constant. Nevertheless, future investigators might be able to design studies comparing subject-generated and experimenter-generated questions. Our observations at Rivermead suggest that many subjects find difficulty in generating appropriate questions. They tend to select questions that fail to elicit the main points in a passage (an example noted was "Is there a man in the story?"). Such patients might be better served if they were taught to *précis* passages and select key points, rather than being assisted to remember prose passages. The latter skill could be taught later, once the patients have become relatively proficient readers.

CONCLUSIONS

In this chapter, four studies are reported in which attempts were made to improve the verbal recall of brain-damaged patients. The first study was an effort to reduce the frequent repetition of two questions by a man with amnesia following a ruptured aneurysm on the anterior communicating artery. He was taught the answers to his questions by means of PQRST. Although this resulted in some experimental success, there was no evidence of clinical success. He learned most of the information that was required of him in the experiment, but he continued to repeat his original questions.

The second study compared two treatment conditions, PQRST and rehearsal, to see whether one was more effective than the other in helping a 59-year-old amnesic man to remember articles from the newspaper. Delayed free recall did not improve with either method. However, when questioned about the articles after a 30-minute delay, he gave more correct answers to the PQRST passages than to the rehearsal passages.

The third study was similar to the previous one, except that in this experiment three patients were included: two with head injuries and one with Korsakoff syndrome. Again, no improvement occurred in delayed free recall, but PQRST resulted in superior performances in all three cases in response to questioning.

The fourth study also compared PQRST with rehearsal, but this time a number of patients with less severe memory impairments were tested. With the exception of immediate recall, when there was a nonsignificant tendency for rehearsal to be the superior strategy, PQRST led to significantly higher scores on all other measures: delayed free recall, percentage retained, immediate questions, and delayed questions.

Once again, I conclude with a brief review of the contributions of the major theoretical disciplines. The responses of L. R., who was able to learn information but not to use it, have been explained by references to work in the field of neuropsychology; a description of the condition by Barbizet (in Walsh, 1978) seems to be particularly appropriate for explaining L. R.'s symptoms. The importance of the condition of the frontal lobes in influencing response to treatment should perhaps be looked at more systematically in the future. The severity of amnesia would also appear to be important when deciding whether or not to use this method for improving free recall. Experiment 4 showed that less impaired subjects were able to retain significantly more information about the prose passages after a 30-minute delay, having used PQRST, than by using rehearsal. The severe amnesics studied in the earlier experiments were unable to improve their free-recall scores, or, indeed, to recall anything with either method unless questioned directly. The explanation provided is that once subjects were "off the floor"—that is, once they could remember something of the passage after a 30-minute delay—then the levels-of-processing principle could be manifested.

While it was evident in these experiments that severity of memory deficit was an important factor, it was equally obvious that other factors, such as IQ, were not. The subject with the highest IQ was M. L. in Experiment 2, yet he was completely unable to remember anything from any passage after a 30-minute delay. In contrast, R. D. in Experiment 4, with an IQ of 67, was able to benefit from the strategy in the delayed condition. Neither were the immediate-recall scores related to success. Indeed, the relatively pure amnesics in Experiments 1, 2, and 3 had higher immediate-recall scores than the eight head-injured patients in Experiment 4.

Cognitive models of human memory and the amnesic syndrome have been employed to find an explanation for the greater success of the PQRST technique in comparison with rote rehearsal. Encoding specificity is invoked to explain why direct questioning resulted in more correct answers following PQRST. It would seem that because the test situation was more similar to the learning situation in PQRST, the subjects remembered more of the answers. In order to explain why the less severely impaired subjects also retained more of the original passages in PQRST, the levels-of-processing paradigm is invoked. It is argued that subjects had to think more carefully when following the stages in PQRST, which meant they had to use a deeper level of processing. One result, which in hindsight should have been predicted from an understanding of cognitive psychology, was the finding in one of the PQRST pilot studies that a multiple-baseline-across-subjects design was impracticable because of excessive interference. The findings reported in Chapter 3 concerning proactive inhibition and prior-list intrusions should have forewarned us. However, once the interference was evident, it was easy to explain by reference to the work quoted in that chapter.

·10·

VISUAL IMAGERY AS A MNEMONIC AID
FOR BRAIN-DAMAGED ADULTS:
A GROUP STUDY

INTRODUCTION

Like Chapter 6, this chapter is concerned with the evaluation of visual-imagery procedures aimed at improving retention or recall in memory-impaired people. However, our attention changes in this chapter from the single-case and small-group studies reported in Chapters 6 to 9, with their descriptions of direct attempts to remediate everyday memory problems, to an investigation of a larger group of subjects who were tested on experimental material. This present study was carried out with the intention of seeking a means whereby we could predict which people would benefit from a given strategy or manipulation. It contains, therefore, an indirect rather than direct implication for rehabilitation; while the findings may suggest which methods of treatment look as though they will be viable for certain kinds of patients, therapists themselves will need to decide how to relate the findings to the actual clinical treatment of individual patients.

Establishing the effectiveness of a given procedure in an experimental setting does not guarantee successful application of the procedure to other nonexperimental situations or tasks. Indeed, evidence from the previous chapters indicates that generalization is unlikely to occur. Nevertheless, such investigations are important in order to determine which circumstances, situations, or procedures *might* lead to improved learning in the memory-impaired.

Some of the visual-imagery techniques for improving learning have been described in Chapter 6. Two others not previously described in detail are peg methods and the method of loci. "Peg methods" are procedures in which a standard set of peg words are learned, and items to be remembered are linked to the pegs by means of visual imagery. The best-known peg system is the rhyming-peg method, whereby the numbers one to ten are associated with rhymes (e.g., "one–bun," "two–shoe," "three–tree," etc.). The first item to be remembered is linked with a bun, the second with a shoe, and so forth. When the items need to be recalled, the pegs are elicited first, and then attempts are made to retrieve the mental images linked to them.

The phonetic-peg system is more complicated, but Lorayne (1979) suggests that it is more flexible and useful than rhyming pegs, once the effort has been made to learn the phonetic pegs themselves. The system is based upon the relationship between numbers and their consonant sounds: For example, 0 is remembered as "Z"—the first sound in "zero"; 1 is represented as a "T," since both 1 and T have one downstroke; and 2 is represented as "N," having two downstrokes. In addition, each sound is remembered as a word. So 1 (T) is remembered as "ties"; 2 (N) is remembered as "Noah"; and 20 (N + Z) is remembered as "nose." Lorayne (1979) provides a detailed account of this system, and Moffat (1984) offers a useful summary.

On a first encounter, the phonetic-peg system appears to be unduly complicated, and most people might regard it as being too difficult to learn and implement. However, there is at least one study testifying to its usefulness with brain-damaged people. Patten (1972) claimed that four out of seven patients with severe verbal-memory deficits benefited in learning experimental material and in remembering practical information. The patients involved took up to 4 weeks to learn the mnemonic. Unfortunately, the lack of data makes it difficult to assess how effectively the procedure worked. One patient, for example, was reported to show improvements in his expressive dysphasia and in his "natural" memory 4 weeks after treatment began. It is hard to believe that learning a peg mnemonic would lead to improvement in general memory functioning and a reduction of dysphasia, so perhaps the improvement was due to some nonspecific factor, such as attention or stimulation.

We (Wilson & Moffat, 1984) have argued that although peg systems may help some mildly head-injured people, they are unlikely to aid those with severe memory impairment. There is no satisfactory evidence that this method has been successfully applied to everyday problems in brain-damaged people or the elderly (Mason & Smith, 1977; A. D. Smith, 1975), although rhyming pegs have helped normal subjects remember such things as new words in a foreign language (Paivio & Desrochers, 1979), and prose learning (Krebs, Snowman, & Smith, 1978).

The method of loci is another visual-imagery technique, which has been used for many centuries. Yates (1966) describes how Simonides of Thessaly, in ancient Greece, was able to recall the names of many people crushed at a banquet by remembering where each guest had been sitting. Yates points out that this was an example of the method of loci (remembering by location). Moffat (1984) provides an alternative explanation when he points out that, as there is no evidence that Simonides deliberately visually encoded where each person was sitting before he was called from the banquet, he may simply have been using location as a retrieval cue.

Perhaps a better example of the method of loci comes from the famous mnemonist Shereshevskii, studied by Luria (1968). One of Schereshevskii's procedures involved forming mental images of items to be remembered, placed at various points along a well-known street—for example, on a window sill, in a doorway, and by the curb. Interestingly, difficulty with retrieval sometimes occurred when the item was visually similar to the background location (e.g., white eggs imagined by a white door). Many locations can be used in the method of loci, such as parts of the body, rooms in one's house, or places at work. This method has been used with non-brain-damaged subjects by Ross and Lawrence (1968), Groninger (1971), and Higbee (1977).

The method of loci has also been employed with some elderly people (Robertson-Tchabo, Hausman, & Arenberg, 1976), with some benefit being noted in experimental situations. However, the elderly did not spontaneously employ this technique on a later occasion, nor is there any evidence for the method being applied outside the laboratory or clinic. As far as is known, there are no previous publications of reports that evaluate this technique with neurologically impaired people. (See Chapter 11 for such a study.)

There are many studies reporting the use of visual-imagery strategies with the memory-impaired. Baddeley and Warrington's (1973) work has already been referred to in an earlier chapter. They found that amnesic subjects were unable to benefit from visual imagery, despite being able to form the images adequately. Jones (1974) used imagery to improve paired-associate recall in people who had undergone unilateral temporal lobectomy. She found that two global amnesics in her study were unable to benefit from imagery.

In 1975, Cermak investigated the use of imagery as an aid to retrieval for six Korsakoff patients and six hospitalized, non-brain-damaged controls. He also used paired-associate learning tasks and three conditions: rote learning, imagery, and cued learning. In the rote-learning condition, subjects simply had to learn the correct response to the stimulus. In the imagery condition, subjects were told how to form an image linking the stimulus to the response word, and were told to try to use this procedure when attempting to recall the response. In the cued-learning condition, a verbal mediator was used, linking the two words (e.g., "wood" was the mediating link for "arrow–tree"). Cermak found that the Korsakoff patients took longer than the controls to learn the lists whatever method was used. However, imagery and cueing were more effective with Korsakoffs than was rote learning when recall was required. When testing involved recognition, only imagery was effective. Cermak concluded that imagery could aid both storage and retrieval for Korsakoff patients, while cueing only aided the retrieval process. A similar finding with non-Korsakoff alcoholics was reported by Binder and Schreiber (1980), who found that alcoholics benefited from both visual imagery and mediation.

Lewinsohn *et al.* (1977) investigated the efficacy of visual imagery on paired-associate learning in a group of 19 brain-damaged patients of mixed etiology and 22 controls. Following this, they went on to test the generality of the findings to a task similar to that encountered in real life—namely, face–name learning. Like Cermak (1975), Lewinsohn *et al.* found that controls did better than patients under all conditions. They also found that visual imagery improved the performance of both brain-damaged and control subjects in the paired-associate task during acquisition and after a 30-minute delay. After a delay of 1 week, however, controls who had used imagery performed no better than controls who had not used imagery. Similarly, brain-damaged patients who had used imagery performed no better than those who had not. In the face–name learning task, imagery was only minimally effective for both groups. A possible weakness in the design of that particular task was contained in the large number of face–name pairs (15 in all). The experiment ceased after two consecutive perfect trials or after 10 trials, whichever was less. Although 15 trials were adequate in the paired-associate word-learning task, it could be argued that words are more discriminable than faces—particularly the highly imageable, medium-frequency words used in this experiment. Had a smaller number of face–name pairs been used, then imagery might have been more effective. If the authors had wanted to emulate a real-life task, choosing a smaller number of names would have been more realistic.

A second weakness lay in the fact that no rehearsal was required during the 1-week delay. Even though, as the authors have pointed out, most new information needs to be retained for at least a week, it might be necessary for brain-damaged people to practice or rehearse the new information regularly in order to retain it. The Lewinsohn *et al.* findings do not provide evidence that imagery is ineffective for learning names; they simply support the view that imagery was an ineffective procedure under the conditions of their experiment. Despite these failings, it is a useful paper with a laudable attempt to relate experimental findings to clinical problems.

THE PRESENT STUDY

The study presented in this chapter was undertaken in an attempt to predict which patients would benefit from visual imagery. Apart from one adaptation, the imagery technique, method, and scoring replicated the work of Jones (1974). She used three lists of 10 paired-associate words; each list contained 7 pairs of concrete words and 3 pairs of abstract words. Our study used only concrete words, because visual imagery employed as a mnemonic strategy in rehabilitation will almost certainly be applied to concrete material. A further point to note about the study by Jones was her finding that performance on recall of abstract pairs in her left temporal lobectomy group was close to floor level. It could be argued that Jones was not in fact using a visual-imagery procedure for the abstract pairs, as no pictures were involved; rather, the words to be remembered were written in colored inks.

Jones selected her patients on the basis of their etiology. However, the memory therapist, working in a setting that contains a variety of brain-damaged adults, will often find it more appropriate to offer treatment on the basis of severity of deficit rather than etiology. Thus severity was taken as the starting point for the present investigation.

Subjects

Thirty-six brain-damaged patients, each referred for a psychological assessment, were asked for immediate and delayed recall of the Logical Memory passages from the Wechsler Memory Scale. On the basis of their delayed-recall scores, they were placed into three groups. Those who failed to recall anything of the passages 1 hour later were placed in the severely impaired group. Those who attained less than 50% of their immediate score were placed in the moderately impaired group. Those who attained 50% or more of their immediate score were placed in the minimally impaired group. This method of scoring is similar but not identical to that used by E. W. Russell (1975). Subject characteristics are shown in Table 10-1.

Method

All patients were tested on three lists of seven paired-associate words. All pairs in each list were "concrete" pairs—that is, rated high in imagery (Paivio, Yuille, & Madigan, 1968). All words were rated medium to high in frequency on the Thorndike and Lorge (1944) ratings.

Table 10-1. Subject Characteristics

Characteristic	Severely impaired (n = 12)	Moderately impaired (n = 12)	Mildly impaired (n = 12)
Sex			
Male	8	8	9
Female	4	4	3
Age (years)			
Mean	35	26	32
SD	15	9	14
Range	17–58	17–43	17–61
Full-scale IQ			
Mean	95	101	104
SD	16	12	13
Range	80–133	83–120	88–131
Diagnosis			
Head injury	8	10	9
CVA	2	0	2
Other[a]	2	2	1
Time after insult (months)			
Mean	12	17	10
SD	8	20	11
Range	3–27	3–30	2–39

[a] The severely impaired group included two people with anoxia following cardiac arrest; the moderately impaired group included two people who had had tumors removed; the mildly impaired group included one person who had had a tumor removed.

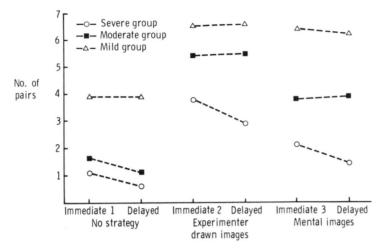

Figure 10-1. Mean scores of each group on immediate and delayed recall.

No pairs began with the same letter, nor did any have semantic or acoustic similarity. Three trials were given for each list. The first list was a baseline list. Subjects were asked to remember which words went together, but were not given any help on how to remember. For the second list, subjects were shown drawings (prepared by me as the experimenter) linking the two words. For example, a soldier was drawn sitting on a table to illustrate "soldier-table." For the third list, subjects were asked to invent their own images by imagining the two words linked together and making a vivid picture in their minds. The lists of words were allocated to the three strategies in a balanced order. Two hours after beginning the test, and without warning, subjects were required to recall the three lists.

Results

As in the study by Jones (1974), the immediate-recall score for each list was the mean number of correct responses for the three trials of that list. For delayed recall, only one trial was given for each list, so the scores were the numbers of correct responses on that trial. Figure 10-1 depicts the mean scores of each group.

From the summary of the analysis of variance (Table 10-2), it can be seen that there was a significant difference between the groups, $F(2, 198) = 129.87$, $p < .001$, and between the lists, $F(2, 198) = 97.23$, $p < .001$. In addition, there was a smaller significant interaction effect between groups and lists, $F(4, 198) = 4.22$, $p < .01$.

In order to determine which particular lists were effective for each group, a series of Newman–Keuls tests was carried out. The data from immediate and delayed conditions were summed for each list, because no significant effect was noted on this factor ($F = 0.93$). The results were as follows:

For the severe group, there was a significant difference between lists 1 and 2 ($p < .01$), and between lists 2 and 3 ($p < .01$), but not between lists 1 and 3. The severely impaired subjects, therefore, were consistently better on list 2—that is, when they had been shown drawings linking the word pairs. They were as poor on list 3 (mental images) as they were when they had no strategy at all.

For the moderately impaired group, there were significant differences between all three lists. List 3 was significantly easier to recall than list 1 ($p < .01$), as was list 2 ($p < .01$). However, list 3 was harder to recall than list 2 ($p < .05$). Thus, this group of subjects was able to benefit from mental imagery, although not to the same extent as they were able to benefit from experimenter-drawn pictures.

Table 10-2. Analysis of Variance: Summary Table

Source	Sum of squares	df	Mean squares	f
A: Groups	496.14	2	248.07	129.87**
B: Lists	371.42	2	185.71	97.23**
C: Times*[a]	1.78	1	1.78	0.93
B·C interaction	0.43	2	0.21	0.10
C·A interaction	9.26	2	4.63	2.42
A·B interaction	32.30	4	8.07	4.22*
A·B·C interaction	3.778	4	0.94	0.49
Within	379.192	198	1.91	
Total	1294.300	215		

[a]Immediate versus delayed recall.
*$p = .01$.
**$p = .001$.

For the mildly impaired group, there were significant differences between lists 1 and 2 ($p < .01$) and between lists 1 and 3 ($p < .01$), but not between lists 2 and 3. This group, then, found mental images and experimenter-drawn images equally beneficial.

Discussion

The findings suggest that people with a severe memory impairment (as judged by their failure to recall anything from a prose passage after an hour's delay) did not find mental imagery a helpful mnemonic strategy, although they were able to benefit from experimenter-drawn images. All subjects were able to understand the task requirements, and to form mental images when they were asked to describe some of the images during the testing. However, the mental images did not lead to better recall than the no-strategy condition. A possible reason why drawn pictures were helpful and mental images were not can be found if we reflect upon the findings reported in Chapter 3, which demonstrated that increased exposure time improved recall from secondary memory but did not influence the recency effect—that is, primary memory. Although the drawn images were exposed for the same time as that allowed for producing mental images, it is possible that in the severely impaired group much of this exposure time was taken up by producing images, leaving little time for any rich, elaborate coding. In contrast, all of the exposure time for the experimenter-generated images could be used for deeper encoding, because no effort was required to form an image. Support for this hypothesis comes from work done with the elderly by Craik and Simon (1980). It is also possible, of course, that the subjects' self-generated images were poorer than those provided for them. A further possibility is that although subjects were *able* to form images, they ceased doing so when not directly prompted each time.

The moderately impaired group—that is, those who recalled between 10% and 49% of the Logical Memory passage after an hour's delay—were able to use mental imagery but did better when the images were drawn for them. Again, the explanation might be that much of the time available in the mental-imagery condition was taken up by producing the image, with correspondingly less time available for elaborate encoding. However, because of this group's less severe handicaps, sufficient encoding took place in the mental-imagery condition for it to be superior to the paired-associate words presented in the no-strategy condition.

Those patients who recalled 50% or more of the prose passage after an hour's delay were equally good at drawn and mental images. The implication here is that mental images were easily and quickly formed, leaving sufficient time for elaborate encoding to take place. These findings are, perhaps, not surprising, given that in other studies researchers have found that global amnesics are unable to benefit from visual imagery (Baddeley & Warrington, 1973; Jones, 1974). The severely impaired group in the present study may be likened to those global amnesics. The moderately impaired group may be seen as analogous to Jones' left temporal lobectomy group, in that they benefited to some extent from imagery, and the minimally impaired group would appear to be like the normal controls in Baddeley and Warrington's study.

The results would also seem to have implications for rehabilitation. For the severely memory-impaired, external aids and environmental changes could play a more profitable role in rehabilitation than visual imagery. When visual images are used, they will perhaps be most helpful when they are drawn by staff members, relatives, or the patients themselves. While it is likely to be true that severely impaired patients will not be able to use mental imagery, those with a moderate degree of impairment may be able to respond to this strategy, since many of this group were better as a result of such intervention than when they had no strategy at all. However, images drawn by others are still likely to be better remembered by this group. For those with a mild degree of impairment, mental imagery seems to be a viable strategy, and may have a large part to play in remembering some kinds of material.

Since this experiment was carried out, a paper has appeared that considers the effects of experimenter- and self-generated images on the memory performance of Korsakoff patients (Howes, 1983). Howes used 12-item paired-associate lists and incorporated some training in the use of visual imagery. She found that both experimenter-generated and self-generated imagery improved performance in comparison with the baseline condition, but that experimenter-generated images were more effective. This is in contrast to other findings with non-brain-damaged patients; for example, Hulicka and Grossman (1967) found that self-generated images were more effective. Howes's results are in keeping with those of the present study. She also stresses that training in visual imagery is important. It is likely that many previous studies have dismissed imagery because too much was expected of the patients in too short a time. On the other hand, therapists do have to make a decision about which techniques to employ with individual patients, and how best to teach these techniques. For the majority of memory-impaired patients, their percentage-retained scores on the Logical Memory passages from the Wechsler Memory Scale would seem to be a simple and satisfactory way of predicting their ability to benefit from visual imagery.

CONCLUSIONS

A total of 36 brain-damaged patients were placed in three groups on the basis of their delayed Logical Memory scores. They were tested for their ability to use imagery as a mnemonic aid. All groups benefited to a greater or lesser extent from experimenter-drawn images. There were striking differences, however, among the groups as far as their ability to remember mental images was concerned. The severely impaired group was unable to do this; the moderately impaired could remember mental images, but not as well as those drawn for them; only the minimally impaired were equally good at both types of imagery. It is suggested that if visual imagery is used for severely impaired patients, then therapists or others should draw the images for them, rather than requiring the patients themselves to generate mental images. For the less severely impaired, training in mental imagery may be worthwhile.

Both this chapter and Chapter 11 describe group studies that were not intended to be investigations into direct attempts at rehabilitation. Instead, both aimed at answering certain questions about the effectiveness of various techniques. Nevertheless, they also drew upon contributions from the three major fields that have been highlighted in Section II. In particular, Chapter 3 focuses upon aspects of the human amnesic syndrome, and refers to studies that have attempted to improve the recall of amnesic patients by inducing them to use visual imagery. Like the patients described in those studies and in earlier chapters of Section III, the severely memory-impaired subjects described in the present chapter were also unable to use mental imagery. They were, however, able to benefit from experimenter-drawn images—a finding that can be explained by the "total time" hypothesis, which posits that length of exposure time influences LTM. However, only subjects in the mildly impaired group were able to make good use of this exposure time in the mental-imagery condition; the severely impaired group apparently spent much of this time forming the images. The performance of the moderately impaired group was in between that of the other two groups. All groups benefited from images drawn for them, so the ability to use visual imagery to improve recall was obviously present.

One finding of interest was the discrepancy between the present results and those from some other studies (e.g., Hulicka & Grossman, 1967), which claimed that self-generated images were more effective than experimenter-generated images. The discrepancy is important because of the implications for treatment of brain-damaged, memory-impaired people. Visual imagery may be an effective intervention strategy, provided that mental imagery is not required. The corollary of this is that relatives of the patients, and staff members working with them, should draw the pictures that will assist learning. This modification of mnemonic techniques using imagery would not have been foreseen on the basis of the earlier studies.

·11·

A COMPARISON OF FOUR MNEMONIC STRATEGIES IN BRAIN-DAMAGED AND NON-BRAIN-DAMAGED SUBJECTS

INTRODUCTION

We have seen in previous chapters that both visual and verbal mnemonics can be used to improve the recall of memory-impaired people. However, there have been few reports comparing the effectiveness of different strategies. Gasparrini and Satz (1979) compared visual and verbal mediation, but, as noted in Chapter 9, there was a methodological flaw in their experiment. When Cermak (1975) compared a visual and a verbal method to increase paired-associate learning in Korsakoff patients, he suggested that imagery helped both recall and recognition, while verbal mediation helped recall only. It is important to find out the comparative effectiveness of various strategies, both for brain-damaged and for non-brain-damaged people, yet no studies appear to exist that compare more than two strategies. Bower (1972) suggests that mnemonics work successfully because they allow previously isolated items to become integrated with each other. While there may be a great deal of evidence to support this suggestion, we do not know whether all mnemonics would achieve this to the same extent. If they do, then individual preferences may be a chief factor in determining which strategy to adopt. If not, then therapists should be encouraging implementation of the more successful strategies. Furthermore, brain-damaged people and normal controls may behave differently. It is known in research on driving ability, for example, that cognitive tests that best predict driving ability in the brain-damaged are not the same tests as those that are most efficient at predicting driving ability in the non-brain-damaged (Sivak, Kewman, & Henson, 1981). Determining any such differences in the effectiveness of memory techniques could be potentially useful in reducing memory failures for both groups. They could also prove to be theoretically interesting in understanding the nature of human memory.

While it is recognized that theory can be helpful to therapists in their work, it is not so clearly recognized that successful treatment might enable theorists to confirm or reject their models. An example of the latter situation has been seen in Chapter 8: In the study reported there, the success of remedial reading via the nonlexical route, together with failure via the lexical route, provided partial evidence for the dual-route model of reading.

THE PRESENT STUDY

The study reported in this chapter represents an attempt to carry out a properly controlled investigation of four mnemonic strategies. It was prompted by a number of issues, including (1) the conflicting evidence that is available to us on the ability of brain-damaged people to benefit from imagery (see Chapters 6 and 10 for discussions of this); (2) the belief of some authors (e.g., Cermak, 1980) that verbal mnemonics are more useful than visual ones for real-life tasks; and (3) the fact that some famous mnemonists such as V. P. (Hunt & Love, 1972) and Aitken (Hunter, 1977) used verbal mnemonics, while others such as Shereshevskii (Luria, 1968) use visual ones.

The four strategies selected were those most commonly used in clinical practice: namely, first-letter cueing, the method of loci, visual imagery, and the story method. All of these have been described in earlier chapters. The first-letter cueing system uses initial letters to act as retrieval cues, and it is commonly used in everyday situations. Gruneberg (1973) points out that 53% of undergraduates use the method for revision of final examinations. Higbee (1978) reminds us that first-letter cueing may be used for learning the names of the cranial nerves: "*On Old Olympus' Towering Tops . . .*" Rawles (1978) also reports that the method was used by Royal Air Force pilots during World War II to enable them to remember action drill. The method of loci or place method is, as noted earlier, an ancient one that can be extremely complex. Rawles (1978), for example, describes a scheme devised in the Middle Ages by Petrus Ravennas in which 100,000 different loci were used.

"Visual imagery" is a general term that refers to many different procedures. The one selected here was an interacting system described by Lorayne and Lucas (1974), whereby the first word to be remembered is imagined and then linked with an image of the second word, the second word with the third, and so on. The linking is achieved by imagining the words interacting in some manner. Winograd and Simon (1980) found that elderly subjects remembered more words when the words were imagined as interacting than when they were not.

The story method is based on Crovitz's (1979) "airplane list," in which the 10 words to be remembered were embedded in a story. Crovitz et al. (1979) attempted to train three brain-damaged patients to produce their own bizarre stories, and concluded that "bizarreness" was not a crucial feature. Gianutsos and Gianutsos (1979) also used the story method to improve recall of brain-damaged people, and Cermak (1980) describes a similar procedure to remember an unusual name. The example he gives is turning "Chowmentowski" into a phrase, "Show men to ski." A colleague of mine recently described the way he used the story method to remember directions for getting to a particular place in London. The streets involved were Cannon Street, Queen Victoria Street, Threadneedle Street, and Broad Street. The story was "A cannon was fired at Queen Victoria, who was threading a needle to mend her drawers before going abroad."

The purpose of the present study was to determine which (if any) of the four mnemonic strategies would be most effective for immediate recall and which for delayed recall, as well as to discover whether brain-damaged and non-brain-damaged subjects would benefit from the same strategies.

Subjects

There were two groups of subjects: 20 brain-damaged individuals and 20 controls. The brain-damaged group consisted of 16 males and 4 females, aged between 15 and 59 years (mean = 31 years, $SD = 13.8$ years). All of the brain-damaged group were patients at Rivermead Rehabilitation Centre. Ten of them had sustained severe head injuries, four had experienced CVAs, three were postencephalitic, two had been treated for a cerebral tumor, and one was diagnosed as having Korsakoff syndrome. The criterion for inclusion in the study was more than three failures on the RBMT (described in Chapter 5). The mean score for this group of 20 subjects on the RBMT was 3.6 (out of a possible total of 12), with a range of 0–8, and a standard deviation of 2.4. The normal controls were recruited from among my friends and colleagues; 7 were males and 13 females. All were aged between 17 and 53 years (mean = 27 years, SD = 11.9 years).

Method

Five lists of 10 words were constructed. The initial letters of the items in each list spelled out a word. The words were "mysterious," "purchasing," "television," "university," and "importance." This was to enable each list to be presented in the first-letter cueing condition. Five stories were also written, one for each list. The format used was similar to Crovitz's (1979) "airplane list." For example, the "university" list story was as follows:

> The first word is "umpire." You can remember that any way you like. The second word is "nose" because the umpire was hit on the nose by a ball. The third word is "iceberg," because the umpire crashed his nose into an iceberg. The fourth word is "vase," because an ancient Egyptian vase was balanced on the iceberg. The fifth word is "elephant," because an elephant picked up the vase with his trunk. The sixth word is "refugee," because a refugee was escaping on the elephant's back. The seventh word is "skylark," because a skylark was flying round and round the refugee's head. The eighth word is "imp," because a mischievous imp trapped the skylark in a net. The next word is "tree," because the imp climbed up a tree to hide. The last word is "yak," because a yak came up to the tree to scratch his back.

In addition, 10 locations, believed to be familiar to each subject, were selected so that each list could be presented in the method of loci. The locations were situated in the subject's own house or apartment and consisted of the following: (1) the front door; (2) the kitchen; (3) the dining room; (4) the sitting room or lounge; (5) the bedroom; (6) the bathroom; (7) the toilet; (8) the window sill; (9) the hall or passage; and (10) the roof.

Brain-damaged subjects were seen individually at Rivermead Rehabilitation Centre. The non-brain-damaged controls were seen in their homes or my own home, or at a local college. It was explained to the controls that they were going to participate in some memory tests to find out ways of helping people to remember.

Each subject was given five lists of words to recall (one with no strategy, one using first-letter cueing, one using method of loci, one using visual imagery, and one using the story method). All subjects had the no-strategy condition first in order to prevent adoption of one of the mnemonic strategies. Following this, the order of the strategies was counterbalanced across subjects. The allocation of lists to strategies was also counterbalanced (apart from the fact that the no-strategy list was always presented first).

The order of presentation for the first 10 subjects can be seen in Table 11-1. The order was repeated for the remaining subjects.

Following the reading of each list, subjects were asked to recall as many words as possible, in any order. Twenty-four hours later, and without warning, subjects were asked to recall as many words as possible from each of the lists they had heard the day before. Instructions for immediate recall were as follows:

1. *No-strategy condition*: "I am going to read a list of words to you, and when I have finished I want you to tell me back as many as possible in any order. I shall say each word twice and give you several seconds before going on to the next word." Subjects were given 5 seconds per word, in order to ensure equivalent exposure for all conditions. Each word was repeated, because of repetition in some of the other conditions. At the end of the reading of each list, the subjects were asked, "Now tell me back as many as you can."

2. *First-letter cueing*: "I am going to read another list of 10 words, but this time the initial letters of the words spell 'mysterious' [or whatever the appropriate word from the experiment happened to be at the time]. Again, when I have finished, tell me back as many of the words as you can, in any order." Exposure time for each word was 5 seconds. At the end of the reading of the list the subjects were asked for the words in any order, but were told that they could use the cue word to help them.

3. *Method of loci*: "This time when I read the words, I shall ask you to imagine each one in a different place in your house or flat. I shall explain more as we go along. Are you ready? [The example given here is the list for "purchasing."] The first word is 'pears'; imagine a pile of pears by your front door. The second word is 'umbrella'; imagine that it is placed in your kitchen. The next word is 'rice'; imagine some rice in your dining room. The next word is 'corned beef'; imagine that in your sitting room or lounge. The next word is 'honey'; imagine a jar of it in your bedroom. The next word is 'antifreeze'; imagine that in your

Table 11-1. Order of Presentation of the Five Lists for the First 10 Subjects

Subject	No strategy		First-letter cueing		Method of Loci		Visual imagery		Story	
	Order	Word	Order	Word	Order	Word	Order	Word	Order	Word
1	1	university	2	mysterious	3	television	4	purchasing	5	importance
2	1	mysterious	5	purchasing	2	importance	3	television	4	university
3	1	purchasing	4	television	5	university	2	importance	3	mysterious
4	1	television	3	importance	4	mysterious	5	university	2	purchasing
5	1	importance	2	university	4	purchasing	5	mysterious	3	television
6	1	university	3	mysterious	5	television	4	purchasing	2	importance
7	1	mysterious	4	purchasing	2	importance	5	television	3	university
8	1	purchasing	5	television	4	university	3	importance	2	mysterious
9	1	television	4	importance	3	mysterious	2	university	5	purchasing
10	1	importance	5	university	3	purchasing	2	mysterious	4	television

Note. The five lists of words (whose initial letters spelled out the words in the table) were as follows:
"university": umpire, nose, iceberg, vase, elephant, refugee, skylark, tree, yak.
"mysterious": matches, yacht, steak, tomatoes, eagle, rope, iodine, olives, uncle, stamp.
"purchasing": pears, umbrella, rice, corned beef, honey, antifreeze, slippers, ice cream, nuts, glue.
"television": trout, envelopes, lamp, eggs, vest, iron, sugar, ink, oranges, nail file.
"importance": injection, milk, potato, ox, rubber, table, armadillo, newspaper, candle, earring.

212

bathroom. The next word is 'slippers'; imagine them in your toilet. The next word is 'ice cream'; imagine a tub of ice cream on the window sill. The next word is 'nuts'; imagine some nuts have spilled out in your hall. The last word is 'glue'; imagine it trickling over the roof." Different words were used in different lists, but the locations were always the same. Subjects who did not have all the rooms required were asked to imagine their parents' houses. At the end of the reading of the list, subjects were asked to "take a mental trip around your house and try to remember what the words were."

4. *Visual imagery*: "This time, when I read the words, I want you to make a picture in your mind of the first word. When I tell you the second word, try to imagine the first and second words interacting in some way. Then link the second with the third, the third with the fourth, and so on. Ready? [The example given here is the list for "importance."] The first word is 'injection.' Have you got a picture of that? Now imagine 'injection' with 'milk.' Have you got that? Now link 'milk' with 'potato' . . . 'potato' with 'ox' . . . 'ox' with 'rubber' . . . 'rubber' with 'table' . . . 'table' with 'armadillo' . . . 'armadillo' with 'newspaper' . . . 'newspaper' with 'candle' . . . 'candle with 'earring.' Earring is the last word. Ready? Now tell me back as many of the words as you can. You can start at the beginning or the end, or anywhere you like."

5. *Story method*: "This time I am going to make the words into a story. It is a rather strange story, but, as with the other lists, I want you to tell me back as many words as you can in any order, once I have finished." The procedure followed was that described earlier in this chapter.

For the 24-hour delayed recall, the instructions were as follows: "Yesterday I read five lists of words to you and asked you to tell me back as many as you could remember. For the first list, I asked you to remember the words without using any particular strategy. Can you tell me as many words from that list as possible? For the second list, I asked you to imagine things in different places in your house. How many words can you remember from that list? Then I read you a list where the initial letters spelled out a certain word. Tell me as many words as you can remember from that list. Next, I asked you to imagine pictures of the words linked together in some way. Tell me as many words as you can from that list. For the last list I made the words into a strange story. Tell me as many words as you can from that list."

Many of the brain-damaged patients were at "floor level" in the delayed-recall condition, so they had the following additional help. After the initial explanation for each list (e.g., "I asked you to remember the words without using any strategy"), each subject was given as much time as he or she wished for free recall, after which I said, "The first word on that list was 'matches' [or whatever the word was]. Can you remember the second word?" Feedback was given as to whether or not the word was correct. If an incorrect response or no response was given, the second word was supplied, and so on through the list. The same procedure was followed for each list.

Scores for both brain-damaged and control subjects were collected from the number of correct responses for each condition.

Results

A three-way analysis of variance was carried out ($2 \times 5 \times 2$ design). The results are shown in Table 11-2. They indicate, first, that there was a significant difference between the groups, $F(1, 380) = 269.00$, $p < .001$; that is, the brain-damaged people did worse than the controls. Second, there was a significant difference between the lists, $F(4, 380) = 15.25$, $p < .001$; that is, some strategies were better than others. Third, there was a significant difference between immediate and delayed recall $F(1, 380) = 349.50$, $p < .001$, with immediate recall being superior. Fourth, there was a smaller significant interaction effect, $F(4, 380) = 3.75$, $p < .01$, between groups and lists; that is,

Table 11-2. Analysis of Variance: Summary Table

Source	Sum of squares	df	Mean squares	F
A: Groups	1076	1	1076	269.00**
B: Lists	244	4	61	15.25**
C: Recall (immediate vs. delayed)	1398	1	1398	349.50**
A·B interaction	60	4	15	3.75*
B·C interaction	30	4	7.5	1.90
A·C interaction	10	1	10	2.50
A·B·C interaction	2	4	0.5	0.01
Within	1532	380	4	
Total	4352	399		

$*p = .01$.
$**p = .001$.

Table 11-3. Newman–Keuls Test Applied to the Data from Normal Controls in the Immediate-Recall Condition

	No strategy	First-letter cueing	Method of loci	Visual imagery	Story
No strategy	—	n.s.	**	**	**
First-letter cueing		—	**	**	**
Method of loci			—	n.s.	*
Visual imagery				—	*
Story					—

*p < .05.
**p < .01.

brain-damaged and non-brain-damaged subjects responded differently to the strategies.

In order to discover which lists were significantly different for each group under immediate and delayed recall, four Newman–Keuls tests were carried out. Table 11-3 shows the results for the normal control subjects in the immediate-recall condition. It can be seen that there was no difference between first-letter cueing and no strategy, or between visual imagery and method of loci. All the other comparisons, however, were significantly different. In particular, the story method was far more successful than either no strategy or first-letter cueing (p's < .01). The story was also superior (although to a lesser degree) to visual imagery and method of loci (p's < .05).

In the delayed-recall condition for the control subjects, the results changed, but not dramatically (see Table 11-4). Again, the story

Table 11-4. Newman–Keuls Test Applied to the Data from Normal Controls in the Delayed-Recall Condition

	No strategy	First-letter cueing	Visual imagery	Method of loci	Story
No strategy	—	n.s.	**	**	**
First-letter cueing		—	n.s.	n.s.	**
Visual imagery			—	n.s.	*
Method of loci				—	*
Story					—

*p < .05.
**p < .01.

method was significantly better than any other method, and it was particularly better than no strategy and first-letter cueing ($p < .01$). However, after a 24-hour delay, the method of loci was not significantly better than the first-letter cueing strategy, although the difference between the two was close to significance at the .05 level.

If we turn now to the brain-damaged group in the immediate-recall condition, we see that the results are strikingly different in comparison with those for the controls. The order of most successful to least successful lists changed (as shown in Table 11-5), but what was perhaps even more striking was that no method was superior to the no-strategy condition. The story was close to being significantly different from the method of loci (difference between totals = 25, significant gap 29 at the .05 level, with $r = 5$ and $q = 3.98$). Thus, for immediate recall, the brain-damaged patients failed to make any convincing gains from any of the mnemonic strategies.

This was not the case in the delayed-recall condition, as can be seen from Table 11-6.

The results indicate that all the strategies helped in delayed recall, but, as with the controls, the story helped most of all. There were no significant differences between visual imagery, method of loci, and first-letter cueing. It will be remembered that control subjects were significantly worse at first-letter cueing than at visual imagery.

In addition to deciding which strategies led to the best performance on each list, it is useful to learn which led to the least forgetting. With the normal subjects, for example, the story may have been superior in the delayed-recall condition simply because more was remembered in the first place. Although therapists may want their patients to retain as much as possible from the beginning of treatment, an equally important aim is to prevent material being forgotten. There

Table 11-5. Newman–Keuls Test Applied to the Data from the Brain-Damaged Patients in the Immediate-Recall Condition

	Method of loci	No strategy	First-letter cueing	Visual imagery	Story
Method of loci	—	n.s.	n.s.	n.s.	n.s.
No strategy		—	n.s.	n.s.	n.s.
First-letter cueing			—	n.s.	n.s.
Visual imagery				—	n.s.
Story					—

Table 11-6. Newman–Keuls Test Applied to the Data from the Brain-Damaged Patients in the Delayed Condition

	No strategy	Visual imagery	Method of loci	First-letter cueing	Story
No strategy	—	*	*	*	**
Visual imagery		—	n.s.	n.s.	**
Method of loci			—	n.s.	*
First-letter cueing				—	*
Story					—

$*p < .05.$
$**p < .01.$

is no evidence that brain-damaged patients forgot more rapidly than the controls, as there was no interaction effect between group and time of recall; that is, there was no A × C interaction in the analysis of variance (shown in Table 11-2).

Newman–Keuls tests were performed in order to compare the percentage-retained scores for each group on the five different lists. The results for the normal subjects (see Table 11-7) indicate that visual imagery, method of loci, and the story all resulted in less forgetting than the no-strategy condition. There is no evidence to show that first-letter cueing led to significantly less forgetting than did no strategy. Differences in forgetting rates among the other strategies would not appear to be significantly different either, although the story method was very close to this in comparison with first-letter cueing at the .05 level of significance.

Table 11-7. Newman–Keuls Test to Compare the Percentage-Retained Scores of Normal Subjects on the Five Different Lists

	No strategy	First-letter cueing	Visual imagery	Method of loci	Story
No strategy	—	n.s.	*	**	**
First-letter cueing		—	n.s.	n.s.	n.s.
Visual imagery			—	n.s.	n.s.
Method of loci				—	n.s.
Story					—

$*p < .05.$
$**p < .01.$

Again, the brain-damaged subjects showed a different pattern of results (see Table 11-8). First-letter cueing was better than no strategy at all. Furthermore, in contrast to the control subjects, the brain-damaged subjects showed as much forgetting with visual imagery as with no strategy at all.

Despite the fact that the story, first-letter cueing, and method of loci were all superior to no strategy for the brain-damaged subjects, they still retained relatively little of the original material. Figure 11-1 shows the mean scores of both groups under all conditions.

Discussion

Not surprisingly, there was a large difference between the performances of the brain-damaged and control subjects. The brain-damaged patients were selected on the basis of memory impairment, so were expected to find the tasks difficult. Nevertheless, they were able to benefit from some of the mnemonic strategies in the delayed-recall condition. We shall return to this later. Perhaps the first question to answer is why the control subjects found the strategies helpful for immediate recall and the brain-damaged, on the whole, did not. The answer probably lies in the fact that, normally, people use both LTM and STM in free-recall tasks; hence the primary and recency effects noted in Chapter 3. Furthermore, most people with amnesia have normal STM but impaired LTM. Although not all the patients in the present study had an amnesic syndrome, they were like amnesics in that most showed normal immediate recall but impaired delayed recall.

Table 11-8. Newman–Keuls Test to Compare the Percentage-Retained Scores of the Brain-Damaged Patients on the Five Different Lists

	No strategy	Visual imagery	Method of loci	First-letter cueing	Story
No strategy	—	n.s.	*	**	**
Visual imagery		—	n.s.	n.s.	*
Method of loci			—	n.s.	n.s.
First-letter cueing				—	n.s.
Story					—

$*p < .05.$
$**p < .01.$

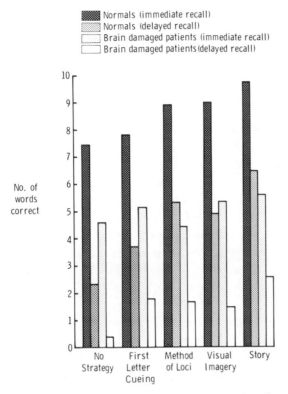

Normals (immediate recall)
Normals (delayed recall)
Brain damaged patients (immediate recall)
Brain damaged patients (delayed recall)

No. of words correct

No Strategy   First Letter Cueing   Method of Loci   Visual Imagery   Story

Figure 11-1. The mean scores of both groups under all conditions.

Thus, they were making far greater use of their STM than of their LTM skills to recall the words. It is also noted in Chapter 3 that any manipulation of memory is likely to affect LTM rather than STM. Given these two pieces of information, it can be seen that the normal subjects were using both STM and LTM for immediate recall. Because of the involvement of LTM, the strategies were able to be influential. On the other hand, because of their almost complete reliance on STM with its resistance to manipulation, the brain-damaged subjects failed to show any significant benefit from the mnemonic strategies. Indeed, some people showed worse performance using mnemonics than they did using no strategy at all.

In the delayed-recall condition, of course, neither group was able to use STM, and again the normal subjects showed better performance. This was no doubt due to unimpaired LTM, which enabled them not only to retain more words to start with, but to recall more words after the delay.

A closer look at the comparative effectiveness of the methods for the control subjects in both the immediate- and delayed-recall conditions shows that the first-letter cueing strategy was not significantly more helpful than no strategy at all. This would appear to confirm Harris (1980b), who has suggested that first-letter mnemonics are helpful only when the material is already known to the subject, and the difficulties encountered are in remembering the correct order. On the other hand, the brain-damaged subjects did find first-letter cueing better than no strategy at all. I have already noted in Chapter 7 that one severely amnesic patient was able to benefit from this strategy, so it is possible that the separate findings are mutually supportive and therefore indicative of genuine influence on the part of first-letter cueing to enable some amnesic patients to learn new material.

The discrepancy between the results of the controls and the brain-damaged subjects may be explained in at least two ways. First, the initial letters provide retrieval cues, which may be less efficient than other methods when LTM is functioning normally, but which are better than nothing at all when the system is functioning abnormally. Second, because the brain-damaged patients were so impaired at delayed recall in the no-strategy condition, it took very little to improve their performance. In contrast, as the controls retained more from the no-strategy list, they needed a relatively bigger increase for any difference to reach significance. In both groups, individual differences were present, so some people (whether brain-damaged or not) did very well with first-letter cueing and some did not. This, of course, was true for other conditions.

In delayed recall, all the mnemonic strategies were better than no strategy at all for the brain-damaged patients. The story was particularly effective, leading to better performance than visual imagery, method of loci, or first-letter cueing. The control subjects in the delayed-recall condition also found the story better than any other strategy. The main reason for the superiority of the story method is probably that visual and verbal methods were combined. Although subjects were not explicitly asked to visualize the story, it is likely that most did so. Informal questioning of some subjects (in both the brain-damaged and control groups) indicated a strong tendency for subjects to picture the items. In addition, the story method may act as a more efficient integration system. In other words, the previously isolated items become memorable because they are associated with one another, as Bower (1972) suggested. In method of loci, visual imagery, and first-letter cueing, each item becomes associated with one other image (a location, another image, or a letter of the alphabet), but there is no common link among all 10 items on a list. In the story method, however, it can be argued that there is no common thread linking one item to the next. Even though the stories are unlikely and far-fetched, there is a coherent whole that is not present in the other mnemonic strategies.

For most subjects, there was little difference in the percentage-retained scores among three of the methods, although all three led to less forgetting than no strategy. However, the three methods did not produce identical effects for both groups. The brain-damaged subjects found the story, first-letter cueing, and method of loci better than no strategy. Furthermore, the story was better than visual imagery. No differences were recorded between first-letter cueing and visual imagery, method of loci and visual imagery, or first-letter cueing and method of loci. The normal controls found story, method of loci, and visual imagery better than no strategy, but their responses to the three mnemonic strategies did not indicate any signs of superiority or preference.

It may be remembered that in the study reported in Chapter 10, there were no significant differences between immediate and delayed recall of the three lists of words used in the experiment. In contrast, there was a large difference between immediate and delayed recall in the present experiment. The reasons for the apparent discrepancy are likely to be multiple and may include the following:

1. Each list was presented three times in the Chapter 10 experiment, allowing for better learning and therefore less decay over time.
2. The delayed recall was after 2 hours in the Chapter 10 experiment and after 24 hours in the present experiment. Again, less decay would be expected over the shorter interval.
3. Fewer lists were used in the Chapter 10 experiment, thereby leading to less interference and a smaller demand on the memory store.

Returning to the questions posed in the introduction to this chapter, we should ask, first, which strategy was most effective for improving immediate free recall. The answer suggests that for the non-brain-damaged subjects the story method was superior, although visual imagery and method of loci were also effective to a lesser extent. There was no difference between visual imagery and method of loci, but as both can be described as imagery techniques, this is not surprising. For the brain-damaged subjects, no method was obviously more effective than any other for improving immediate free recall, although the story method was close to significance at the .05 level when compared with method of loci. Second, which method was most effective for delayed recall? The answer would be the story method, and this was true for both groups. The final question is whether or not both groups found the same strategies effective. To some extent, they did: The story was the most effective strategy after a 24-hour delay. Furthermore, both groups found visual imagery and method of loci better than no strategy in the delayed-recall condition. In other ways, however, the two groups differed. The brain-damaged subjects found none of the methods significantly better than no strategy at all in the immediate-recall condition, whereas the control subjects benefited from three methods: story, visual imagery, and method of loci. It should also be noted that in the delayed-recall condition, the brain-damaged subjects found first-letter cueing, better than imagery or method of loci while the controls did not.

CONCLUSIONS

A comparison of four mnemonic strategies for improving the recall of brain-damaged and non-brain-damaged subjects is reported here. Five lists of words were presented to brain-damaged and control subjects. One list required no strategy other than rote rehearsal; another required subjects to use the method of loci in order to assist remembering the words; A third list required visual imagery; a fourth list required first-letter cueing; and a fifth list required remembering words embedded in a story. The no-strategy condition was always presented first, but the allocation of words to a particular list was controlled so that each list was applicable to any strategy. In addition, the order of presentation for each mnemonic strategy was also controlled. Subjects were asked for both immediate and delayed free recall, the delay being 24 hours.

In general, the story method, which combines visual and verbal encoding, was found to be the most effective method for both groups.

There were significant differences between the groups and between the lists. There was also a significant difference between immediate and delayed recall, as well as on interaction effect between groups and lists. Brain-damaged subjects failed to benefit from any strategy in immediate recall, whereas control subjects found three strategies helpful. In delayed recall, the story method was the most effective strategy for both groups.

The fact that the mnemonic strategies helped the control subjects in both the immediate- and delayed-recall conditions, whereas they were of assistance to the brain-damaged patients only in the delayed-recall condition, has been explained by reference to the nature of STM and LTM. The controls were using both STM and LTM for immediate recall, while the brain-damaged, with their impaired LTM abilities, were relying almost exclusively on their reasonably intact STM skills until forced into using the damaged LTM system when asked to recall after a delay. In retrospect, this experiment may have produced more useful results if the brain-damaged patients had been given extra learning time in order to ensure that more information had entered the LTM store. This kind of manipulation has been recommended by Meudell and Mayes (1982).

In addition, it can be argued that the strategies might have been more effective if they had been taught one step at a time and if the manipulation of the material had not been performed mentally. Thus the first-letter cueing list could have been written down and a fading procedure could have been introduced to aid learning. In the method of loci, pictures of various rooms could have been shown, accompanied by drawings of the appropriate items to be remembered. A three-dimensional model of a house might have been even more effective. The visual-imagery pairs could have been drawn in a similar fashion to that described in Chapter 10. The story method could have been presented by means of words *and* pictures.

Individual differences emerged for both groups, with some people showing a marked preference for method of loci and others for visual imagery or first-letter cueing. However, the majority of subjects recalled more information when using the story technique. The masking of individual differences is, of course, one of the disadvantages of using group studies; this problem has been discussed in the introduction to this volume.

·IV·
CONCLUSIONS

·12·

AFTERWORD: THEORY AND PRACTICE IN COGNITIVE REHABILITATION

INFLUENCE OF THEORY

Throughout this book, it has been suggested that knowledge of theoretical and laboratory work from three major areas of psychology will enable the clinician to pursue clearer directions in the field of memory rehabilitation. Neuropsychology can help to increase understanding of the organization of the brain, and thus can enable therapists to improve selection of particular patients for specific treatment strategies. Patients with marked frontal lobe damage, for example, may be expected to respond differently from patients with purely temporal lobe damage when practicing certain therapeutic techniques. L. R., described in Chapter 9, is an example of a patient with frontal lobe damage who was able to learn but not to use the information taught to him. In contrast, F. D., described in Chapter 7, had no obvious frontal lobe deficits and was able to learn and to adapt one strategy (first-letter cueing) to other problems not selected for treatment.

Knowledge about specific disorders may also influence selection of treatment strategies and exercise some influence on decisions as to how long to continue with a particular technique. For example, patients with degenerative disorders such as Alzheimer disease may be taught to use internal memory strategies in the early stages of their illness before proceeding to external aids during the middle stages. In the terminal stages, relatives could be taught to make environmental changes to facilitate accommodation on the part of the patient to as normal a life as possible.

On the basis of the series of studies contained in Section III of this volume, it is not feasible to conclude that patients with different diagnoses respond differently to treatment. This is partly due to the fact that some diagnostic categories, such as postencephalitis or anoxia following cardiac arrest, were represented by too few patients.

227

Furthermore, most patients were treated on the basis of severity or the *nature* of the memory deficit, rather than its *cause*. Nevertheless, knowledge about diagnostic categories can help therapists indirectly. Head-injured patients, for example, may improve slowly for a long time, whereas postencephalitic patients are unlikely to show changes to the same extent when tested some months after the illness. L. T., described in Chapter 8, still appears to be improving several years after her head injury whereas M. L., the postencephalitic man described in Chapter 6, and 9, has shown no such change. Of course there is a big difference in the ages of these patients, and this might account for some difference in reaction to treatment; however, the findings that head-injured patients continue improving receives support from the work of Lezak (1979) and others. Therapists will probably need to take account of each individual patient's diagnosis, but should not let that diagnosis alone dictate which procedures to use.

An understanding of neuropsychological assessment procedures and the ability to use them will, unlike knowledge about etiology, play important roles in cognitive rehabilitation. Treatment needs to take account of patients' strengths and weaknesses. The overall level of intellectual functioning of an individual patient may influence that patient's understanding of, and active participation in, treatment. Perceptual problems will preclude or postpone some treatment approaches, as we have observed in the cases of O. E. (see Chapter 6) and L. T. (see Chapter 8). Chapter 5 has demonstrated that an assessment of the memory deficit itself requires a combined neuropsychological and behavioral approach; and, as has been seen in Chapter 10, the severity of the memory deficit itself is also an important consideration in therapy.

From the field of cognitive psychology come models of human memory that can be used in order to further understanding of the functioning and dysfunctioning of patients' memory skills. A knowledge of such models might have prevented the psychiatrist quoted by Baddeley (1984) from believing that a patient with severe memory impairment following carbon monoxide poisoning was suffering from hysteria because her pattern of deficits did not fit into his mistaken conceptualization of memory!

Cognitive psychology also provides theoretical interpretations of the human amnesic syndrome, and from some of these we might, in certain cases, obtain guidance on possible ameliorative strategies. For example, Butters and Cermak (1975) believe that amnesia is due to inadequate coding or processing. Although evidence is, on the whole, against this hypothesis, it would appear to be true that procedures requiring deeper encoding improve the recall of patients with milder memory deficits. The PQRST strategy, described in Chapter 9, might owe its success for the less impaired subjects described in Experiment 4 to the deeper levels of processing required from them.

The third contribution from cognitive psychology lies in the body of knowledge that relates to the learning abilities of amnesic patients. Because of theories that have been developed within the field of cognitive psychology, we are able to hypothesize that the ability of O. E. to learn names if they are associated with motor movements (see Chapter 6) may have been due to procedural learning. O. E. was unable to explain when, where, or how he learned the names, but if asked what a particular motor movement meant, he was able to provide the correct name. Conversely, if asked to show the appropriate movement for any given name, he could do so. If ways can be found to "proceduralize" other tasks, then therapists working with the memory-impaired might begin to stride rather than inch forward.

Behavioral psychology provides cognitive rehabilitation with assessment techniques that are complementary to neuropsychological assessments, and are crucial for the understanding of problems seen outside test situations. The influence of behavioral assessment is evident throughout much of this book. The RBMT (described in Chapter 5), for example, is an attempt to combine the strengths of both neuropsychological and behavioral measures. The patients in Chapter 6 were all tested on nonexperimental, meaningful material that was also part of the treatment process—another feature of behavioral assessment. F. D. in Chapter 7 was given a series of simulated or analogue situations in order to assess both his everyday memory deficits and his response to treatment.

Behavioral treatment techniques, as pointed out in Chapter 4, are often indistinguishable from behavioral assessment procedures. The examples given in the preceding paragraph also testify to this. A further example is given in Chapter 8, where a behavior modification program was drawn up to teach L. T. the letters of the alphabet. The principle of breaking behaviors down into small units in order to improve learning has been demonstrated in Chapters 6 and 8. The most important contribution from behavioral therapy or behavior modification is the structure it provides for designing a treatment. The series of steps to be followed enables therapists to attend to a wide variety and complexity of problems.

The other major contribution from behavioral psychology is the provision of single-case experimental designs. These are invaluable tools for the rehabilitation therapist. Investigating the sucess of imagery with the patients in Chapter 6, or examining the success and failure of different strategies with F. D. in Chapter 7, or evaluating the effectiveness of L. T.'s program in Chapter 8 would have been far more difficult and less satisfactory without the flexible multiple-baseline designs.

DETERMINING FUTURE DIRECTIONS

Costs and Benefits

As we consider future developments in cognitive rehabilitation, we must ask whether research, as illustrated by the studies in Section III of this book, can be justified in terms of cost and benefits. In answer to this question, it needs to be pointed out that too little is known about the effectiveness of rehabilitation techniques, and that many of the practices recommended in textbooks and courses have not been properly evaluated (if at all). The studies reported in Section III have been inspired by two basic beliefs: (1) Whatever the problem and however severe it is, there is always something that can improve matters; and (2) every treatment procedure carried out should be properly evaluated. Following on from the second belief, I should add that each properly evaluated treatment procedure should be regarded as a piece of research, which might possibly contain within it a finding that could extend our knowledge of general principles and/or methodological skills applicable to the whole field of cognitive rehabilitation.

Cost–benefit analysis is an important consideration. On the one hand, clinical psychologists and other therapists working in memory therapy could be considered expensive personnel who might be better employed working with patients whose response to treatment could be demonstrated to be more dramatic. On the other hand, the severely memory-impaired are very disabled members of society, who are likely to make long-term demands on their nations' resources. If treatment can make the difference between long-term institutional care and living at home, then the initially expensive therapy will have been worthwhile. If treatment of the memory-impaired allows immediate relatives to continue employment, and/or if it helps to cut down on expensive psychiatric and social services, then the intensive therapy required for the rehabilitation techniques described in this book can be justified.

Cost–benefit analysis should address itself to decisions concerning treatment of individuals or groups. If it can be demonstrated that the latter produce measurable improvements, then obviously group treatment programs should be introduced, as these will have certain economic advantages over individual treatment programs. Some studies of group therapy have been conducted, particularly in the area of reality orientation therapy with the elderly (e.g., Citrin & Dixon, 1977; Goldstein et al., 1982). Like the studies reported in this book, the reports on reality orientation therapy suggest that it is possible to teach some new items of information, but that generalization effects fail to occur. A study of group treatment of younger brain-damaged people, mostly with severe head injuries (Wilson, Cooper, & Kennerley, 1983) demonstrated some minimal recovery in general memory functioning following group treatment. What are awaited with interest are results from studies that set out formally to compare individual and group treatments.

Indeed, this leads into one last point concerning cost–benefit analysis, and this is a recommendation to all interested parties that efforts to build bridges between and among theory, research, and treatment should continue, because the knowledge engendered by sharing ideas may lead to improvements in the daily living of our patients, which in turn might increase certain levels of independence that could lead to financial savings. Also, money spent on investigating treatment ought to lead to more *effective* treatment. What cannot be tolerated is mindless, ineffective treatment that eventually leads to more expensive forms of caring.

Unless we try to help the severely cognitively impaired and discover which if any of our strategies is of any value, then rehabilitation is likely to remain the Cinderella of medicine. Aiming too high by attempting to restore memory functioning to its previous level should, on the whole, be avoided, because in many (if not most) cases such a goal will not be achieved, and we shall be left wondering just how far we *can* go in improving the abilities of brain-damaged patients. By pushing forward a little at a time, we can scrutinize findings to see what is viable and what is not.

Once the effectiveness of a particular approach has been established, then less expensive personnel may be able to implement it. The British National Health Service, for example, uses volunteer helpers in many of its centers. Volunteers could quite easily take over a great deal of the work described in this volume—for example, teaching letters of the alphabet to patients like L. T., or helping patients to learn the PQRST strategy. However, volunteers are unlikely to be able to design experiments to find out whether or not they are pursuing useful methods. Guidelines and monitoring from a trained therapist could support individual treatments and could thereby help to reduce the cost of many rehabilitation techniques.

In some of the studies reported in this book, the efforts have paid handsome dividends. F. R. E. and L. T. have improved considerably. Even F. D. with a pure amnesic syndrome, has to some degree been able to make use of the information and strategies taught to him. It is not easy to predict which patients will respond to intensive rehabilitation, but all deserve the chance to do as well as they possibly can.

Finally, brain-damaged people exist in large numbers. In many cases, they are still young. Those who survive a severe head injury are likely to be under the age of 26 years, and will go on to live a normal (or nearly normal) life span. In many cases, their lives have been saved by impressive and sophisticated techniques. In order that those lives should be improved qualitatively, we have a duty to explore the possibility of applying equally sophisticated techniques to rehabilitation. The studies in this volume represent, I hope, a few short steps in that direction.

APPENDICES

APPENDIX A. SCORING OF THE RBMT IN
THE PILOT STUDY

Each item was scored pass or fail as follows:

1-2. Remembering a first name and surname. Recall of first name and recall of surname were scored separately. If the subject correctly recalled both names when asked, and without help, 2 points were scored. If the subject recalled only one name without help, 1 point was scored; otherwise, no points were scored.

3. Remembering a hidden belonging. If the subject requested his or her belonging and remembered where this was hidden, 1 point was scored; otherwise, no points were scored.

4. Remembering an appointment. If the subject asked the appropriate question when the alarm sounded, and without a reminder, 1 point was scored; otherwise, no points were scored.

5. Immediate remembering of a route. If all five parts of the route were reproduced, *in the correct order*, 1 point was scored; otherwise, no points were scored.

6. Delayed remembering of a route. Scored as for immediate remembering of a route.

7. Remembering an errand. If the envelope was left at the correct place in *both* the immediate and delayed routes, 1 point was scored; otherwise, no points were scored.

8. Learning a new skill. The subject had to complete all six steps alone, on or before the third trial, in order to score a point.

9. Orientation. One point was scored if the subject was correct on *all* of the following questions: year, month, day of week, place and city of location, and age. Otherwise, no points were scored. (Note: In the pilot study, fewer questions were asked than are indicated in the description of the RBMT in Chapter 5.)

10. Date. One point was scored if the subject gave the correct date.

11. Face recognition. In order to score 1 point, the subject had to select all five faces correctly, with no false positives.

12. *Picture recognition.* In order to score 1 point, the subject had to select all 10 pictures correctly, with no false positives.

The maximum possible number of points was 12.

APPENDIX B. MEMORY CHECKLIST USED AT RIVERMEAD

Patient _____   Department _____

Date _____   Filled in by _____

| | 9:00 A.M. | 10:45 A.M. | 1:30 P.M. | 3:15 P.M. |
| | 10:30 A.M. | 12:00 NOON | 3:00 P.M. | 4:30 P.M. |

A.   *Forgetting things:* Did he/she

(1) Forget *things* he/she *was told* yesterday or a few days ago, and have to be reminded of them?

(2) Forget *where* he/she had *put something* or lose things around the Department?

(3) Forget *where* things are *normally kept* or look for things in the wrong places?

(4) Forget *when* something had happened—for instance, whether it was yesterday or last week?

(5) Forget *to take things* with him/her, or leave things behind and have to go back for them?

(6) Forget *to do things* he/she said he/she would do?

(7) Forget *important details* of what he/she had done the day before?

(8) Forget *details* of his/her daily routine?

(9) Forget a *change* in his/her daily routine?

(10) Forget the *names* of people he/she has met before?

B.   *In Conversation:* Did he/she

(1) *Ramble on* about unimportant or irrelevant events?

| 9:00 A.M. | 10:45 A.M. | 1:30 P.M. | 3:15 P.M. |
| 10:30 A.M. | 12:00 NOON | 3:00 P.M. | 4:30 P.M. |

(2) Find words on *"the tip of the tongue,"* knowing the words but not quite able to find them?

(3) Get *details* of what someone said *confused*?

(4) Tell a *story* or *joke* he/she had told before?

(5) Forget what he/she had already said, perhaps *repeating* what he/she had just said, or saying, "What was I talking about?"?

C. *Actions:* Did you observe the patient

(1) Having difficulty with *picking up a new skill*—e.g., playing a game or learning to use a new gadget?

(2) *Checking up* on whether he/she had done things he/she intended to do?

(3) *Getting lost* on a journey or in a building where he/she has been before?

(4) Forgetting what he/she was originally doing *after becoming distracted* by something else?

Number of patients in room:
Number of therapists in room:
Any other comments or observations:

APPENDIX C. AN EXAMPLE OF ONE OF THE PARAGRAPHS USED IN EXPERIMENTS 2 and 3 IN CHAPTER 9

Proper nouns were changed from the actual story in the newspaper.

Railway signalman Lionel Morgan was yesterday jailed for the maximum 2 months for being drunk on duty. A court was told he had been celebrating his 53rd birthday and finally fell asleep at the Whitstable junction. Five trains were stranded on his 12-mile section of the main London/Victoria to Margate line, magistrates at Herne Bay, Kent, heard.

APPENDIX D. EXAMPLES OF THE QUESTIONS AND ANSWERS USED FOR THE PARAGRAPH IN APPENDIX C

Questions	Answers
1. What was the man's name?	Lionel Morgan.
2. What was his job?	Railway signalman.
3. For how long was he jailed?	Two months.
4. Why was he jailed?	For being drunk/Drunk on duty.
5. Where did he work?	Whitstable.
6. What was the line he worked on?	London–Margate/Victoria–Margate.
7. How old was he?	53.
8. Where was the court hearing held?	Herne Bay.

Answers were scored 1 or 0. Half points were also awarded for near-correct answers—for example, "Lionel Mills" instead of "Lionel Morgan"; "London–Victoria" instead of "London (and/or Victoria) to Margate."

APPENDIX E. EXAMPLE OF ONE OF THE STORIES IN EXPERIMENT 4 IN CHAPTER 9

A Harrier jet/crashed/near/a housing estate/in Nottingham/at noon/today./ The pilot ejected/safely/when his plane caught fire/and began spiraling/out of control./ It narrowly missed/the roof tops/of a row of houses/and exploded/in a patch of waste ground./ Many windows/were shattered,/and several people/were treated for shock./

APPENDIX F. EXAMPLES OF QUESTIONS, ANSWERS, AND SCORING FOR THE STORY IN APPENDIX E

Questions	Answers	Maximum score
1. What kind of jet was in the story?	Harrier.	1 point.
2. What happened to it?	It caught fire,/spiraled/ out of control,/and crashed/in waste ground./	5 points.
3. What happened to the pilot?	He ejected/safely./	2 points.
4. What happened nearby?	Windows were shattered,/and people were treated for shock./	2 points.

REFERENCES

Adams, M. R., & Hotchkiss, J. (1973). Some reactions and responses of stutterers to a miniaturized metronome and metronome therapy: Three case reports. *Behavior Therapy, 4,* 565–569.

Albert, M. L. (1979). Alexia. In K. M. Heilman & E. Valenstein (Eds.), *Clinical neuropsychology.* New York: Oxford University Press.

Albert, M. L., Feldman, R. G., & Willis, A. L. (1974). The "subcortical dementia" of progressive supranuclear palsy. *Journal of Neurology, Neurosurgery and Psychiatry, 37,* 121–130.

Albert, M. S., Butters, N., & Brandt, J. (1981). Patterns of remote memory in amnesic and demented patients. *Archives of Neurology, 38,* 495–500.

Albert, M. S., Butters, N., & Levin, J. (1979). Temporal gradients in the retrograde amnesia of patients with alcoholic Korsakoff's disease. *Archives of Neurology, 36,* 211–216.

Anastasi, A. (1982). *Psychological testing* (5th ed.). New York: Collier/Macmillan.

Angelergues, R. (1969). Memory disorders in neurological disease. In P. J. Vinken & G. W. Bruyn (Eds.), *Handbook of clinical neurology* (Vol. 3). Amsterdam: North-Holland.

Apuzzo, M. L. J., Chikovani, O. K., Gott, P. S., Teng, E. L., Zee, C., Giannotta, S. L., & Weiss, M. H. (1982). Transcallosal, interfornical approaches for lesions affecting the third ventricle: Surgical considerations and consequences. *Neurosurgery, 10,* 547–554.

Assal, G., Probst, A., Zander, E., & Rabinowicz, T. (1976). Syndrome amnésique per infiltration tumorale. *Archives Suisses de Neurologie, Neurochirugie et Psychiatrie, 119,* 317–324.

Atkinson, R. C., & Shiffrin, R. M. (1968). Human memory: A proposed system and its control process. In K. W. Spence & J. T. Spence (Eds.), *The psychology of learning and motivation* (Vol. 2). New York: Academic Press.

Ayllon, T., & Azrin, N. H. (1965). The measurement and reinforcement of the behavior of psychotics. *Journal of the Experimental Analysis of Behavior, 8* 357–383.

Baddeley, A. D. (1966). The influence of acoustic and semantic similarity on long-term memory for word sequences. *Quarterly Journal of Experimental Psychology, 18,* 302–309.

Baddeley, A. D. (1973). Theories of amnesia. In R. A. Kennedy & A. L. Wilkes (Eds.), *Studies in long-term memory,* London: Wiley.

Baddeley, A. D. (1982a). Amnesia: A minimal model and an interpretation. In L. Cermak (Ed.), *Human memory and amnesia.* Hillsdale, NJ: Erlbaum.

Baddeley, A. D. (1982b). Implications of neuropsychological evidence for theories of normal memory. *Philosophical Transactions of the Royal Society, 298,* 59–72.

237

Baddeley, A. D. (1984). Memory theory and memory practice. In B. Wilson & N. Moffat (Eds.), *Clinical management of memory problems*. London: Croom Helm.

Baddeley, A. D., & Hitch, G. J. (1974). Working memory. In G. A. Bower (Ed.), *The psychology of learning and motivation* (Vol. 8). New York: Academic Press.

Baddeley, A. D., & Warrington, E. K. (1970). Amnesia and the distinction between long and short-term memory. *Journal of Verbal Learning and Verbal Behaviour, 9*, 176–189.

Baddeley, A. D., & Warrington, E. K. (1973). Memory coding and amnesia. *Neuropsychologia, 11* 159–165.

Baddeley, A. D., & Wilson, B. A. (1983, April). *Differences among amnesias and between amnesics: The role of single case methodology in theoretical analysis and practical treatment*. Paper presented at the Princeton Amnesia Conference, Princeton, NJ.

Baddeley, A. D., & Wilson, B. A. (in press). Amnesia, autobiographical memory and confabulation. In D. Rubin (Ed.), *Autobiographical memory*. Cambridge, England: Cambridge University Press.

Baer, D. M., Wolf, M. M., & Risley, T. R. (1968). Some current dimensions of applied behavior analysis. *Journal of Applied Behavior Analysis, 1*, 91–97.

Bahrick, H. P. (1984). Memory for people. In J. E. Harris & P. Morris (Eds.), *Everyday memory, actions and absentmindedness*. London: Academic Press.

Basmajian, J. V. (1981). Biofeedback in rehabilitation: A review of principles and practices. *Archives of Physical and Medical Rehabilitation, 62*, 469–475.

Beauvois, M. F., & Dérouesné, J. (1979). Phonological alexia: Three dissociations. *Journal of Neurology, Neurosurgery and Psychiatry, 42* 1115–1124.

Bender, M. B. (1956). Syndrome of isolated episode of confusion with amnesia. *Journal of Hillside Hospital, 5*, 212–215.

Bennett-Levy, J. (1982). *Long-term effects of severe closed head injury on cognitive function: Evidence from an unselected sample of young adults*. Unpublished manuscript.

Bennett-Levy, J., & Powell, G. E. (1980). The Subjective Memory Questionnaire (SMQ): An investigation into the self-reporting of "real life" memory skills. *British Journal of Social and Clinical Psychology, 19* 177–183.

Benson, D. F., Marsden, C. D., & Meadows, J. C. (1974). The amnesic syndrome of posterior cerebral artery occlusion. *Acta Neurologica Scandinavica, 50*, 133–145.

Benson, F., & Geschwind, N. (1969). The alexias. In P. J. Vinken & G. W. Bruyn (Eds.), *Handbook of neurology* (Vol. 4). Amsterdam: North-Holland.

Benton, A. L. (1968). Differential behavioral effects in frontal lobe disease. *Neuropsychologia, 6*, 53–60.

Benton, A. L. (1974). *The revised Visual Retention Test*. New York: Psychological Corporation.

Benton, A. L. (1979). Visuoperceptive, visuospatial and visuoconstructive disorders. In K. M. Heilman & E. Valenstein (Eds.), *Clinical neuropsychology*. New York: Oxford University Press.

Binder, L. M., & Schreiber, V. (1980). Visual imagery and verbal mediation as memory aids in recovering alcoholics. *Journal of Clinical Neuropsychology, 2*, 71–74.

Bloomquist, E. R., & Courville, C. B. (1947). The nature and incidence of traumatic lesions of the brain: A survey of 350 cases with autopsy. *Bulletin of the Los Angeles Neurological Society, 12*, 174–183.

Booraem, C. D., & Seacat, G. F. (1972). Effects of increased incentive in corrective therapy. *Perceptual and Motor Skills, 34,* 125–126.

Boudin, G., Brion, S., Pepin, B., & Barbizet, J. (1968). Syndrome de Korsakoff d'etiologie arteriopathique. *Revue Neurologique, 119,* 341–348.

Bower, G. H. (1972). A selective review of organizational factors in memory. In E. Tulving & W. Donaldson (Eds.), *Organization of memory.* New York: Academic Press.

Bradley, L. (1981). A tactile approach to reading. *British Journal of Special Education, 8,* 32–36.

Brain, W. R. (1963). The neurological complications of neuroplasms. *Lancet, 1,* 179–184.

Brierley, J. B. (1977). The neuropathology of amnesic states. In C. W. M. Whitty & O. Zangwill (Eds.), *Amnesia.* London: Butterworths.

Brierley, J. B., Corsellis, J. A. N., Hierons, R. & Nevin, S. (1960). Subacute encephalitis of later adult life, mainly affecting the limbic areas. *Brain, 83,* 357–368.

Broadbent, D. E., Cooper, P. F., Fitzgerald, P., & Parkes, K. R. (1982). The Cognitive Failures Questionnaire (CFQ) and its correlates. *British Journal of Clinical Psychology, 21,* 1–16.

Broca, P. (1861). Nouvelle observation d'aphemie produite par une lesion de la moitié posterieure des deuxième et troisième circonvolutions frontales. *Bulletin de la Société Anatomique de Paris, 6,* 398–407.

Brooks, D. N. (1972). Memory and head injury. *Journal of Nervous and Mental Disease, 155,* 350–355.

Brooks, D. N. (1974). Recognition memory and head injury. *Journal of Neurology, Neurosurgery and Psychiatry, 37,* 794–801.

Brooks, D. N. (Ed.). (1984). *Closed head injury: Psychological, social and family consequences.* Oxford: Oxford University Press.

Brooks, D. N., & Baddeley, A. D. (1976). What can amnesics learn? *Neuropsychologia, 14,* 111–122.

Brooks, D. N., & Lincoln, N. B. (1984). Assessment for rehabilitation. In B. Wilson & N. Moffat (Eds.), *Clinical management of memory problems.* London: Croom Helm.

Broome, A. K. (1980). Clinical psychology within obstetrics and gynaecology. *Bulletin of the British Psychological Society, 33,* 357–359.

Butters, N. (1979). Amnesic disorders. In K. M. Heilman & E. Valenstein (Eds.), *Clinical neuropsychology.* New York: Oxford University Press.

Butters, N. (1984). The clinical aspects of memory disorders: Contributions from experimental studies in amnesia. *Journal of Clinical Neuropsychology, 6,* 17–36.

Butters, N., & Cermak, L. (1975). Some analyses of amnesic syndromes in brain damaged patients. In R. L. Isaacson & K. H. Pribram (Eds.), *The hippocampus,* (Vol. 2) New York: Plenum Press.

Butters, N., & Cermak, L. (1976). Neuropsychological studies of alcoholic Korsakoff patients. In G. Goldstein & C. Neuringer (Eds.), *Empirical studies of alcoholism.* Cambridge, MA: Ballinger.

Butters, N., & Cermak, L. (1980). *Alcoholic Korsakoff's syndrome: An information-processing approach to amnesics.* New York: Academic Press.

Butters, N., Sax, D., Montgomery, K., & Tarlow, S. (1978). Comparison of the neuropsychological deficits associated with early and advanced Huntington's disease. *Archives of Neurology, 35,* 585–589.

Cameron, A. S., & Archibald, Y. M. (1981). Verbal memory deficit after left fornix removal: A case report. *International Journal of Neuroscience, 12,* 201.

Carr, J. (1980). Imitation, discrimination and generalisation. In W. Yule & J. Carr (Eds.), *Behaviour modification for the mentally handicapped.* London: Croom Helm.

Carr, S., & Wilson, B. A. (1983). Promotion of pressure relief exercising in a spinal injury patient: A multiple baseline across settings design. *Behavioural Psychotherapy, 11,* 329–336.

Cautela, J. R., & Upper, D. (1978). The Behavioral Inventory Battery: The use of self report measures in behavioral analysis and therapy. In M. Hersen & A. S. Bellack (Eds.), *Behavioral assessment.* New York: Pergamon Press.

Cermak, L. S. (1975). Imagery as an aid to retrieval for Korsakoff patients. *Cortex, 11,* 163–169.

Cermak, L. S. (1976). The encoding capacity of a patient with amnesia due to encephalitis. *Neuropsychologia, 14,* 311–326.

Cermak, L. S. (1980). Comments on imagery as a therapeutic mnemonic. In L. W. Poon, J. L. Fozzard, L. S. Cermak, D. Arenberg, & L. W. Thompson (Eds.) *New directions in memory and aging.* Hillsdale, NJ: Erlbaum.

Cermak, L. S., & Butters, N. (1973). Information processing deficits of alcoholic Korsakoff patients. *Quarterly Journal of Studies on Alcohol, 34,* 1110–1132.

Cermak, L. S., Butters, N., & Moreines, J. (1974). Some analyses of the verbal encoding deficit in alcoholic Korsakoff patients. *Brain and Language, 1,* 141–150.

Cermak, L. S., & O'Connor, V. (1983). The anterograde and retrograde retrieval ability of a patient with amnesia due to encephalitis. *Neuropsychologia, 21,* 213–234.

Ciminero, A. R., Calhoun, K. S., & Adams, H. E. (Eds.). (1977). *Handbook of behavioral assessment.* New York: Wiley.

Citrin, R. S., & Dixon, D. N., (1977). Reality orientation: A milieu therapy used in an institution for the aged. *Gerontologist, 17,* 39–43.

Claparede, E. (1951). Recognition and "me-ness." In D. Rapaport (Ed.), *Organization and pathology of thought.* New York: Columbia University Press. (Original work published 1911)

Cohen, N. J., & Corkin, S. (1981, October). *The amnesic patient H. M.: Learning and retention of a cognitive skill.* Paper presented at the meeting of the *Society for Neuroscience,* Los Angeles.

Coltheart, M. (1972). Visual information processing. In P. C. Dodwell (Ed.), *New Horizons in psychology* (Vol. 2). Harmondsworth, England: Penguin.

Coltheart, M. (1980). Deep dyslexia: A right hemisphere hypothesis. In M. Coltheart, K. E. Patterson, & J. C. Marshall (Eds.), *Deep dyslexia.* London: Routledge & Kegan Paul.

Coltheart, M. (1981). Disorders of reading and their implications for models of normal reading. *Visible Language, 15,* 245–286.

Coltheart, M. (1982). The psycholinguistic analysis of acquired dyslexias: Some illustrations. In D. E. Broadbent & L. Weiskrantz (Eds.), *The neuropsychology of cognitive function.* London: The Royal Society.

Coltheart, M. (1985). Cognitive neuropsychology and reading. In M. Posner & O. S. M. Marin (Eds.), *Attention and performance* (Vol. 11). Hillsdale, NJ: Erlbaum.

Coltheart, M., Patterson, K. E., & Marshall, J. C. (1980). (Eds.), *Deep dyslexia*. London: Routledge & Kegan Paul.

Conrad, R. (1964). Acoustic confusions and immediate memory. *British Journal of Psychology, 55*, 75–84.

Corkin, S. (1965). Tactually-guided maze learning in man: Effects of unilateral cortical excisions and bilateral hippocampal lesions. *Neuropsychologia, 3*, 339–351.

Corkin, S. (1968). Acquisition of motor skills after bilateral medial temporal lobe excision. *Neuropsychologia, 6*, 255.

Corkin, S. (1979). Hidden-figure test performance: Lasting effects of unilateral penetrating head injury and transient effects of bilateral cinglotomy. *Neuropsychologia, 17*, 585–605.

Corkin, S., Cohen, N. J., & Sagar, H. J. (1983). Memory for remote personal and public events after bilateral medial temporal lobectomy. *Society for Neuroscience Abstracts, 9*, 28.

Corsi, P. M. (1969, April). *Verbal memory impairment after unilateral hippocampal lesions*. Paper presented at the 40th Annual Meeting of the Eastern Psychological Association, Philadelphia.

Craik, F. I. M. (1979). Conclusions and comments. In L. S. Cermak, F. I. M. Craik, & N. J. Hillsdale (Eds.), *Levels of processing in human memory*. Hillsdale, NJ: Erlbaum.

Craik, F. I. M., & Lockhart, R. S. (1972). Levels of processing: A framework for memory research. *Journal of Verbal Learning and Verbal Behaviour, 11*, 671–684.

Craik, F. I. M., & Simon, E. (1980). Age differences in memory: The roles of attention and depth of processing. In L. W. Poon, J. L. Fozard, L. S. Cermak, D. Arenberg, & L. W. Thompson (Eds.), *New directions in memory and aging*. Hillsdale, NJ: Erlbaum.

Craik, F. I. M., & Tulving, E. (1975). Depth of processing and the retention of words in episodic memory. *Journal of Experimental Psychology: General, 104*, 268–294.

Craik, F. I. M., & Watkins, M. J. (1973). The role of rehearsing in short-term memory. *Journal of Verbal Learning and Verbal Behaviour, 12*, 599–607.

Crovitz, H. (1979). Memory retraining in brain damaged patients: The airplane list. *Cortex, 15*, 131–134.

Crovitz, H., Harvey, M., & Horn, R. (1979). Problems in the acquisition of imagery mnemonics: Three brain damaged cases. *Cortex, 15*, 225–234.

Dailey, C. A. (1956). Psychological findings five years after head injury. *Journal of Clinical Psychology, 12*, 349–353.

Davidoff, J., & Wilson, B. A. (1985). A case of visual associative agnosia showing a disorder of pre-semantic categorisation. *Cortex, 21*, 121–134.

Davies, J. M., Davis, K. R., Kleinman, G. M., Kirchner, H. S., & Taveras, J. M. (1978). Computerised tomography of herpes simplex encephalitis with clinico-pathological correlation. *Radiology, 129*, 409–417.

Dejong, R. N., Itabashi, H. H., & Olson, J. R. (1969). Memory loss due to hippocampal lesions: Report of a case. *Archives of Neurology, 20*, 339–348.

Delay, J., & Brion, S. (1969). *Le syndrome de Korsakoff*. Paris: Masson.

Delay, J., & Brion, S., & Derouesne, C. (1964). Syndrome de Korsakoff et etiologie tumorale. *Revue Neurologique, 111*, 97–133.

De Renzi, E., & Vignolo, L. A. (1962). The token test: A sensitive test to detect receptive disturbances in aphasics. *Brain, 85*, 665–679.

Diller, L., (1980). Development of a perceptual remedial program. In L. Ince (Ed.), *Behavioral psychology in rehabilitation medicine.* Baltimore: Williams & Wilkins.

Diller, L., & Weinberg, J. (1977). Hemi-inattention in rehabilitation: The evolution of a rational remediation program. In E. A. Weinstein & R. P. Friedland (Eds.), *Advances in neurology* (Vol. 18). New York: Raven Press.

Dott, N. M. (1938). Surgical aspects of the hypothalamus. In W. E. Clark, J. Beattie, G. Riddoch, & N. M. Dott (Eds.), *The hypothalamus.* Edinburgh: Oliver & Boyd.

Drachman, D. A., & Adams, R. D. (1962). Herpes simplex and acute inclusion-body encephalitis. *Archives of Neurology, 7,* 45-63.

Dunn, L. M., & Dunn, L. M. (1981). *Peabody Picture Vocabulary Test—Revised.* Circle Pines, MN: American Guidance Service.

Ebbinghaus, H. E. (1964). *Memory: A contribution to experimental psychology.* New York: Dover. (Original work published 1885)

Edgington, E. S. (1982). Nonparametric tests for single-subject multiple schedule experiments. *Behavioral Assessment, 4,* 83-91.

Edwards, A. E., & Rosenberg, B. (1966). An automated branching device for the assessment and training of visual discrimination. *Perceptual and Motor Skills, 22,* 488-490.

Eisler, R. M. (1978). The behavioral assessment of social skills. In M. Hersen & A. S. Bellack (Eds.), *Behavioral assesment.* New York: Pergamon Press.

Elithorn, A. (1965). Psychological tests. An objective approach to the problem of task difficulty. *Acta Neurologica Scandinavica, 41,* (Suppl. 13, Part 2), 661-667.

Ellis, A. W. (1984). *Reading, writing and dyslexia: A cognitive analysis.* Hillsdale, NJ: Erlbaum.

Emmelcamp, P. M. G. (1974). Self observation versus flooding in the treatment of agorophobia. *Behaviour Research and Therapy, 12,* 229-237.

Erickson, R. C., Poon, L. W., & Walsh-Sweeney, L. (1980). Clinical memory testing of the elderly. In L. W. Poon, J. L. Fozard, L. S. Cermak, D. Arenberg, & L. W. Thompson (Eds.), *New directions in memory and aging.* Hillsdale, NJ: Erlbaum.

Erickson, R. C., & Scott, M. L. (1977). Clinical memory testing: A review. *Psychological Bulletin, 84,* 1130-1149.

Evans, C. D. (Ed.). (1981). *Rehabilitation after severe head injury.* Edinburgh: Churchill Livingstone.

Eysenck, H. J. (1959). Learning theory and behaviour therapy. *Journal of Mental Science, 105,* 61-75.

Eysenck, H. J. (Ed.). (1960). *Behavior therapy and the neuroses.* New York: Pergamon Press.

Eysenck, M. W. (1979). Depth, elaboration and distinctiveness. In L. S. Cermak & F. I. M. Craik (Eds.), *Levels of processing in human memory.* Hillsdale, NJ: Erlbaum.

Fedio, P., & Van Buren, J. M. (1974). Memory deficits during electrical stimulation of the speech cortex in conscious man. *Brain and Language, 1,* 29-42.

Field, J. G. (1960). Tables for use with Wechsler's intelligence scales. *Journal of Clinical Psychology, 16,* 3-7.

Fisher, C. M., & Adams, R. D. (1964). Transient global amnesia. *Acta Neurologica Scandinavica, 40* (Suppl. 9), 7-83.

Frederikson, L. W., & Frederikson, C. B. (1975). Teacher-determined and self-determined token reinforcement in a special education classroom. *Behavior Therapy, 6,* 310-314.

Gade, A. (1982). Amnesia after operations on aneurysms of the anterior communicating artery. *Surgical Neurology, 18,* 46–49.

Gaffan, D. (1972). Loss of recognition memory in rats with lesions to the fornix. *Neuropsychologia, 10,* 327–341.

Galton, F. (1907). *Inquiries into the human faculty and its development* (2nd ed.). New York: E. P. Dutton.

Gardner, H. (1977). *The shattered mind: The person after brain damage.* London: Routledge & Kegan Paul.

Gasparrini, B., & Satz, P. (1979). A treatment for memory problems in left hemisphere CVA patients. *Journal of Clinical Psychology, 1,* 137–150.

Geschwind, N. (1975). The borderland of neurology and psychiatry: Some common misconceptions. In F. Benson & D. Blumer (Eds.), *Psychiatric aspects of neurological disease.* New York: Grune & Stratton.

Geschwind, N., & Fusillo, M. (1966). Color-naming deficits in association with alexia. *Archives of Neurology, 15,* 137–146.

Gianutsos, R., & Gianutsos, J. (1979). Rehabilitating the verbal recall of brain injured patients by mnemonic training: An experimental demonstration using single case methodology. *Journal of Clinical Neuropsychology, 1,* 117–135.

Glasgow, R. E., Zeiss, R. A., Barrera, M., & Lewinsohn, P. M. (1977). Case studies on remediating memory deficits in brain damaged individuals. *Journal of Clinical Psychology, 33,* 1049–1054.

Goldfried, M. R., & Sprafkin, J. N. (1976). Behavioral personality assessment. In J. T. Spence, R. C. Carson, & J. W. Thibaut (Eds.), *Behavioral approaches to therapy.* Morristown, NJ: General Learning Press.

Goldstein, G. (1984). Methodological and theoretical issues in neuropsychological assessment. In B. A. Edelstein & E. T. Couture (Eds.), *Behavioral assessment and rehabilitation of the traumatically brain-damaged.* New York: Plenum Press.

Goldstein, G., Turner, S. M., Holzman, A., Kanagy, M., Elmore, S., & Barry, K. (1982). An evaluation of reality orientation therapy. *Journal of Behavioral Assessment, 4,* 165–178.

Goodkin, R. (1966). Case studies in behavioural research in rehabilitation. *Perceptual and Motor Skills, 23,* 171–182.

Grafman, J. (1984). Memory assessment and remediation. In B. A. Edelstein & E. T. Couture (Eds.), *Behavioral assessment and rehabilitation of the traumatically brain-damaged.* New York: Plenum Press.

Groninger, L. D. (1971). Mnemonic Imagery and forgetting. *Psychonomic Science, 23,* 161–163.

Gruneberg, M. M. (1973). The role of memorization techniques in finals examination preparation—a study of psychology students. *Educational Research, 15,* 134–139.

Gunzburg, H. C. (1973). *Social competence and mental handicap* (2nd ed.). London: Bailliere Tindall.

Haber, R. N., & Standing, L. G. (1969). Direct measures of short-term visual storage. *Quarterly Journal of Experimental Psychology, 21,* 43–54.

Hall, J. F. (1971). *Verbal learning and retention.* Philadelphia: J. B. Lippincott.

Hall, P. (1963). Korsakoff's syndrome following herpes-zoster encephalitis. *Lancet, 1,* 752.

Harris, J. E. (1980a). Memory aids people use: Two interview studies. *Memory and Cognition, 8,* 31–38.

Harris, J. E. (1980b). We have ways of helping you remember. *Concord: The Journal of the British Association for Service to the Elderly, No. 17*, 21–27.

Harris, J. E. (1984). Remembering to do things: A forgotten topic. In J. E. Harris & P. Morris (Eds.), *Everyday memory, Actions and Absentmindedness*. London: Academic Press.

Harris, J. E., & Morris, P. E. (Eds.). (1984). *Everyday memory: Actions and absentmindedness*. London: Academic Press.

Hasher, L., & Zacks, R. T. (1979). Automatic and effortful processes in memory. *Journal of Experimental Psychology, General, 108*, 356–388.

Hassler, R., & Riechert, T. (1957). Uber einen fall von doppelseitiger fornicotonie bei sogenannter temporaler epilepsie. *Acta Neurochirurgie, 5*, 330–340.

Hay, L. R. (1982). Teaching behavioral assessment to clinical psychology students. *Behavioral Assessment, 4*, 35–40.

Hay, W. M., Hay, L. R., Angle, H. V., & Nelson, R. O. (1979). The reliability of problem identification in the behavioral interview. *Behavioral Assessment, 1*, 41–49.

Haynes, S. N. (1978). *Principles of behavioral assessment*. New York: Gardner Press.

Heathfield, K. W. G., Croft, P. B., & Swash, M. (1973). The syndrome of transient global amnesia. *Brain, 96*, 729–736.

Hecaen, H., & Ajuriaguerra, J. (1956). *Troubles mentaux au cours des tumeurs intracraniennes*. Paris: Masson.

Hecaen, H., & Albert, M. L. (1978). *Human neuropsychology*. New York: Wiley.

Heilbrun, A. (1962). Issues in the assessment of organic brain damage. *Psychological Reports, 10*, 511–515.

Heilman, K. M. (1979). Neglect and related disorders. In K. M. Heilman & E. Valenstein (Eds.), *Clinical neuropsychology*. New York: Oxford University Press.

Heilman, K. M., & Sypert, G. W. (1977). Korsakoff's syndrome resulting from bilateral fornix lesions. *Neurology, 27*, 490–493.

Herrmann, D., & Neisser, U. (1978). An inventory of everyday memory experiences. In M. M. Gruneberg, P. Morris, & R. Sykes (Eds.), *Practical aspects of memory*. London: Academic Press.

Hersen, M., & Barlow, D. H. (1976). *Single case experimental designs: Strategies for studying behavior change*. New York: Pergamon Press.

Hersen, M., & Bellack, A. S. (Eds.). (1978). *Behavioral assessment*. New York: Pergamon Press.

Higbee, K. L. (1977). *Your memory: How it works and how to improve it*. Englewood Cliffs, NJ: Prentice-Hall.

Higbee, K. L. (1978). The pseudolimitations of mnemonics. In M. M. Gruneberg, P. E. Morris, & R. N. Sykes (Eds.), *Practical aspects of memory*. London: Academic Press.

Hilgard, E. R. (1969). Pain as a puzzle for psychology and physiology. *American Psychologist, 24*, 103–114.

Howes, J. L. (1983). Effects of experimenter and self-generated imagery on the Korsakoff patient's memory performance. *Neuropsychologia, 21*, 341–349.

Hulicka, I. M., & Grossman, J. L. (1967). Age group comparisons for the use of mediators in paired associate learning. *Journal of Gerontology, 22*, 46–51.

Hunt, E., & Love, T. (1972). How good can memory be? In A. W. Melton & E. Martin (Eds.), *Coding processes in human memory*. New York: Wiley.

Hunter, I. M. L. (1977). An exceptional memory. *British Journal of Psychology, 68*, 155–164.

Huppert, F. A., & Piercy, M. F. (1976). Recognition memory in amnesic patients. *Cortex, 12,* 3–20.

Huppert, F. A., & Piercy, M. (1978a). Dissociation between learning and remembering in organic amnesia. *Nature, 275,* 317–318.

Huppert, F. A., & Piercy, M. (1978b). The role of trace strength in recency and frequency judgements by amnesic and control subjects. *Quarterly Journal of Experimental Psychology, 30,* 346–354.

Huppert, F. A., & Piercy, M. (1981). Learning and forgetting in amnesia. In L. S. Cermak (Ed.), *Human memory and amnesia.* Hillsdale, NJ: Erlbaum.

Hussian, R. A. (1981). *Geriatric psychology: A behavioural perspective.* London: Van Nostrand Reinhold.

Ince, L. P. (1969). A behavioural approach to motivation in rehabilitation. *Psychological Record, 19,* 105–111.

Ince, L. P. (1976). The use of relaxation training and a conditional stimulus in the elimination of epileptic seizures in a child: A case study. *Journal of Behavior Therapy and Experimental Psychiatry, 7,* 39–42.

Ince, L. P. (Ed.). (1980). *Behavioral psychology in rehabilitation medicine.* Baltimore: Williams & Wilkins.

Iwatha, B. A., & Lorentzson, A. M. (1976). Operant control of seizure-like behaviour in an institutionalized retarded adult. *Behavior Therapy, 7,* 247–251.

Jacoby, L. L., & Witherspoon, D. (1982). Remembering without awareness. *Canadian Journal of Psychology, 36,* 300–324.

Jaffe, P. G., & Katz, A. N. (1975). Attenuating anterograde amnesia. *Journal of Abnormal Psychology, 84,* 559–562.

Jastak, J. F. (1949). A rigorous criterion of feeblemindedness. *Journal of Social Psychology, 44,* 367–378.

Jones, M. (1974). Imagery as a mnemonic aid after left temporal lobectomy: Contrast between material specific and generalised memory disorders. *Neuropsychologia, 12,* 21–30.

Joynt, R. J., & Shoulson, I. (1979). Dementia. In K. M. Heilman & E. Valenstein (Eds.), *Clinical neuropsychology.* New York: Oxford University Press.

Kahn, E. A., & Crosby, E. C. (1972). Korsakoff's syndrome associated with surgical lesions involving the mamillary bodies. *Neurology, 22,* 117–125.

Kanfer, F. H. (1970). Self-regulation: Research issues and speculations. In C. Neuringer & M. L. Michael (Eds.), *Behavior modification in clinical psychology.* New York: Appleton-Century-Crofts.

Kanfer, F. H., & Saslow, G. (1969). Behavioral diagnosis. In C. Franks (Ed.), *Behavior therapy: Appraisal and status.* New York: McGraw-Hill.

Kapur, N. & Pearson, D. (1983). Memory systems and memory performance of neurological patients. *British Journal of Psychology, 74,* 409–415.

Kazdin, A. E. (1974). Self monitoring and behavioral change. In M. J. Mahoney & C.E. Thorensen (Eds.), *Self-control: Power to the person.* Monterey, CA: Brooks/Cole.

Kazdin, A. E. (1979). Fictions, factions and functions of behavior therapy. *Behavior Therapy, 10,* 629–654.

Kazdin, A. E. (1982). *Single case research designs.* New York: Oxford University Press.

Kern, J. M. (1984). Relationships between obtrusive laboratory and unobtrusive naturalistic behavioral fear assessments: Treated and untreated subjects. *Behavioral Assessment, 6,* 45–60.

Keschner, M., Bender, M. B., & Strauss, I. (1938). Mental symptoms associated with brain tumor: A study of 530 verified cases. *Journal of the American Medical Association, 110*, 714–718.

Kiernan, C. C. (1973). Functional analysis. In P. Mittler (Ed.), *Assessment for learning in the mentally handicapped*. London: Churchill Livingstone.

Kimura, D. (1963). Right temporal lobe damage. *Archives of Neurology, 8*, 254–271.

Kinsbourne, M. (1972). Behavioral analysis of the repetition deficit in conduction aphasia. *Neurology, 22*, 1126–1132.

Kinsbourne, M., & Warrington, E. K. (1962). A disorder of simultaneous form perception. *Brain, 85*, 461–486.

Kinsbourne, M., & Wood, F. (1975). Short-term memory processes and the amnesic syndrome. (Eds.), *Short-term memory*. New York: Academic Press.

Klonoff, H., & Paris, R. (1974). Immediate, short-term and residual affects of acute head injuries in children: Neuropsychological and neurological correlates. In R. M. Reitan & L. A. Davison (Eds.), *Clincial neuropsychology: Current status and applications*. Washington, DC: V. H. Winston & Sons.

Klove, H., & Cleeland, C. S. (1972). The relationship of neurophysiological impairment to other indices of severity of head injury. *Scandinavian Journal of Rehabilitation Medicine, 4*, 55–60.

Kratochwill, T. R. (Ed.). (1978). *Single subject research: Strategies for evaluating change*. New York: Academic Press.

Krebs, E. W., Snowman, J., & Smith, S. H. (1978). Teaching new dogs old tricks: Facilitating prose learning through mnemonic training. *Journal of Instructional Psychology, 5*, 33–39.

Landauer, T. K., & Bjork, R. A. (1978). Optimum rehearsal patterns and name learning. In M. M. Gruneberg, P. E. Morris, & R. N. Sykes (Eds.), *Practical aspects of memory*. London: Academic Press.

Lavender, A. (1981). A behavioural approach to the treatment of epilepsy. *Behavioural Psychotherapy, 9*, 231–243.

Lazarus, A. A. (1971). *Behavior therapy and beyond*. New York: McGraw-Hill.

Lazarus, A. A. (1973). Multimodal behavior therapy: Treating the "BASIC ID." *Journal of Nervous and Mental Disease, 156*, 404–411.

Levin, H. S., Benton, A. L., & Grossman, R. B. (1982). *Neurobiological consequences of closed head injury*. New York: Oxford University Press.

Lewinsohn, P. M., Danaher, B.G., & Kikel, S. (1977). Visual imagery as a mnemonic aid for brain-injured persons. *Journal of Consulting and Clinical Psychology, 45*, 717–723.

Lezak, M. D. (1976). *Neuropsychological assessment*. New York: Oxford University Press.

Lezak, M. D. (1979). Recovery of memory and learning functions following traumatic brain injury. *Cortex, 15*, 63–72.

L'Hermitte, F., & Signoret, J. L. (1972). Analyse neuropsychologique et differentiation des syndromes amnésiques. *Revue Neurologique, 126*, 161–178.

Lick, J. R., & Katkin, E. S. (1978). Assessment of anxiety and fear. In M. Hersen & A. S. Bellack (Eds.), *Behavioral assessment*. New York: Pergamon Press.

Lidvall, H. E., Linderoth, B., & Norlin, B. (1974). Causes of the postconcussional syndrome. *Acta Neurologica Scandinavica, 50*, (Suppl. 56).

Lishman, W. (1978). *Organic psychiatry*. Oxford: Blackwell Scientific Publications.

Loftus, M., & Wilson, B. A. (1984). *Memory therapy with a Korsakoff patient: A multiple baseline design.* Unpublished manuscript.

Longwill, A. (1980, July). *A behavioral approach to treatment compliance in diabetes.* Paper presented at the First World Congress on Behavior Therapy, Jerusalem.

Lorayne, H. (1979). *How to develop a super power memory.* Wellingborough, England: A. Thomas.

Lorayne, H., & Lucas, J. (1974). *The memory book.* New York: Ballantine Books.

Luria, A. R. (1959). Disorders of "simultaneous perception" in a case of bilateral occipito-parietal brain injury. *Brain, 82,* 437–449.

Luria, A. R. (1968). *The mind of a mnemonist.* New York: Basic Books.

Mair, W. P. G., Warrington, E. K., & Weiskrantz, L. (1979). Memory disorder in Korsakoff's psychosis. *Brain, 102,* 749–783.

Malamud, N., & Skillicorn, S. A. (1956). Relationship between the Wernicke and the Korsakoff syndrome. *Archives of Neurology and Psychiatry, 76,* 585–596.

Marcel, A. J. (1980). Surface dyslexia and beginning reading: A revised hypothesis of the pronunciation of print and its impairments. In M. Coltheart, K. E. Patterson, & J. C. Marshall (Eds.), *Deep dyslexia.* London: Routledge & Kegan Paul.

Marshall, J. C., & Newcombe, F. (1973). Patterns of paralexia: A psycholinguistic approach. *Journal of Psycholinguistic Research, 2,* 175–199.

Marzillier, J. S. (1980). Cognitive therapy and behavioural practice. *Behaviour Research and Therapy, 18,* 249–258.

Marzillier, J., & Winter, K. (1978). Success and failure in social skills training: Individual differences. *Behaviour Research and Therapy, 16,* 67–84.

Mason, S. E., & Smith, A. D. (1977). Imagery in the aged. *Experimental Aging Research, 3,* 17–32.

Mayes, A. R., & Meudell, P. R. (1981a). How similar is the effect of aging in amnesics and normal subjects following forgetting? *Cortex, 17,* 113–124.

Mayes, A. R., & Meudell, P. R. (1981b). How similar is immediate memory in amnesic patients to delayed memory in normal subjects? A replication, extension and reassessment of the amnesic cueing effect. *Neuropsychologia, 19,* 647–654.

Mayes, A. R., Meudell, P. R., & Neary, D. (1978). Must amnesia be caused by either encoding or retrieval disorders? In M. M. Gruneberg, P. E. Morris, & R. N. Sykes (Eds.), *Practical aspects of memory.* London: Academic Press.

Mayes, A. R., Meudell, P. R., & Neary, D. (1980). Do amnesics adopt inefficient encoding strategies with faces and random shapes? *Neuropsychologia, 18,* 527–540.

McCarty, D. (1980). Investigation of a visual imagery mnemonic device for acquiring face–name associations. *Journal of Experimental Psychology and Human Learning Memory, 6,* 145–155.

McEntee, W. J., Biber, M. P., Perl, D. P., & Benson, F. D. (1976). Diencephalic amnesia: A reappraisal. *Journal of Neurology, Neurosurgery and Psychiatry, 39,* 436–441.

McGinnis, D. J., & Smith, D. E. (1982). *Analyzing and treating reading problems.* New York: Macmillan.

McHugh, P. R., & Folstein, M. F. (1975). Psychiatric syndromes of Huntington's chorea: A clinical and phenomenologic study. In F. Benson & D. Blumer (Eds.), *Psychiatric aspects of neurological disease.* New York: Grune & Stratton.

McKenna, P., & Warrington, E. K. (1983). *The Graded Naming Test.* Windsor, England: National Foundation for Educational Research-Nelson.

McKinlay, W. W., & Brooks, D. N. (1984). Methodological problems in assessing psycho-social recovery following severe head injury. *Journal of Clinical Neuropsychology, 6*, 87–99.

Meichenbaum, D. H. (1977). *Cognitive behavior modification.* New York: Plenum.

Meudell, P. R., & Mayes, A. R. (1982). Normal and abnormal forgetting. In A. W. Ellis (Ed.), *Normality and pathology in cognitive functions.* London: Academic Press.

Meudell, P. R., Northen, B., Snowden, J. S., & Neary, D. (1980). Long term memory for famous voices in amnesic and normal subjects. *Neuropsychologia, 18*, 133–139.

Miller, E. (1978). Is amnesia remediable? In M. M. Gruneberg, P. E. Morris, R. N. Sykes (Eds.), *Practical aspects of memory.* London: Academic Press.

Miller, E. (1980). Psychological intervention in the management and rehabilitation of neuropsychological impairments. *Behaviour Research and Therapy, 18*, 527–535.

Miller, E. (1984). *Recovery and management of neuropsychological impairments.* Chichester: Wiley.

Miller, G. A. (1956). The magical number seven, plus or minus two: Some limits on our capacity for processing information. *Psychological Review, 63*, 81–97.

Milner, B. (1959). The memory defect in bilateral hippocampal lesions. *Psychiatric Research Reports, 11*, 43–52.

Milner, B. (1963). Effects of different brain lesions on card sorting. *Archives of Neurology, 9*, 90–100.

Milner, B. (1965). Visually guided maze learning in man: Effects of bilateral hippocampal, bilateral frontal, and unilateral cerebral lesions. *Neuropsychologia, 33*, 17–38.

Milner, B. (1966). *Amnesia following operation on the temporal lobes.* In C. W. M. Whitty & O. Zangweill (Eds.), *Amnesia.* London: Butterworths.

Milner, B. (1967). Brain mechanisms suggested by studies of temporal lobes. In F. L. Darley (Ed.), *Brain mechanisms underlying speech and language.* New York: Grune & Stratton.

Milner, B. (1968). Visual recognition and recall after right temporal lobe excision in man. *Neuropsychologia, 6*, 191–209.

Milner, B. (1970). Memory and the medial temporal regions of the brain. In K. H. Pribam & D. E. Broadbent (Eds.), *Biology of memory.* New York: Academic Press.

Milner, B. (1971). Interhemispheric differences in the localisation of psychological processes in man. *British Medical Bulletin: Cognitive Psychology, 27*, 272–277.

Milner, B. (1972). Disorders of learning and memory after temporal lobe lesions in man. *Clinical Neurosurgery, 19*, 421–446.

Milner, B. (1974). Hemispheric specialization: Scope and limits. In F. O. Schmitt & F. G. Worden (Eds.) *The neurosciences: Third research program.* Cambridge, MA: MIT Press.

Milner, B., Corkin, S., & Teuber, J. L. (1968). Further analysis of the hippocampal amnesic syndrome: A 14 year follow-up study of H. M. *Neuropsychologia, 6*, 215–234.

Mischel, W. (1968). *Personality and assessment.* New York: Wiley.

Moffat, N. (1984). Strategies of memory therapy. In B. A. Wilson & N. Moffat (Eds.), *Clinical management of memory problems.* London: Croom Helm.

Mohr, J. O., Leicester, J., Stoddard, L. T., & Sidman, M. (1971). Right hemianopia with memory and color deficits in circumscribed left posterior cerebral artery territory infarction. *Neurology, 21*, 1104–1113.

Moore, B. E., & Ruesch, J. (1944). Prolonged disturbances of consciousness following head injury. *New England Journal of Medicine, 230,* 445-452.

Moore, P., & Carr, J. (1976). Behaviour modification programme to teach dressing to a severely retarded adolescent. *Communication, 11*(2), 20-27.

Morganstern, K. P. (1978). Behavioral interviewing: The initial stages of assessment. In M. Hersen & A. S. Bellack (Eds.), *Behavioral assessment.* New York: Pergamon Press.

Morton, J., & Patterson, K. E. (1980). A new attempt at an interpretation, or an attempt at a new interpretation. In M. Coltheart, K. Patterson, & J. C. Marshall (Eds.), *Deep dyslexia.* London: Routledge & Kegan Paul.

Moscovitch, M. (1982). Mulitple dissociation of function in amnesia. In L. Cermak (Ed.), *Human memory and amnesia.* Hillsdale, NJ: Erlbaum.

Moyer, S. B. (1979). Rehabilitation of alexia: A case study. *Cortex, 15,* 139-144.

Murphy, G., & Goodall, E. (1980). Measurement error in direct observation: A comparison of common recording methods. *Behaviour Research and Therapy, 18,* 147-150.

Neisser, U. (1978). Memory: What are the important questions? In M. M. Gruneberg, P. E. Morris, & R. N. Sykes (Eds.), *Practical aspects of memory.* London: Academic Press.

Nelson, H. E., & O'Connell, A. (1978). Dementia: The estimation of levels of premorbid intelligence using the new Adult Reading Test. *Cortex, 14,* 234-244.

Nelson, R. O., & Hayes, S. C. (1979a). The nature of behavioral assessment: a commentary. *Journal of Applied Behavior Analysis, 12,* 491-500.

Nelson, R. O., & Hayes, S. C. (1979b). Some current dimensions of behavioral assessment. *Behavioral Assessment, 1,* 1-16.

Newcombe, F., & Marshall, S. C. (1981). On psycholinguistic classifications of the acquired dyslexias. *Bulletin of the Orton Society, 31,* 29-46.

Newcombe, F., & Ratcliff, G. (1979). Long term psychological consequences of cerebral lesions. In M. S. Gazannig (Ed.), *Handbook of behavioral neurobiology, (Vol. 2, Neuropsychology).* New York: Plenum Press.

Nielsen, J. M. (1958). *Memory and amnesia.* Los Angeles: San Lucas Press.

Norrman, B., & Svahn, K. (1961). A follow-up study of severe brain injuries. *Acta Psychiatrica Scandinavica, 37,* 236-264.

Oldfield, R. C., & Wingfield, A. (1965). Response latencies in naming objects. *Quarterly Journal of Experimental Psychology, 17,* 273-281.

Oppenheimer, D. R. (1968). Microscopic lesions in the brain following head injury. *Journal of Neurology, Neurosurgery and Psychiatry, 31,* 229-306.

Paivio, A. (1969). Mental imagery in learning and memory. *Psychological review, 76,* 241-263.

Paivio, A., & Desrochers, A. (1979). Effects of an imagery mnemonic on second language recall and comprehension. *Canadian Journal of Psychology, 33,* 17-28.

Paivio, A., Yuille, J. C., & Madigan, S. A. (1968). Concreteness, imagery and meaningfulness values for 925 nouns. *Journal of Experimental Psychology Monographs, 76,* (Pt. 2), 1-25.

Parkin, A. J. (1984). Amnesic syndrome: A lesion-specific disorder? *Cortex, 20,* 479-508.

Patten, B. M. (1971). Transient global amnesia syndrome. *Journal of the American Medical Association, 217,* 690-691.

Patten, B. M. (1972). The ancient art of memory. *Archives of Neurology, 26*, 25–31.

Patterson, G. R., Weiss, R. L., & Hops, H. (1976). Training of marital skills: Some problems and concepts. In H. Leitenberg (Ed.), *Handbook of behavior modification*. New York: Appleton-Century-Crofts.

Patterson, K. E. (1981). Neuropsychological approaches to the study of reading. *British Journal of Psychology, 72*, 151–174.

Patterson, K. E. (1982). The relation between reading and phonological coding: Further neuropsychological observations. In A. W. Ellis (Ed.), *Normality and pathology in cognitive functions*. London: Academic Press.

Penfield, W., & Milner, B. (1958). Memory deficit produced by bilateral lesions in the hippocampal zone. *Archives of Neurology and Psychiatry, 79*, 475–497.

Piercy, M. (1978). Experimental studies of the organic amnesic syndrome. In C. M. Whitty & O. Zangwill (Eds.), *Amnesia*. London: Butterworths.

Peterson, L. R. (1966). Short-term verbal memory and learning. *Psychological Review, 73*, 193–207.

Postman, L., & Phillips, L. W. (1965). Short term temporal changes in free recall. *Quarterly Journal of Experimental Psychology, 17*, 132–138.

Powell, G. E. (Ed.). (1981). *Brain function therapy*. Aldershot, England: Gower Press.

Premack, D. (1959). Towards empirical behavior laws: 1. Positive reinforcement. *Psychological Review, 66*, 219–233.

Prisko, L. (1963). *Short-term memory in focal cerebral damage*. Unpublished doctoral dissertation, McGill University, Montreal.

Quinsey, V. L., & Chaplin, T. C. (1984). Stimulus control of rapists and non-sex offenders sexual arousal. *Behavioral Assessment, 6*, 169–176.

Rachman, S., & Hodgson, R. (1974). Synchrony and desynchrony in fear and avoidance. *Behaviour Research and Therapy, 12*, 311–318.

Ramachandran, V. S. (1976). Learning-like phenomena in stereopsis. *Nature, 262*, 382–384.

Randt, C. T., Brown, E. R., & Osborne, D. P. (1980). A memory test for longitudinal measurement of mild to moderate deficits. *Clinical Neuropsychiatry, 2*, 184–194.

Raven, J. C. (1960). *Guide to the Standard Progressive Matrices*. London: Lewis.

Rawles, R. E. (1978). The past and present of mnemotechny. In M. M. Gruneberg, P. E. Morris, & R. N. Sykes (Eds.), *Practical aspects of memory*. London: Academic Press.

Rimm, D., & Masters, J. (1979). *Behavior therapy: Techniques and empirical findings*. New York: Academic Press.

Rizzo, E. M. (1955). Sulla sindroma di Korsakoff. *Rassegna di Studi Psichiatrici, 44*, 801–816.

Robbins, F. C. (1958). The clinical and laboratory diagnosis of viral infections of the central nervous system. In W. C. Fields & R. J. Blathner (Eds.) *Viral encephalitis*. Springfield, IL: Charles C Thomas.

Robertson-Tchabo, E. A., Hausman, C. P., & Arenberg, D. (1976). A classical mnemonic for older learners: A trip that works. *Educational Gerontologist, 1*, 215–226.

Robinson, F. B. (1970). *Effective study*. New York: Harper & Row.

Rose, F. C., & Symonds, C. P. (1960). Persistent memory defect following encephalitis. *Brain, 83*, 195–212.

Ross, J., & Lawrence, K. A. (1968). Some observations on memory artifice. *Psychonomic Science, 13*, 107–108.

Rowntree, D. (1983). *Learn how to study.* New York: Harper & Row.

Russell, E. W. (1975). A multiple scoring method for the assessment of complex memory functions. *Journal of Consulting and Clinical Psychology, 43,* 800–809.

Russell, W. R. (1932). Cerebral involvement in head injury. *Brain, 55,* 549–603.

Russell, W. R. (1971). *The traumatic amnesias.* London: Oxford University Press.

Russell, W. R., & Nathan, P. W. (1946). Traumatic amnesia. *Brain, 69,* 280–301.

Russell, W. R., & Smith, A. (1961). Post traumatic amnesia in closed head injuries. *Archives of Neurology, 5,* 4–17.

Sachs, E. (1950). Meningiomas with dementia as the first and presenting feature. *Journal of Mental Science, 96,* 998–1007.

Sakitt, B. (1976). Iconic memory. *Psychological Review, 83,* 257–276.

Sanders, H. I., & Warrington, E. K. (1971). Memory for remote events in amnesic patients. *Brain, 94,* 661.

Sanders, H. I., & Warrington, E. K. (1975). Retrograde amnesia in organic amnesic patients. *Cortex, 11,* 397–400.

Sarno, M. T., & Levita, E. (1981). Some observations on the nature of recovery in global aphasia after stroke. *Brain and Language, 13,* 1–12.

Schacter, D., & Crovitz, H. (1977). Memory function after closed head injury: A review of the quantitative research. *Cortex, 13,* 105–176.

Schonell, F. J., & Schonell, F. E. (1963). *Diagnostic attainment testing.* Edinburgh: Oliver & Boyd.

Scoville, W. B. (1968). Amnesia after bilateral mesial temporal lobe excision: Introduction to case H. M. *Neuropsychologia, 6,* 211–213.

Scoville, W. B., & Milner, B. (1957). Loss of recent memory after bilateral hippocampal lesions. *Journal of Neurology, Neurosurgery and Psychiatry, 20,* 11–21.

Selecki, B. R. (1964). Cerebral mid-line tumours involving the corpus callosum among mental hospital patients. *Medical Journal of Australia, 2,* 954–968.

Series, C., & Lincoln, N. B. (1978). Behaviour modification in physical rehabilitation. *Occupational Therapy, 41,* 222–224.

Shallice, T. (1979). Neuropsychological research and the fractionation of memory systems. In L. Nilsson (Ed.), *Perspectives in memory research.* Hillsdale, NJ: Erlbaum.

Shallice, T. (1982). Specific impairments of planning. *Philosophical Transactions of the Royal Society of London* (Series B), *298,* 199–209.

Shallice, T., & Warrington, E. K. (1970). Independent functioning of verbal memory stores: A neuropsychological study. *Quarterly Journal of Experimental Psychology, 22,* 261–273.

Shallice, T., & Warrington, E. K. (1977). Auditory-verbal short term memory impairment and conduction aphasia. *Brain and Language, 4,* 479–491.

Shallice, T., & Warrington, E. K. (1980). Single and multiple component central dyslexic syndromes. In M. Coltheart, K. E. Patterson, & J. C. Marshall (Eds.), *Deep dyslexia.* London: Routledge & Kegan Paul.

Shuttleworth, E. C., & Wise, G. R. (1973). Transient global amnesia due to arterial embolism. *Archives of Neurology, 29,* 340–342.

Siegel, S. (1956). *Nonparametric statistics for the behavioral sciences.* New York: McGraw-Hill.

Singh, N. N., Beale, I. L., & Dawson, M. J. (1981). Duration of facial screening and suppression of self-injurious behavior: Analysis using an alternating treatments design. *Behavioral Assessment, 3,* 411–420.

Sisler, G., & Penner, H. (1975). Amnesia following severe head injury. *Canadian Psychiatric Association Journal, 20*, 333–336.

Sivak, M., Kewman, D. G., & Henson, D. L. (1981). Driving and perceptual/cognitive skills: Behavioral consequences of brain damage. *Archives of Physical Medicine and Rehabilitation, 62*, 476–483.

Smith, A. (1962). Ambiguities in concepts and studies of "brain damage" and "organicity." *Journal of Nervous and Mental Disease, 135*, 311–326.

Smith, A. D. (1975). *Interaction between human aging and memory.* Georgia Institute of Technology Progress Report, No. 2.

Smith, E. (1974). Influence of site of impact on cognitive impairment persisting long after severe closed head injury. *Journal of Neurology, Neurosurgery and Psychiatry, 37*, 719–726.

Snodgrass, J. G., & Vanderwart, M. (1980). A standardized set of 260 pictures: Nouns for name agreement, image agreement, familiarity and visual complexity. *Journal of Experimental Psychology: Human Learning and Memory, 6*, 174–215.

Sobell, M. B., & Sobell, L. C. (1978). Assessment of addictive behavior. In M. Hersen & A. S. Bellack (Eds.), *Behavioral assessment.* New York: Pergamon Press.

Sperling, G. (1960). The information available in brief visual presentations. *Psychological Monographs, 74*, 1–29.

Sprofkin, B. E., & Sciarra, D. (1952). Korsakoff psychosis associated with cerebral tumors. *Neurology, 2*, 427–434.

Squire, L. R. (1981). Two forms of human amnesia: An analysis of forgetting. *Journal of Neuroscience, 1*, 635–630.

Squire, L. R. (1982). Comparisons between forms of amnesia: Some deficits are unique to Korsakoff's syndrome. *Journal of Experimental Psychology: Learning, Memory and Cognition, 8*, 560–571.

Squire, L. R., & Chace, P. M. (1975). Memory functions six to nine months after electroconvulsive therapy. *Archives of General Psychiatry, 32*, 1557–1564.

Squire, L. R., & Cohen, N. J. (1982). Remote memory, retrograde amnesia, and the neuropsychology of memory. In L. S. Cermak (Ed.), *Human memory and amnesia.* Hillsdale, NJ: Erlbaum.

Squire, L. R., & Moore, R. Y. (1979). Dorsal thalamic lesion in a noted case of human memory dysfunction. *Annals of Neurology, 6*, 303–306.

Squire, L. R., & Zola-Morgan, S. (1983). The neurology of memory: The case for correspondence between the findings for human and non-human performance. In J. A. Deutsch (Ed.), *The physiological basis of memory.* New York: Academic Press.

Starr, A., & Phillips, L. (1970). Verbal and motor memory in the amnesic syndrome. *Neuropsychologia, 8*, 75–82.

Strauss, I., & Keschner, M. (1935). Mental symptoms in cases of tumor of the frontal lobe. *Archives of Neurology and Psychiatry, 33*, 986–1005.

Sundberg, N. D., & Tyler, L. E. (1962). *Clinical Psychology.* New York: Appleton-Century-Crofts.

Sunderland, A., Harris, J. E., & Baddeley, A. D. (1983). Do laboratory tests predict everyday memory? A neuropsychological study. *Journal of Verbal Learning and Verbal Behaviour, 22*, 341–357.

Sunderland, A., Harris, J. E., & Baddeley, A. D. (1984). Assessing everyday memory after severe head injury. In J. E. Harris & P. Morris (Eds.), *Everyday memory, actions and absentmindedness.* London: Academic Press.

Sunderland, A., Harris, J. E., & Gleave, J. (1984). Memory failures in everyday life after severe head injury. *Journal of Clinical Neuropsychology, 6,* 127–142.

Sweet, W. H., Talland, G. A., & Ballantine, H. T. (1966). A memory and mood disorder associated with ruptured anterior communicating aneurysm. *Transactions of the American Neurological Association, 91,* 346–348.

Sweet, W. H., Talland, G. A., & Ervin, F. R. (1959). Loss of recent memory following section of the fornix. *Transactions of the American Neurological Association, 84,* 876–882.

Talland, G. A. (1965). *Deranged memory.* New York: Academic Press.

Talland, G. A., Sweet, W. H., & Ballantine, H. T. (1967). Amnesic syndrome with anterior communicating artery aneurysm. *Journal of Nervous and Mental Disease, 145,* 179–192.

Taylor, G. P., & Persons, R. W. (1970). Behavior modification techniques in a physical medicine and rehabilitation center. *Journal of Psychology, 74,* 117–124.

Teuber, H. L., Milner, B., & Vaughan, H. G. (1968). Persistent anterograde amnesia after stab wound of the basal brain. *Neuropsychologia, 6,* 267–282.

Theanders, S., & Granholm, L. (1967). Sequelae after spontaneous subarachnoid haemorrhage with special reference to hydrocephalus and Korsakoff's syndrome. *Acta Neurologica Scandinavica, 43,* 479–488.

Thorndike, E. L., & Lorge, I. (1944). *The Teacher's word book of 30,000 words.* New York: Teachers' College Press.

Tulving, E. (1972). Episodic and semantic memory. In E. Tulving & W. Donaldson (Eds.), *Organization of memory.* New York: Academic Press.

Vernon, P. E. (1977). *The Graded Word Spelling Test.* London: Hodder & Stoughton.

Victor, M., Adams, R. D., & Collins, G. H. (1971). *The Wernicke-Korsakoff syndrome.* Oxford: Blackwell Scientific Publications.

Victor, M., Angevine, J. B., Mancall, E. L., & Fisher, C. M. (1961). Memory loss with lesions of hippocampal formation. *Archives of Neurology, 5,* 244–263.

Wallace, L. (1982). The heart of the matter: A clinical psychologist in coronary care. *Bulletin of the British Psychological Society, 35,* 379–382.

Walsh, B. F., & Lamberts, F. (1979). Errorless discrimination and picture fading as techniques for teaching sight words to TMR students. *American Journal of Mental Deficiency, 83,* 473–479.

Walsh, K. (1978). *Neuropsychology: A clinical approach.* Edinburgh: Churchill Livingstone.

Walton, J. N. (1953). The Korsakoff syndrome in spontaneous subarachnoid haemorrhage. *Journal of Mental Science, 99,* 521–530.

Walton, J. N. (1971). *Essentials of neurology.* London: Pitman Medical & Scientific Publishing.

Warrington, E. K. (1974). Deficient recognition memory in organic amnesia. *Cortex, 10,* 284–291.

Warrington, E. K. (1982). Neuropsychological studies of object recognition. *Philosophical Transactions of the Royal Society of London* (Series B), *298,* 15–33.

Warrington, E. K., (1984). *The Recognition Memory Test.* Windsor, England: National Foundation for Educational Research-Nelson.

Warrington, E. K., & Sanders, H. I. (1971). The fate of old memories. *Quarterly Journal of Experimental Psychology, 23,* 432–442.

Warrington, E. K., & Taylor, A. M. (1973). The contribution of the right parietal lobe to object recognition. *Cortex, 7,* 152–164.

Warrington, E. K., & Weiskrantz, L. (1968). New method of testing long-term retention, with special reference to amnesic patients. *Nature, 217,* 972–974.

Warrington, E. K., & Weiskrantz, L. (1970). Amnesic syndrome: Consolidation or retrieval? *Nature, 228,* 628–630.

Warrington, E. K., & Weiskrantz, L. (1973). An analysis of short-term and long-term memory deficits in man. In J. Deutsch (Ed.), *The physiologial basis of memory.* New York: Academic Press.

Warrington, E. K., & Weiskrantz, L. (1982). Amnesia: A disconnection syndrome? *Neuropsychologia, 20,* 233–248.

Watkins, O. C. (1975). *The origin of the build-up of proactive inhibition effect.* Paper presented at the meeting of the Experimental Psychology Society, London.

Wechsler, D. (1945). A standardized memory scale for clinical use. *Journal of Psychology, 19,* 87–95.

Wechsler, D. (1955). *Wechsler Adult Intelligence Scale.* New York: Psychological Corporation.

Weddell, J. M., & Beresford, S. A. (1979). *Planning for stroke patients: A four year descriptive study of home and hospital care.* London: Her Majesty's Stationery Office.

Weinberg, M. A., Diller, L., Gordon, W. A., Gerstman, L. J., Lieberman, A., Lakin, P., Hodges, G. & Ezrachi, O. (1979). Training sensory awareness and spatial organization in people with right brain damage. *Archives of Physical Medicine and Rehabilitation, 60,* 491–496.

Weiskrantz, L. (1978). A comparison of hippocampal pathology in man and other animals. In *Functions of the septo-hippocampal system* (Ciba Foundation Symposium 58). Amsterdam: Elsevier North-Holland.

Weiskrantz, L., & Warrington, E. K. (1979). Conditioning in amnesic patients. *Neuropsychologia, 17,* 187–194.

Whiteley, A. M., & Warrington, E. K. (1977). Prosopagnosia: A clinical psychological and anatomical study of three patients. *Journal of Neurology, Neurosurgery and Psychiatry, 40,* 395–403.

Whitty, C. W. M., & Lishman, W. A. (1966). Amnesia in cerebral disease. In C. W. M. Whitty & O. Zangwill (Eds.), *Amnesia.* London: Butterworths.

Wickens, D. D. (1970). Encoding categories of words: An empirical approach to meaning. *Psychological Review, 77,* 1–15.

Williams, M. (1953). Investigations of amnesic defects by progressive prompting. *Journal of Neurology, Neurosurgery and Psychiatry, 16,* 14.

Williams, M. (1968). The measurement of memory in clinical practice. *British Journal of Social and Clinical Psychology, 7,* 19–34.

Williams, M., & Pennybacker, J. (1954). Memory disturbances in third ventricle tumours. *Journal of Neurology, Neurosurgery and Psychiatry, 17,* 173–182.

Wilson, B. A. (1981a). A survey of behavioural treatments carried out at a rehabilitation centre for stroke and head injuries. In G. E. Powell, *Brain function therapy.* Aldershot, England: Gower Press.

Wilson, B. A. (1981b). Teaching a man to remember people's names after removal of a temporal lobe tumour. *Behavioural Psychotherapy, 9,* 338–344.

Wilson, B. A. (1982). Success and failure in memory training following a cerebral vascular accident. *Cortes, 18,* 581–594.

Wilson, B. A. (1984a). Memory therapy in practice. In B. A. Wilson & N. Moffat (Eds.), *Clinical management of memory problems.* London: Croom Helm.

Wilson, B. A. (1984b). Cognitive rehabilitation after brain damage. Ph.D. thesis, University of London.

Wilson, B. A. (1985). Adapting Portage for neurological patients. *International Rehabilitation Medicine, 7,* 6–8.

Wilson, B. A. (in press). Identification and remediation of everyday problems in memory impaired adults. In O. Parsons, N. Butters, & P. Nathan (Eds.), *Neuropsychology of alcoholism: Implications for diagnosis and treatment.* New York: Guilford Press.

Wilson, B. A., & Baddeley, A. D. (in press). Single case methodology and the remediation of acquired dyslexia. In G. Pavlides & D. Fisher (Eds.), *Dyslexia: Neuropsychology and treatment.* London: Wiley.

Wilson, B. A., Cooper, Z., & Kennerley, H. (1983, December). *An investigation of the effectiveness of group training on memory functioning in adults with acquired brain damage.* Paper presented at the meeting of the Society for Research in Rehabilitation, London.

Wilson, B. A., & Moffat, N. (1984). Rehabilitation of memory for everyday life. In J. Harris & P. Morris (Eds.), *Everyday memory, actions and absentmindedness.* London: Academic Press.

Wilson, B. A., & Moore, P. (1979). A chaining procedure to teach a retarded deaf child to wear her hearing aid. *British Journal of Mental Subnormality, 25,* 88–90.

Wilson, B. A., & Powell, G. (in press). Treatment of neurological problems. In S. Lindsay & G. Powell (Eds.), *Handbook of clinical psychology.* Aldershot, England: Gower Press.

Wilson, B. A., White, S., & McGill, P. (1983, June). *Remediation of acquired dyslexia following a gun shot wound.* Paper presented at the Second World Congress on Dyslexia, Halkidiki, Greece.

Wilson, R. S., Koller, W., & Kelly, M. P. (1980). The amnesia of transient global amnesia. *Journal of Clinical Neuropsychology, 2,* 259–266.

Winocur, G., & Kinsbourne, M. (1978). Contextual cueing as an aid to Korsakoff amnesica. *Neuropsychologia, 16,* 671–682.

Winocur, G., & Weiskrantz, L. (1976). An investigation of paired-associate learning in amnesic patients. *Neuropsychologia, 14,* 97–110.

Winograd, E., & Simon, E. W. (1980). Visual memory and imagery in the aged. In L. W. Poon, J. L. Fozard, L. S. Cermak, D. Arenberg, & L. W. Thompson (Eds.), *New directions in memory and aging.* Hillsdale, NJ: Erlbaum.

Wolpe, J. (1958). *Psychotherapy by reciprocal inhibition.* Stanford, CA: Stanford University Press.

Wong, S. E., & Liberman, R. P. (1981). Mixed single-subject designs in clinical research: Variations of the multiple baseline. *Behavioral Assessment, 3,* 297–306.

Woolsey, R. M., & Nelson, J. S. (1975). A symptomatic destruction of the fornix in man. *Archives of Neurology, 32,* 566–568.

Wowern, F. von (1966). Post traumatic amnesia and confusion as an index of severity in head injury. *Acta Neurologica Scandinavica, 42,* 373–378.

Yarnell, P. R., & Lynch, S. (1973). The "ding" amnestic states in football trauma. *Neurology, 23,* 196–197.

Yates, F. A. (1966). *The art of memory.* London: Routledge & Kegan Paul.

Yuille, J. C., & Paivio, A. (1967). Latency of imaginal and verbal mediators as a function of stimulus and response concreteness-imagery. *Journal of Experimental Psychology, 75,* 540–544.

Yule, W., & Carr, J. (1980). *Behaviour modification and the mentally handicapped child.* London: Croom Helm.

Yule, W., & Hemsley, D. (1977). Single case method in medical psychology. In S. Rachman (Ed.), *Contributions to medical psychology* (Vol. 1). New York: Pergamon Press.

Zaidel, D., & Sperry, R. W. (1974). Memory impairment after commissurotomy in man. *Brain, 97,* 263–272.

Zlutnick, S. I., Mayville, W. T., & Moffat, S. (1975). Modification of seizure disorders: The interruption of behavior chains. *Journal of Applied Behavioral Analysis, 8,* 1–12.

INDEX

Numbers in italic indicate material in figures and tables.